Nov 20/2014

To Greg
With my very best
wishes for your
continued success in photo-
journalism

Jack.

The Heritage of
Canadian Military Music

THE HERITAGE OF

Canadian Military Music

Jack Kopstein
and
Ian Pearson

Vanwell Publishing Limited
St. Catharines, Ontario

Vanwell Publishing acknowledges the financial support of the Government of Canada through the Book Publishing Industry Development Program for our publishing activities.

Design: Jay Tee Graphics
Cover: Linda Moroz-Irvine

Vanwell Publishing Limited
1 Northrup Crescent
P.O. Box 2131
St. Catharines, Ontario L2R 7S2
sales@vanwell.com
tel: 905-937-3100
fax: 905-937-1760

Printed in Canada

National Library of Canada Cataloguing in Publication

Kopstein, Jack
   The heritage of Canadian military music / Jack Kopstein and Ian Pearson. — 1st ed.

Includes bibliographical references, discography and index.
ISBN 1-55125-050-0

   1. Bands (Music)—Canada—History. 2. Military music—Canada—History and criticism. 3. Canada—Armed Forces—Bandmasters—Biography. I. Pearson, Ian V. II. Title.

ML1313.K825 2002   784.8'4'0971   C2002-902326-2

The Heritage of Canadian Military Music

Frederick Charles Ashton

1927–1998

Frederick Charles Ashton was born in Toronto and lived there all his life. His military career began at an earlier age learning to play trumpet in the Boys' Brigade. He later enlisted as a Trumpeter in the 7th Toronto Regiment, RCA (Reserve Army) and transferred to The Royal Canadian Army Service Corps playing in the Trumpet Band. He enlisted in the Canadian Infantry Corps of the Regular Army until demobilization when he joined the Bugle Band of The Queen's Own Rifles of Canada and also played in the bands of the Royal Canadian Electrical Mechanical Engineers (Militia) and the Royal Canadian Army Medical Corps (Militia).

Fred was a founding member of The International Military Music Society, Canadian Branch in 1978, serving as Secretary and later the Chairman. Over the years he became renowned in Canada for his extensive knowledge of and interest in Canadian military bands.

Foreword

I was a small boy in the early forties during the Second World War and like most youngsters growing up at the time, I was exposed to military music on a daily basis. In those days, we simply couldn't get enough despite the fact that the radio programs and the films at the time were full of it. We always listened attentively, we stood a little straighter when we heard a band play and that music touched a primeval chord that lay within us all and it did it like no other music ever could.

Even as a youngster, I knew it was part of the government's policy of stirring up Canadian patriotism at a time when that was desperately needed. The sounds of military music brought forth in every Canadian a sense of national pride that was so vitally important during the war and in some ways stimulated a sense of our ultimate invincibility in terms of the outcome of the war. There were other elements, of course, that raised the level of national pride and helped maintain morale during the war but military band music lay at the heart of it all.

Like everyone of my generation, the sound of that music had a profound impact on me and it still does well over half a century later. I was and still am enormously grateful for the opportunity to be exposed to military bands during my early years because it instilled a love of military music in me and great admiration for the people who play it. I still stand a little taller when I hear a band and that tingle still runs up my spine and the hair on the back of my neck still rises a little. The simple fact is that everyone is stirred by the sound of a military band. The pity is that more Canadians won't admit it.

When I was serving in The Black Watch, The Royal Canadian Regiment and the Airborne Regiment no parade, no matter how small, was complete without a band. Although few of us would admit it, the sound of a band on parade gave us new life and spirit. Simply put, we were better when the band was with us.

As something of a military sideline (which has now become much more than that) I found myself producing military Tattoos. It was that experience that gave me the opportunity to work with Canada's military band musicians. In the process I not only got to know them, I developed great respect for their ability and great affection for them as individuals.

I also began to realize that there was immense talent there not only as accomplished musicians but also that creative talent as composers which like so many other aspects of military music, has never been given the recognition in Canada that skill deserves. Perhaps, that inherent modesty is typically Canadian but the talent of Canadian Forces' musicians has never really been recognized even by the Canadian Forces.

The late Jim Gaffer, and more recently Jack McGuire, a retired RCN Director of Music, along with many other Canadian military band musicians, have composed marches that will stand with any in the world. Although they are not being given the credit now they deserve, they will certainly be recognized in the years ahead. Sadly, I suspect that recognition will not come from Canada but rather from the USA or Europe.

Alden Nowlan, a well known Canadian poet who died a number of years ago used to sit in his cluttered den on Windsor Street in Fredericton, with a glass of gin in his hand, and his stereo blaring out marches. His tastes were universal – German and French marches, Sousa, of course, but above all those great British marches that are still the foundation of the repertoire of every Canadian Military Band.

In the early 1970s when I was commanding 2RCR in Gagetown, I frequently sat with him as he played those old recordings. While he listened, he cursed the military bureaucrats whom he always referred to as "cellophane wrapped young technocrats" and blamed them for the lack of interest in bands and things ceremonial that was developing within the Canadian Forces at the time.

"Don't those damn fools in Ottawa realize," he said, as the speakers of his stereo thundered out those marches he loved so much, "that one small band is worth a thousand cannons."

I didn't know at the time but learned later he was paraphrasing a 19th century General. Although I still don't know who said it, a more accurate statement about the value of military bands has never been made.

During one of the sessions in his study, he turned to me and said in a loud voice over the sound of an Alford march.

"If you ever end up running the army, promise me you'll fire all of the technocrats and the bean counters who know the price of everything and the value of nothing. Then get rid of those damn fools that have put all of you people into silly green uniforms and give us more bands."

That, of course, never happened but if it ever had, I would have followed Alden's advice to the letter.

Jack Kopstein and Ian Pearson have filled a gap in this book that is badly needed in this country. They have recorded the history of Canadian Military Music and in so doing have, to some degree, corrected an omis-

Mr. Robert Blight — Central Band of the Canadian Forces in re-photo-
graphing old photographs;

Mr. Wilf Anthony, Oshawa, Ontario;

Music Library Queens University, Kingston, Ontario;

New Brunswick Museum, St. John, New Brunswick;

Oshawa Community Archives, Oshawa, Ontario;

Peterborough Centennial Museum And Archives, Peterborough,
Ontario;

Petty Officer Phil Andrews (HMCS York) , Whitby, Ontario;

Pipe Major Archie Cairns, Former Senior Pipe Major of the Canadian
Forces;

Provincial Archives of New Brunswick, Fredericton, New Brunswick;

Public Archives of Nova Scotia, Halifax, Nova Scotia;

Regiments of the Canadian Forces;

Robert McLaughlin Gallery, Oshawa, Ontario (includes the Thomas
Bouckley Collection);

Royal Canadian Artillery Museum, Shilo, Manitoba;

Royal Canadian Mounted Police Centennial Museum, Regina,
Saskatchewan;

Scugog Shores Museum and Archives, Port Perry, Ontario;

Staff of the Directorate of History, Canadian Forces, Ottawa, Ontario;

The Nova Scotia Tattoo, Halifax, Nova Scotia;

Town of Whitby Archives, Whitby, Ontario;

Uxbridge-Scott Museum and Archives, Uxbridge, Ontario.

CHAPTER 1

The Early Years

"Noble and manly music invigorates the spirit strengthens the wavering man, and incites him to great and worthy deeds"

Homer: The Iliad, 1000 B.C.

The Evolution of the Military Band

References to Military Bands, or at least to groups of instrumentalists performing for military purposes, can be found in records dating back to biblical times. An example of this would be the siege of Jericho by the Children of Israel, when "the armed men went forth led by the priests who blew trumpets." The army of the Israelites used these trumpets for their military ceremonies and displays, and they are frequently mentioned in the Book of Joshua. The Hebrews used a number of instruments in various military and religious services, however, it appears that flutes (*'ugab*), drums (*tof*) and trumpets (*hazozra*) comprised the usual military band. These instruments, used individually or in combination, were directed solely to producing signals for the arrival of priests, or as a prelude to battle. It is unlikely that these primitive instruments produced anything more than cacophony.

The ancient Greeks held music in high esteem. Along with their development of an alphabetical system of musical notation came a number of important musical instruments, the *aulos*, or reed pipe, later known as the oboe, and the *syrinx*, pipes built in different lengths. Bards who accompanied singers used these instruments, and this was probably the first attempt at forming a band.

Before the twelfth century, popular music was almost entirely in the hands of roving musicians known as troubadours, who associated with actors and acrobats. If a new melody grew up like a wildflower, these fifers, fiddlers or minstrels took it up and made it known far and wide. Although these musicians were social outcasts, it was not considered a breach of etiquette to allow them into houses of low or high degree to learn from them the latest ballad or dance tune. On all great occasions, court feasts or church festivities, great numbers of troubadours flocked together for the exercise of their merry calling. But their associating as a band was a matter of momentary convenience, and their performances consisted only of playing melodies of songs, dances and march tunes.

Trumpets and kettledrums were strictly forbidden to ordinary minstrels, being reserved for the exclusive use of princes and men of high rank. These instruments predominated in the bands that officially performed on state occasions or at royal banquets. It is said that in 1587, King Henry VIII's band consisted of ten trumpets, sixteen trombones and four drums. In 1620, the Elector of Saxony had twenty court trumpeters and three kettledrums, with apprentices being trained to perform on each instrument. Other courts had their trumpet-corps and their respective numbers were considered an indication of the importance, wealth and power of the court. In the German Empire they formed the Guild of Royal Trumpeters and Army Kettledrummers, under the protection and jurisdiction of the Elector of Saxony.

As early as the thirteenth century, those pipers who settled in towns in Germany, France and England, and who felt the ignominious position of being classed with the wandering vagabonds, formed *Innungen*, or corporations, for their mutual protection. The first of these, The Brotherhood of St. Nicolas, was instituted at Vienna in 1288. This guild was imitated during the next two centuries by most of the large imperial towns, which established regular bands of "Townpipers" under the leadership of a *Stadpfeifer*, who had to provide all music at civic or private festivities. Although the town bands had only poor instrumentation, consisting mostly of fifes, flutes, *schalmei* (a form of oboe), *bombards* (a bass flute) *zinken* or cornetti, bagpipes, viols and drums, yet they formed the basis from which modern bands originated.

The use of musical instruments in war by the ancients as an incentive to the courage of the troops rather than a means of conveying signals, began in earnest in the fourteenth century. Here we find for the first time undoubted evidence of the sounding of trumpets on a field of battle, during the Battles of Crécy 1346 (France) and Neville's Cross 1346 (England), spectacular English victories over the French and Scots in 1346. For the next two centuries the instrument used in signalling seems to have been the trumpet alone. In 1347, however, King Edward VII is said to have entered Calais with a fine procession of trumpets, drums, schalmei and bells.

In pieces written for bands about three centuries ago we find a rather peculiar habit of keeping different classes of instruments separated; flutes, reed instruments, trumpets and hunting horns mostly were treated as forming distinct bands. Until the seventeenth century, music played by bands of trumpeters was learned by ear and transmitted without notation. The mercenary troops of Austrian Emperor Charles V and French King François I had large bands of trumpets and kettledrums in the Battles of Marignano (1515) and Pavia (1525). It is said that the clash of the instruments was as fierce as that of the weapons. By the seventeenth century, we find trombones or *sacbut* in general use and, combining with flutes, oboes and bassoons, trumpets and drums, a very decent degree of band music began to emerge. Music now began to be noted down and we are able to trace its progress as we come nearer the eighteenth century. Bands separated more distinctly into three classes — the full orchestra, addressing itself to the cultivated musical intellect, and the military and brass bands, that appealed to the masses. The inclusion of the newly developed clarinet, ideally suited to wind-band music, caused the oboe to be pushed into second place. The French horn was also now included in bands.

In 1763, Frederick the Great of Prussia first defined the composition of the military band. It included the following instruments: oboes, clarinets, horns and bassoons in pairs, and later a flute and one or two trumpets, as well as a contrabassoon. The band of Louis XIV (1643-1715), organized by Lully, consisted of oboes, bassoons and drums. Around 1800, the vogue of Turkish music resulted in the adoption of noise-making instruments such as cymbals, triangles and military glockenspiels. Infantry regiments under Napoleon had bands consisting of one piccolo, one high clarinet (probably either A-flat or E-flat clarinets), sixteen regular clarinets (probably pitched in B-flat or C), four bassoons, two serpents, two trumpets, one bass trumpet, four horns, three trombones, two side drums, one bass drum and two pairs of cymbals.

Some of the early band music exemplified the most developed form of wind-band writing before valved brass instruments altered its tone colour. A good example is the "Grand March in E-flat" by Sir Henry Bishop (1786-1855), scored for one flute, two oboes, four clarinets, two trumpets, two horns, two bassoons, bass trombone, serpent and ophicleide. A landmark in the development of military music was a performance in Berlin on May 12, 1838, in honour of the Russian emperor. The conductor was Wilhelm Wieprecht (1802-1872), the organizer of Prussian military music. Here he conducted the massed bands of thirty-two infantry and cavalry units, totalling one thousand wind instruments and two hundred drummers.

15

Around 1783, the Duke of York first introduced the military band into England from Germany. Prior to this the Royal Artillery had a number of men who were trained as musicians, as did the Guards, in 1662, the Band of the Scots Guards consisted of drums, fifes and bagpipes. Charles II, during his exile in France, was struck by the Band of Oboes (*Hautbois*), and when he returned in 1660, he introduced these Hautbois into the Grenadier Guards. Nearly seventy-five years passed without further development of the band in England, and by 1783, there were only eight bandsmen in the three regiments of Guards — two oboes, two clarinets, two horns and two bassoons. Although they were excellent performers, they were civilian members of the military and thus could decline to perform. The officers, who were responsible for their pay, wanted a band they could utilize on all occasions, and a letter was sent to the Duke of York, Colonel-in-Chief of the Coldstream Guards, requesting a full-time band. The duke consented, and, with the approval of the King raised a band consisting of twenty-four members, including clarinets, horns, bassoons, trumpets, trombones, serpents and drums. This was the forerunner of the present military band in England and the Commonwealth.

This innovation met with instant and universal approval and regiments of the line were allowed by the War Office to raise similar bands at their own expense. They permitted a certain number of men from the ranks to be trained as musicians, but ordered that all expenses such as music, instruments and pay for the bandmaster should be borne by the officers. Therefore, as time proved, the entire welfare of the bands depended entirely on the enthusiasm and pockets of the officers of the regiments. Regiments spent enormous amounts of money on their bands, importing some of the finest instrumentalists in Europe, building and establishing vast music libraries and outfitting the musicians in the most expensive and resplendent uniforms. It was a good system because it created a strong rivalry among the regiments, however it lacked a proper central organization to co-ordinate the band activities. The famous Scutari Incident in 1854, where massed bands struck up "God Save the Queen" in several different keys, finally brought to light the inadequacies and musical indifference present in the officer-supported regimental bands. This stirred the Commander-in-Chief of the British Army, the Duke of Cambridge, into action. He suggested that a military school of music be organized and provided by the government to train bandmasters and young instrumentalists. The first military music class was established at Kneller Hall, Twickenham, on March 3, 1857.

The immediate effect was to raise the standard of British military bands and to standardize the instrumentation of bands, allowing composers and arrangers to write for a set musical ensemble. Early in the twentieth century great discrepancies still existed in the number and variety of instruments used by different bands, and, in 1921, a final established order was agreed upon and adopted by all bands in England, with other Commonwealth countries following suit.

British Military Bands in Canada

In the period following the taking of Quebec by the British in 1759, British regiments garrisoned many Canadian towns and cities. These regiments had official establishments for fife-and-drum corps. The trumpet had become associated with mounted troops.

By 1783, the regiments began to adopt the practice of enlisting musicians unofficially for service in their units and paid for by subscription by the officers.

As the regiments were drafted for service in the new world they were often accompanied by their regimental bands. The bands usually consisted of flutes, oboes, clarinets, horns and bassoons. Shortly thereafter, trumpets and trombones were added. This size of group was ideal for parades and dinners and provided a much-needed incentive for marching troops. The pace for marching during this period never exceeded sixty paces per minute. Many of the instruments were in their rudimentary state. The clarinets were five-keyed instruments and the flutes (open-hole type) were associated with fifes. Valved brass instruments were not invented until much later in the nineteenth century, and, as a result, the horns and trumpets relied exclusively on playing notes of the natural harmonic series. Eventually there were a great number of regimental bands that could be heard in the major populated areas such as Halifax, Quebec, Montreal and Toronto.

The bands stationed in Canada were tremendously popular because of their diversity. In addition to their normal military functions of parades and mess dinners, they assisted at theatrical productions, provided the nucleus of an orchestra for concerts and played for church services. One of the most important activities of the regimental bands was performances at public concerts. The concerts were staged in the outdoors in summer and in concert halls during winter and were the highlights of what can be described as a drab existence for the military and civilian population. They were warmly received and became the backbone of cultural activity in Canada.

In August 1791, the Royal Fusiliers came to Canada to be stationed at Quebec. They were accompanied by what the press described as "their

17

grand band of military musicians." The band had been raised and financed by Prince Edward Augustus (later the Duke of Kent, Queen Victoria's father) at a cost assessed at £800 per year. The band provided subscription concerts that were the highlights of Quebec's concert activity until the regiment moved to Halifax in 1794. Prince Edward Augustus had a special bandstand constructed that is preserved to this day. Other bands which appeared in garrison towns included the 60th Royal American Regiment Band in Montreal and the 41st Regiment Band in Niagara-on-the-Lake.

A record of the early British bands in Canada exists in the diary of Mrs. Simcoe. In 1790, Colonel John Graves Simcoe was appointed Lieutenant Governor of Upper Canada. He and Mrs. Simcoe arrived in the colony on November 11, 1791, and she began to document in her diary the daily life in Canada at that time. The following extracts from her diary help to provide an insight into ceremonial and cultural aspects of musical life.

Monday, November 21, 1791:

I went to a subscription concert of Prince Edward's Band of the 7th Fusiliers. The music was thought excellent. The band costs the Prince eight hundred a year.

Sunday, November 27, 1791:

I went to church. The service is performed in a room occasionally used as Council Chamber. Prince Edward always goes to church and his band plays during the service.

Monday, November 28, 1791:

I went to a concert and afterward to a dance at the Fusiliers Barracks.

At Niagara...
Wednesday, April 3, 1793:

Immediately after I have dined I rise [from] the table, one of the officers attends me home and the Band plays on the parade before the house till six o'clock. The music adds cheerfulness to this retired spot and we feel much indebted to the Marquis of Buckingham for the number of instruments he presented to the Regiment.

Monday, March 14, 1794:

In a magazine we met with a very pretty hymn sung by Sicilian Mariners. It sounds charming played by the Band on the water. The Master of the Band is a German who boasts of having performed before the King of Prussia in the great church of Strasbourg.

With the outbreak of the Crimean War in March 1854, British regiments, which had been the garrison troops on duty in Canada, received orders to sail for England. It was to be two years before their return to Canada. Their absence was felt most particularly in Montreal. The residents became starved for entertainment. They missed the bands and the parades and the theatricals that had been provided at the Artillery and Theatre Royal. The entry of the 39th Regiment in 1856 was met with a thunderous ovation. The long winters without the music of the bands were over for the time being.

By 1859, the British forces in Canada had been reduced to fewer than 3,000 troops. In Montreal there was but one regiment, the Seventeenth, numbering 821 men. This was soon reduced to 370 men and a battery of artillery. In 1860, the Prince of Wales visited Canada and one of the largest crowds in Montreal's history gathered at Logan's Farm to watch the Prince review the troops gathered for this momentous occasion.

The troops were representative of the British regulars and the Canadian Volunteer Militia. On completion of the grand review, the Prince departed by barge, and it is said the strains of the Royal Canadian Rifles wafted cheerily from the shore.

Many of the British military musicians remained in Canada when the troops departed, taking their retirement in the New World. Other bandsmen returned after completing their service in the army. The influence of these military musicians helped to nurture the military band movement

2nd Battalion Band, the Duke of Wellington's Regiment (West Riding). Cold weather dress in Canada, 1888. (*Courtesy of The Duke of Wellington's Regiment [West Riding]*)

in Canada. Their expertise helped to maintain and further cultural activity.

The Victorian era in Canada heralded what was to become the golden age of bands. The military bands played a prominent part in helping the country grow by acting as ambassadors of music for the Department of Militia and, more importantly, in the development of cultural activities. Bandmasters such as George Robinson in Hamilton and J. J. Gagnier in Montreal acted as the catalysts for the band movement, and, as a result, it became a nation-wide phenomenon.

An abstract of militia inspection reports for 1869-70 shows the existence of some forty-six bands in the Canadian militia. The report reveals the number of musicians and comments on their proficiency. For example:

> 29th Battalion (Hamilton Light Infantry)
> A fair band of 11 musicians;
> [29th Waterloo Battalion of Infantry]

> 45th Bn (RCA Militia)
> One of the best bands in the district with 21 performers;
> [45th West Durham Battalion of Infantry, converted to artillery in 1936]

> 65th Bn (Fredericton, NB)
> Brass band with 15 musicians just organized.
> [65th Battalion Mount Royal Rifles]

The Early Campaigns

The bands served a need by militia units to build morale among their volunteers and to develop esprit de corps. The biggest problem they faced was a lack of trained musicians. The band instrumentation was often unbalanced, and the bandmasters had difficulty in trying to field the musicians when they were needed. The inability of bands to perform properly gave rise to numerous complaints by their commanding officers to the Minister for Militia.

> They were late for parade and appeared without a drum.(Commanding Officer, Midland Battalion [Regimental Report 1885]).

> The bandmaster was improperly attired in morning suit and was no doubt drunk (Commanding Officer, Fourteenth Battalion Volunteer Militia Rifles).

Bands, however, had a part in the early campaigns. From the time of the Fenian Raids comes this account of the militia leaving to defend homes:

62nd Saint John Battalion of Infantry Band, Charlottetown, PEI, 1875. (*New Brunswick Museum, Edith Magee 57.99*)

On my way to school I had to pass the Grand Trunk Station. Upon this particular morning in May 1866 the alluring sound of the fife and drum led me to cross the railway tracks and join the crowd at the platform. The volunteers of Peel had been called to repel the Fenian invasion. The band struck up the tune of Tramp Tramp Tramp the boys are marching. The men began to sing, and the crowd cheered and the train pulled out for Toronto and as we feared the front." From Brock to Currie [Wm. Perkins Bull, Toronto, 1935, 237].

The historian of the Ninetieth Regiment (Winnipeg Rifles) had this to say about that band during the Riel Rebellion:

The brass band, particularly during the last few months of the campaign, for its playing improved wonderfully and was the pride and joy of the force. There was almost a row in the artillery lines because some members of Colonel Otter's force ventured to speak disparagingly of the 90th Band. In the field, particularly during the fight at Fish Creek, the bandsmen performed invaluable service as an ambulance corps. (Chambers *The 90th Regiment*, 1906, 53).

T. S. Marquis, in his book *Canada's Sons on Kopje and Veldt*, recalls how the RCR Band, a volunteer band, cheered the men on their way to South Africa aboard the *Sardinian* during the Boer War. "Through it all Bandmaster Tresham's band which had by now, by dint of constant practice, become to the minds of the soldiers a not unworthy rival to Sousa and had kept the spirits of all buoyant with airs of the pine and maple."

A Canadian infantry sergeant recorded an example of what band music can do for tired troops, especially when soldiering is based on a strong regimental spirit.

> It was early June 1900 and the capital of the Boer Republic, Pretoria had fallen. The troops of the Empire had campaigned from Cape Town. They were now about to enter the city; the Commander-in-Chief himself took the salute. It was the climax of the campaign, we were foot sore and weary and as we wheeled around the corner from Western Road the band struck up The Boys of the Old Brigade and I thought it was the sweetest music I had ever heard. I hope everyone else experienced as much being stirred up as I did.

The Queen's Own Rifles of Canada provided troops for the Canadian contingent during the South African campaign in 1900. A most interesting personality who emerged from the Boer War was a young bugler named Douglas Williams, who led the historic charge at Paardeberg. His personal story has taken an honoured place in the history of the QOR and he described the final charge dramatically:

> Bayonets were fixed, straps were tightened and we were ready. Soon I hear the Cornwalls (Duke of Cornwall's Light Infantry) getting orders to charge and looking back saw them coming on the run. The order came from the center for the Canadians to charge. It was plain that by the time the order had gotten the length of our line (about half a mile) that the Cornwalls would be past us, and not wanting any regiment to beat us at the finish, when we had led all day, I jumped up and blew the Canadian Regimental Call and then the charge! I sounded four times, namely to the right, left, rear and the front.

One of Canada's most poignant battle scenes is the painting entitled *The Dawn of Majuba, 1900*. This painting actually depicts the victory of six companies of the Royal Canadian Regiment over the Boers at Paardeberg on February 27, 1900. Dr. McCormick, formerly a corporal with the South African Service in 1899-1900, described the scene. Dr. McCormick said, "We continued to fire on Cronje's position in darkness and at dawn we opened up a steady stream of fire and suddenly white flags

22

appeared and the bugler began to signal cease firing and all down the lines our boys began to cheer."

The blowing of the bugle at Paardeberg may have been the last hurrah for bugle calls under wartime conditions. The whistle replaced bugles in the First World War.

The earliest reference to a bugler in Canada sounding reveille is contained in the following extract: "The bright chill of an April morning in 1793 and the Queen's Rangers building new quarters at Queenston where the gallant Brock was to fall two decades later in the defence of Canada and the bugles sounded at five every morning..."

The militia in Halifax had to keep a tight rein on the Halifax Rifles Bugle Band as shown in the following extract:

Militia General Orders
Headquarters, Halifax NS
Adjutant General's Office
May 14, 1860

His Excellency, the Lieutenant Governor and Commander in Chief, has been pleased to issue the following orders:

The buglers of the Volunteer Companies are not to sound the Assembly on any occasion whatever, except when practising on the ground appointed for that purpose, or drill outside the city.

Band of #3 Company, Royal Artillery, Halifax Citadel 1900. (*Public Archives of Nova Scotia,* [*Notman Collection 12505*] N-5129)

The historian for the 12th Regiment, [Queen's York Rangers] was not very complimentary to the battalion buglers when remarking on the number of personnel coming to summer camp in 1885. He said, "that at our annual camp the Captains bring over to Niagara about two Lieutenants, three sergeants, three corporals, the indispensable and inharmonious bugler and twenty or thirty private citizens."

The bugling must have improved, as after orders had been received to draft four companies of York Rangers for active service in the North West Territories, where a fierce rebellion was taking place, the Toronto *Globe* noted on April 1, 1885:

> ROUSING THE RANGERS
> A Midnight Assembly on the Bugle Call
> The Call Responded to Promptly
>
> The resonant tones of a bugle sounding assembly on Monday night, rousing many slumbering citizens in the northern, western and eastern parts of the city.

Later that month, fired by the massacre at Frog Lake, the men of the 92nd Battalion (Winnipeg Light Infantry) were among the many military units based at Calgary and preparing to march out to protect the scattered prairie settlements and hunt down Big Bear and his forces. The strident notes of the bugle band sounded reveille at half past four, and, breaking camp, they marched twenty-five miles their first day.

Following Confederation in 1867, Canadian militia units sprang up in every corner of the country. In the summer of 1873, the entire seven troops of the 8th Princess Louise's New Brunswick Hussars assembled in camp in Sussex. The camp, which ran for twelve days, was a tough grind, and the daily routine of soldiering at the time was documented by a young subaltern, Lieutenant H.R. Emberson, in a diary.

> When it got dark you could sit around the camp and you'd see row after rows of tents.... and every tent was like a little triangle of light. They used candles to light them. At ten o'clock you'd hear the bugles sound lights out...Then you'd hear the last post. Everybody would get quiet when the bugler played the last post. It's strange the sort of hush there is in that music. You'd always get a feeling way down inside when it came across the camp there in the night.

Before the Great War

In the annual Canadian militia department report for the year ending December 31, 1898, Major General Edward Hutton stated, "A good permanent band is much required which should form a Military School of Music for improving the existing militia bands...Its service should be available for public occasions in Ottawa and other cities of the Dominion." A year later he could report that such a band had been formed at the Royal Canadian Artillery Quebec Garrison and that its proficiency already warranted courses of instruction in military music for band sergeants and musicians belonging to bands of the active militia.

The Royal Canadian Artillery evolved from the two regular garrison batteries formed in 1871 and in earlier militia units. It was the first element of the Permanent Active Militia, better known as the Permanent Force, to have a full-time military band.

The bandmaster of the Royal Canadian Artillery Garrison Band was Joseph Vezina, who, although largely self taught, had studied harmony under Calixa Lavallée, the composer of "O' Canada." Joseph Vezina was to emerge as one of the great pioneers of Canadian band music and can be considered the father of military bands in the regular armed forces.

General Hutton's concerns for a permanent band were well founded. The comptroller for Governor General Lord Minto had frequently complained that "Their Highnesses were not satisfied with the quality of the music provided by the militia band."

The original establishment for the RCGA band was one bandmaster, one sergeant, one corporal and twenty-two bandsmen. Instrumentation, unfortunately, was not an exact science as yet, and the instrumental imbalance is obvious in a photograph from 1903 which shows one bandmaster, three clarinets, one alto sax, two alto horns, seven cornets, two trombones, two baritones and two drummers.

During its formative years the RCGA Band was often called upon to play concerts for troops at the various camp locations such as Valcartier and Petawawa. Each year they journeyed to Ottawa for numerous parades, concerts and garden parties. Under the guidance of Bandmaster Vezina and with the patronage of General Hutton, the band increased dramatically in size. By 1904, it had developed a suitable balanced instrumentation — one piccolo, one E-flat clarinet, eight B-flat clarinets, one bassoon, two alto horns, five cornets, three trombones, one baritone, two basses and three drummers.

By the time of the First World War the Permanent Force had two artillery bands — the RCA Garrison Band in Quebec and the Royal Canadian Horse Artillery Band, stationed in Kingston, Ontario. The

RCHA band had been established on October 23, 1905 with a complement of twenty-five including the Bandmaster. On December 1, 1905, General Order Number 280 authorized the band's formation.

Prior to 1905, the band had consisted of a small number of volunteers under the direction of Trumpet Major K. L. McKinnon. He worked most conscientiously during the band's first two years of official status to train and develop the RCHA Band. In 1908, it was decided to appoint a bandmaster from the Imperial Army, and Alfred Light, the Band Sergeant from the Royal Hampshire Regiment Band was selected. He took over in May of that year. The band in its early years became very popular in Eastern Canada for both its distinctive dress and high standard of music.

In 1910 the RCA band came under the direction of Bandmaster Charles O'Neill, a graduate of the Royal Military School of Music, Kneller Hall. It massed with the RCHA Band on various occasions. The practice had started with the inception of the RCHA Band and both bands were employed at various summer camps during training sessions of the Canadian Field Artillery. The original proposal had been that the bands perform alternately, but it was later decided that they should be massed for all their engagements, and there were often sixty musicians on parade or in concert.

I. S. C. BAND.

Infantry Corps School Band, Fredericton, NB, 1884. (*Provincial Archives of New Brunswick, P132-4*)

The first permanent infantry band to be established before the First World War was the Royal Canadian Regiment Band, officially recognized on June 21, 1905, in Halifax. The RCR had a long history of unofficial military bands beginning in 1884 when the School of Infantry was formed in Fredericton. Sergeant Charles Hayes was credited with forming the first band from 'A' Company the RCR. The band is shown in a photograph taken in 1885 with two clarinets, six cornets, two alto horns, one trombone, one baritone, two basses and two drummers.

Later, in 1888, a band was formed in London, Ontario, under Bandmaster Robert Fisher, and it became a prominent institution in London between 1888 and 1891.

In 1905, the Royal Garrison Regiment of the British Army was relieved by the RCR who took over garrison duties in Halifax. This action prompted the militia department to give careful consideration to the formation of a fully authorized military band. The authorization was approved on June 21, 1905, with an establishment of one bandmaster, one sergeant, one corporal and twenty-two musicians.

Michael Ryan, a native of Quebec City, was selected bandmaster. He had lived most of his earlier life in India and had become a band boy at the age of fifteen. Later he became a bandmaster and formed and trained the 3rd Battalion West Indies Regiment Band. In 1901, he took a six-month furlough and returned to Canada for a visit to Halifax. He was urged to take over the band while on leave and did so on a voluntary basis for the entire period of his leave. On the conclusion of his leave he returned to his unit, then stationed in Bermuda. In 1905, he retired from the British army and was invited to become the bandmaster of the RCR Band. He was appointed to the rank of Warrant Officer First Class. Ryan took over a very small group of untrained musicians and struggled along for several months with his ensemble. In 1906 he had a stroke of extremely good luck, and the band suddenly doubled in size. Thirty men from the Manchester Regiment in England came to Canada and this was known as the "Manchester Draft." This group of well-trained musicians constituted the nucleus of the RCR Band up to end of the First World War.

In 1908, the RCR Band, under the baton of Bandmaster Ryan, visited the Plains of Abraham at Quebec City to play with several hundred other musicians for a review of Canadian troops by the Prince of Wales, marking the Tercentenary of Quebec celebrations.

During this same year and the next the band performed at the Canadian National Exhibition, sharing the bandstand with the Winnipeg City Band. In 1911, the band was chosen to represent Canada at the Coronation of King George V, and, in honour of the occasion, Ryan was promoted to the rank of Honorary Lieutenant. A photograph of the band taken in 1909 at the Canadian National Exhibition indicates the depth of the instrumentation — two flutes, ten clarinets, two bassoons, seven cornets, two saxes, two trumpets, four horns, five trombones, two euphoniums, four basses and four percussionists.

The CNE in Toronto offered the permanent bands a splendid opportunity to perform in a concert atmosphere. The bands also were able to determine their musical standing by comparison with other bands that came from across Canada and Europe. Military band historian Fred Ashton said, "There were two main forms of activities involving bands during less than three weeks of operation of the CNE each year. Concerts were one form. Spectacles, such as tattoos or pageants in the old grandstand shows, were the other." Concerts by guest bands were a great feature for those who loved band music. Audiences could look forward to the performances in the band shell in the afternoon and evening. The visit of the Coldstream Guards Band, who performed for a week in 1903, drew crowds estimated at more than forty thousand. A photo of an afternoon concert shows a huge crowd surrounding the bandstand.

Reference has been made to the Quebec Tercentenary celebrations held in July 1908. The coordinator for all events was Joseph Vezina, former bandmaster of the RCGA Band. There were military parades and pageants, culminating with a grand review on the Plains of Abraham. Over fifteen thousand regular and militia personnel took part in this festivity. The massed bands numbered over five hundred, and no doubt this was the most colourful spectacle ever to take place in Canada up to that point in our history. It would be over fifty-nine years before a comparable military display appeared again, and that was the Canadian Forces Tattoo of 1967.

CHAPTER 2

Bands Before the First World War

Bands attached to reserve military units and made up entirely of part-time musicians came into existence because of the departure of the British garrisons prior to 1867 and Confederation.

The first military band in Hamilton was started in 1865 by the Independent Artillery Company. It had been a brass band known as the Sons of Temperance. The artillery band held together for several years but by the time the 13th Battalion was formed it had disappeared. It was restarted as the band of the 13th Battalion and Peter Grossman was appointed as Bandmaster, a position he held until he retired in 1869. The band then came under the baton of George Robinson, a graduate of Kneller Hall in England who had served with the Rifle Brigade in Canada. He took over the band in 1869 and held the position for the next half century. He developed it into one of the finest militia bands in Canada which would become the Royal Hamilton Light Infantry Band. Mr. Robinson would become the senior Bandmaster in Canada with a reputation as Canada's finest military bandmaster.

The Band of the Royal Regiment of Canada maintains the distinction of being the country's longest-serving band. On July 6, 1863, upon presentation of colours to the Royal Regiment, the unit also obtained a set of drums and instruments. The Royal Regiment performed an historical concert on July 1, 1867, at Queen's Park in Toronto as part of the ceremonies marking Confederation. Until February of 1888, when Captain John Waldron of Halifax was appointed to the position, the band had no regular bandmaster.

The most well-known and popular militia band in Canada was that of the 48th Highlanders, organized in 1892. Bandmaster John Griffin formed this band, however, in 1896, Captain John Slatter became the director, remaining so for fifty years. The band traveled extensively throughout

Governor General's Foot Guard Band, Parliament Buildings, Ottawa, 1872. (Public Archives Canada C-642)

Queen's Own Rifles Band, 1878, Conductor William Carey, seated, in civilian clothes. (Fred Ashton, Toronto)

Band of No. 5 Company, 41st Battalion 1869-70. (Public Archives of Canada C363)

Victoria Volunteer Rifle Corps Band, Victoria, BC, 1876. (Kopstein Collection)

Royal Canadian Regiment Band at the Western Fair, London, Ontario, 1899. (Kopstein Collection)

Canada and the United States playing at fairs and exhibitions. In Canada it played for a host of visiting dignitaries including the Prince of Wales and King George V. The 48th, the original kilted band in Canada, was the only band on the North American continent playing in full highland uniforms.

The Band of the Queen's Own Rifles was formed in Toronto in 1862 under the direction of Alfred Maul. In September 1879, Mr. John Bayley became leader, and under his direction the band rapidly gained international recognition, touring Canada from east to west, and charming "their way through the United States." In 1890, under G. L. Timpson, the band made a triumphal tour of England. Later, under the superb leader Captain R. B. Hayward, the band would capture many contests at the Canadian National Exhibition and establish itself as a first-rate militia band.

The Band of the Governor General's Foot Guards (GGFG) in Ottawa was formed in 1872 under J. Bonner. By 1900, the band had grown to thirty-five performers, and the director was Joseph Miller Brown, a world famous cornetist. The band made its first trip to the United States in 1906 when it visited New York City. In 1909 the band performed for the Champlain Tercentenary and was inspected by the American President William Howard Taft.

Among the early militia bands associated with Quebec was the Band of the 9th Battalion Rifles "Voltigeurs" in Quebec organized and trained by the eminent Quebec bandmaster George Vezina in 1869. Another Quebec

Royal Marines Band with the Westminster Rifle Company behind, Vancouver, BC, July 1887. (Public Archives of Canada C11726)

34th Battalion Band, Oshawa, 1892. (Mr. Wilf Anthony, Oshawa, Ontario)

The Halifax Garrison Artillery Band, 1895. (The Royal Canadian Artillery (RCA) Museum, Shilo, Manitoba)

43rd Regiment Band, Burlington, Vermont, 1903. (Ed Hall, Ottawa)

band of distinction was that of the 'B' Battery of the Canadian artillery that Mr. Vezina led from 1879 to 1910. The 'B' Battery band, which was called the Royal Canadian Garrison Artillery Band, comprised many professionally trained musicians from France and England. Eventually this band became the first permanent military band in Canada.

The City of Winnipeg has a long tradition of bands and bandsmen. The Ontario Rifles, who came to Winnipeg with Wolseley during the Red River troubles of 1869, brought musicians who were the nucleus of the first military band in Winnipeg. The Royal Winnipeg Rifles had a band in 1901 under the leadership of Fred Sandford, and the Winnipeg Light Infantry Band was formed in 1912.

This letter shows that there were financial hazards in sponsoring a band:

To the Officers
Governor General's Foot Guards
Ottawa, Ontario

Gentlemen,
It is the first time in our experience that we have to write a dozen times to Officers in Her Majesty's service for payment of a debt which they cannot and do not dispute. The instruments for which this debt (40/9/6

15th Light Horse Band with the Irish Guards Band, 1904. (Glenbow Archives Canada NA 3063-3)

plus 14/7/6 interest) was incurred have been, and as far as we know, are now actually in use in the band.

Besson & Co. Ltd.
London, England

Following Confederation in Canada in 1967, most militia units made the decision to raise regimental bands. As in Britain the financial burden of having a band was the responsibility of the regimental officers, who were duty bound to provide subscriptions for the purchase of instruments, music and accessories. When this particular issue of payment was resolved is a matter of conjecture. However, since no payment date is documented in the file, it can be concluded that Besson & Co. did finally receive payment for this overdue account.

The Band of the New Brunswick Regiment of Fencible Infantry (1803-1810) would later become known as the 104th (New Brunswick) Regiment of Foot (1810-1817) and finally the New Brunswick Fencibles (1813-1816). They are mentioned as early as 1805 in a letter by Mrs. Hunter. Describing the arrival of recruits from Upper Canada she wrote "they sounded bugles, had the band, fifes and drums." The Fencibles Band had two drummers for each company and the Grenadier Company had twenty drummers and two fifers. The band, it appears, had made quite a name for itself in 1807 as the New Brunswick Assembly decided to honour the group with the purchase of a silver trumpet.

Royal Canadian Regiment Band, Captain M. Ryan, Director of Music. Halifax, NS, 1911. (Public Archives Canada PA28468)

103rd Regiment (Calgary Rifles) Band church parade, Calgary, Alberta, May 4th, 1913. (Alberta Archives NA 2621-2)

Royal Canadian Horse Artillery Band, Petawawa, Ontario, 1909. (RCA Museum, Shilo, Manitoba)

59th Battalion Band, Peterborough, Ontario. (Peterborough Museum and Archives)

Band of the 34th Battalion, Whitby, Ontario, 1880. (Public Archives of Canada C27419)

A most interesting view of bands of the time is provided by the New Brunswick Museum in an engraving from 1860. It depicts the arrival of the Prince of Wales on August 2, 1860 at Saint John harbour alighting to a mounted guard of honour accompanied by a band. The instruments depicted in this drawing were of the American Civil War style with over the shoulder bass and baritone instruments and keyed bugles.

Another engraving from the late 1880s reveals the band had increased in size and had taken on the look of a brass band with four cornets, a mellophone, four alto horns, two baritones, two basses and three drums. Using the engravings and regimental histories the band would be identified as the forerunners of the 8th Canadian Hussars.

F. S. Meighen of Montreal, a patron of the arts and later a general in the Canadian Army, was responsible for the organization of the Band of the Canadian Grenadier Guards. This band was founded on April 26, 1913, under the distinguished musician and bandmaster J. J. Gagnier. The band

Captain Charles O'Neill, Royal 22e Regiment. (Jacques Gauthier)

was made up of many professional and semi-professional musicians and was formed with the intention of accompanying the troops on parade and for mess dinners. However, the band is best remembered as a concert band. Under Mr. Gagnier's capable leadership, the band earned for itself international renown both in concert hall and in recordings.

The Canadian Grenadier Guards band was somewhat of a family affair in its formative years. Amongst the member musicians were several Gagniers. They included Lucien (flute), Aland (bassoon), Armand (clarinet), Guillaume (French horn), Ernest (French horn) and René (euphonium).

Many of the British military musicians remained in Canada when the troops departed, taking their retirement in the New World. Other bandsmen returned after completing their service in the army. The influence of these military musicians helped to nurture the military band movement in Canada. Their expertise helped to maintain further cultural activity.

13th Regiment Band, Quebec City, Quebec, July 1908. (Public Archives of Canada: PA 24755)

91st Regiment, Canadian Highlanders, Hamilton, Ontario, 1907. (Pearson Collection)

13th Regiment, Dundurn Castle, Hamilton, Ontario, 1901. (Royal Hamilton Light Infantry)

34th Battalion Band, circa 1900. (Robert McLaughlan Gallery, Thomas Buckley Collection 2245)

CHAPTER 3

The Great War
1914–1918

At the beginning of the First World War in 1914, the Canadian Army's strength stood at thirty-one hundred members. Within a few months over thirty-two thousand volunteers had stepped forward to serve Canada in this conflict. Although the war establishment had no provision for regimental bands during the organization of the first Canadian contingent to go overseas, many of the units unofficially formed their own bands.

The permanent militia supplied three of the kilted battalions, the 13th, 15th and 16th with pipe bands. The entire City of Edmonton Pipe Band volunteered to serve with the Princess Patricia's Canadian Light Infantry and was accepted. Traditionally, the only musicians allowed were the six pipers of the Highland Regiments but by the time the Canadian Expeditionary Force (CEF) was ready to sail, many battalions had received permission to take their bands overseas. In November 1914, in an option granted by the Minister of Militia and Defence, Sir Sam Hughes, the establishment of every CEF battalion was increased by one bandmaster and twenty-four men. The option was exercised by many units.

While the CEF contingent assembled at Camp Valcartier, both permanent artillery bands, the RCHA and RCGA, played through the lines. A number of RCHA musicians had made application to serve overseas in the firing lines, and the Commander of Military District No. 3 in Kingston promptly replied by advising the bandmaster, Captain Light, "You will kindly point out to these men that their patriotism in volunteering for active service has been noted and is much appreciated. The authorities, however, consider their services are of more value to the Empire in their present appointments. It has been estimated that one hundred men have been enlisted for, and through the music of, each bandsman retained at home."

Royal Newfoundland Regiment Band, England, 1914. (Kopstein Collection)

Once the CEF had landed in England and taken up residence on Salisbury Plain the problem of what to do with men under training became a matter of great concern to commanding officers. There was a good deal of sports and games during daylight hours to keep the men occupied, but it was difficult to find entertainment in the hours between dinner and First Post or Lights Out. The decision to begin concert programs was taken and this proved to be a very successful outlet for the men under training. It was also an incentive for musicians and bands to perform for live audiences.

The 76th Overseas Battalion had been given authority to raise a band for overseas service and on July 30, 1915, the band began accepting volunteers. The bandmaster was Arthur Wellesley Hughes, a very well known musician and composer of marches. Bandmaster Hughes worked extremely hard as described in this extract from the historical record of the 76th Band:

> Hughes began work with the band long before reveille until, with words horrible dictu, long after retreat. Yet day by day we all felt that a brighter tone, a more lilting tune, a snappier cadence was given by *OUR BAND* and after several overtures, marches, selections had been given at concerts, at least the chrysalis of immaturity was broken in fuller life and splendid vigour with harmony resonance and interpretation. The Battalion constantly burst itself in cheering and applause, as it realized what a band means to the Battalion.

44

The Queen's Own Rifles Band experienced manpower problems during the war, and the conductor, H. Barrow, worked under great pressure to carry on his commitments. The band was constantly disrupted by men going into active service. Many of the militia bands were called out on a moment's notice to provide marching music for volunteers heading for overseas duty.

On August 22nd, 1914, the GGFG Band led the first contingent to Union Station in Ottawa. This band was unique in that it was able to maintain a strong militia-band representation throughout the war. This was due to the fact that a number of musicians in the band were older, unable to enlist and thus could turn out for special occasions. As well, many of the musicians worked for the Department of Militia, and as civil servants they were needed in Ottawa to support the war effort.

The Winnipeg Grenadiers Band was also able to maintain a very good band with a balanced instrumentation during the war. During 1915 and 1916, they appeared on numerous parades and concerts in Manitoba with a thirty-three-piece band comprised of one flute, ten clarinets, two saxes, five trumpets, four horns, three trombones, one bassoon, two euphonium, two basses and three drums. Sam Barraclough, one of Winnipeg's most renowned band directors, was leader of the 90th Regiment Band in 1916. The 144th Band was led by Charles Newman. In 1917, after the Americans had entered the war, the Winnipeg Grenadiers toured the Minnesota Iron Range to spur the miners to a greater war effort.

82nd Battalion Band CEF, Calgary, 1915. (Glenbow Archives NA 3877-3)

76th Battalion Band, CEF, Niagara Camp October 21st, 1915. Bandmaster is A.W. Hughes. (Kopstein Collection)

45th Battalion Band, France, 1918. Bandmaster is H.A. Gray. (Glenbow Archives NA1507-6)

In the spring of 1916, the government secured a large tract of land near Barrie, Ontario, on the Angus Plain, and created Camp Borden. By the summer of 1916 there were over forty thousand soldiers under canvas in this area, which soon became known as the Dust Bowl. The concentration of white tents was considered spectacular. In the calm of the evening the bands throughout the camp would play their regimental marches followed by Last Post, first it would be sounded by the headquarter's bugler and then taken up, one after another, by the battalion buglers until it died away in the still night air.

A description of the first tattoo held in Camp Borden on August 16, 1916, appeared in the *Orillia Packet*:

As darkness gathered, the different regimental bands stood ready to move, each accompanied by torch bearers. At the proper signal, when the appointed time arrived, these bands moved out into place, the torches shining out against the darkness, and the band itself playing in each case its own regimental march. As each new band approached the assembly ground the bands already in position took up the march of the newcomer. The result of this was gradually to increase the volume of sound, so that when the last of the twenty-eight bands marched forward, the effect was very marked.

The article went on to say:

The bands began by playing "O' Canada" and followed that with "We'll Never Let The Old Flag Fall" and it was not quite easy to analyze the well of emotion which swept over the throng...In the second part of the program, the playing by twenty-eight bands of "Keep The Home Fires Burning" brought out the love of home in these men, whose faces are turned towards the east and toward the day of battle...But perhaps the most emotional part of the program was the rendering of "Abide With Me." At this time the evening glow had died out of the west and the deep blue sky above our heads, dotted with bright stars, was the stately roof of our open air cathedral. All the torches except four were put out, the band played the air, and then for the second verse the men's voices carried the words. The effect of it all was very impressive.

The Royal Canadian Regiment Band, France, 1916. Conductor is Lieutenant Jones. (Public Archives of Canada 3576-16)

South Alberta Light Horse, 1918. (Glenbow Archives)

Canadian Army Massed Bands, Canadian National Exhibition, August, 1916. (Kopstein Collection)

The Musical Director at Camp Borden was Captain John Slatter, Supervisor of Bands and Buglers. Captain Slatter was the Director of the 48th Highlanders and was second only in seniority to Captain George Robinson of the 13th Royal Regiment Band (later Royal Hamilton Light Infantry). Captain Slatter trained sixty-three bands in Camp Borden during the war, and his contribution earned for him the Order of the British Empire.

Captain Slatter helped to arrange a massed band concert at the CNE in August 1916, and a large photograph was recently unearthed showing a lineup of bandmasters and each of the bands in formation. In 1914, Captain Slatter also contributed orders and special regulations for bandmasters and musicians in the ninth edition of the *Guide for Canadian Militia*, the manual for Canadian Infantry compiled by Major General Otter.

BANDMASTER

1. The bandmaster should be the sole instructor of the band, subject only to the directions of the Commanding Officer and Band Committee President; no other should interfere in the practice or public playing of the band.
2. The Bandmaster should make such suggestions to the President of the Band Committee as he may consider beneficial to the band, with a view to their being forwarded to the Commanding Officer.
3. He should have charge of the clothing, appointments, music and instruments, being responsible to the committee for their safe keeping. He should inspect the instruments at regular intervals, reporting to the President whenever an instrument is broken or out of order and be particular in the care of the music, not permitting any copies of it to be taken without the special sanction of the Commanding Officer. He should have a Sergeant to assist him.

The daily pay for the bandmaster if he was a Warrant Officer was $1.75. However, if he was an Acting Warrant his stipend was $1.50.

The regulations for bands on parade were very carefully outlined in General Otter's guide and some of the information is worth quoting:

1. No Battalion, except when ordered to contrary should march past to any other than its own.
2. No band when marching by itself and unaccompanied by troops will play.
3. When the brigade marches past, the bands should be brigaded under the senior bandmaster and play the particular air belonging to each battalion as it passes the saluting point, or if specially ordered the same air for all.

191st Battalion Band CEF, 1916. (Glenbow Archives NA 3057-2)

116th Q. O. R. Battalion Band, 1917. (Kopstein Collection)

Similarly the orders for bandsmen were very detailed and gave very little room for manipulation:

1. Whenever the band is ordered to play at mess or any public assembly, it should be properly dressed.
2. No bandsmen should engage to play in uniform without the consent of the President of the Band Committee, and the band should not play in uniform without the consent of the Commanding Officer.
3. A bandsman habitually misbehaving should be sent to his duty in the rank, as the band must be necessarily composed of well conducted men.

In 1914, the Royal Canadian Regiment was detailed for duty in Bermuda to relieve the Duke of Cornwall's Light Infantry, a British regi-

Royal Canadian Horse Artillery Band, Victory Bond Drive, Ottawa, Ontario, 1918. (Kopstein Collection)

ment which returned to England for war mobilization. The regimental band accompanied the troops to Bermuda under Bandmaster Michael Ryan.

The unit returned to Canada in August 1915 and remained in Halifax for only one week prior to sailing for Europe on August 26, 1915. On the twenty-third of August the band gave a farewell performance to the citizens of Halifax, and the concert drew a capacity crowd. The Halifax *Herald* described the band's performance as a "Crowd Pleaser" with standing ovations and encores throughout the musical evening.

In France, by 1916, every infantry battalion in the Canadian Corps had at least one band. Some of the engineers and pioneers also had bands, as did the Divisional Headquarters. These bands played for the troops in and out of the trenches, performed at concerts and occasionally went on tour. Massed bands, especially massed pipe bands, played on ceremonial occasions.

The Honour Roll for the First World War shows that numerous musicians who transferred from their respective bands to the CEF were killed or wounded in action. Many received decorations for their gallant actions. The highest award in the Commonwealth, the Victoria Cross, was posthumously awarded to Walter Lloyd Algie, a euphonium player in the 48th

7th Canadian Infantry Battalion (British Columbia Regiment Band), July, 1918. (Public Archives of Canada PA 2835)

Highlanders Band. Many others were mentioned in dispatches and received merit awards. The RCR Band was mentioned in the following dispatch taken from official sources:

> From about 2:30 on, the German Artillery devoted itself to an intense bombardment of the captured position, with the heaviest weight of fire being concentrated on Mount Sorrel itself and on the original Canadian line. The woods and trenches were continuously rocketed with shrapnel and high explosive and many casualties resulted. All through the night the regimental band under Sergeant Young displayed great devotion in carrying wounded men to the rear.

On the home front, the RCGA band was kept extremely busy and was often ordered to various locations to assist with recruiting campaigns. The band was the subject of much newspaper coverage, such as this from the Montreal *Star* of August 16, 1916: "The band of the Royal Canadian Garrison Artillery, stationed at the Citadel in Quebec City, is justly known as one of the best bands in North America. Its repertoire is remarkable and it is doubtful if a more diversified series of programs is given by any other band in the country." The article went on to describe the affection held for the band with the unofficial title of State Band because of its numerous ceremonial appearances in Ottawa. Charles O'Neill was mentioned prominently in this article.

The reaction to the declaration of war in Europe was reflected in newspaper accounts of that era. The London *Free Press* reported on August 5, 1914, that all western Ontario was stirred by the news that Canada had joined the melee in Europe. "The streets were in a turmoil for hours after the fateful announcement and at 10:40 enthusiasts in London started a procession on Richmond Street, with four Union Jacks and a trombone player from the 7th Regiment Band as a basis and it soon became a big parade, with shouting and singing down the streets. An eyewitness account in the Toronto *Globe* of August 6, 1914, said: "I shall always remember the night the war was declared. We all went down to the armouries. We were there in the hundreds. The 48th Band came out and played 'Rule Britannia' and that was the spark that ignited the whole thing."

Scenes of men marching off to combat were repeated over and over during the months of the war. These sad moments were described in very emotional and poignant terms and always accompanied by mention of patriotic airs. Colonel Francis Ware, the diarist of the 7th Regiment in London, recounts the Regiment parading to the station, the troops marching up Dundas Street between lines of cheering citizens with the band playing "The Maple Leaf Forever." "And far ahead we could hear the shouts of 'Here They Come' from the crowd," he said. Later, at the railway station, the troops quickly entrained and the band played the national anthems "O Canada" and "God Save The Queen." The train pulled out with everyone striving through misty eyes to catch the last glimpse of their loved ones.

182nd Battalion Band, Camp Niagara, 1916. (Town of Whitby Archives 29-002-021)

146th Battalion Band, Niagara Falls, April 1917. (The Oshawa Community Archives A978.23)

It was an exciting time for Canadians. Few could resist the call to the colours, and Canadian bands helped to foster the spirit of loyalty and patriotism by performing rousing national airs and thrilling marches. Canadian poet, Richard LeGallienne, in his poem "War" captured the sombre spirit of music against a backdrop of death and destruction.

> War I abhor, and yet how sweet
> The sound along the marching Street
> Of drum and fife, and I forget
> Wet eyes of Widows, and forget
> Broken old mothers, and the whole
> Dark butchery without a soul.

A Bell Telephone Company employee named Bert Remington described his war experience in the book, *The Great War and Canadian Society*. Remington was a Boy Scout bugler in Montreal who decided to try to enlist as a bugler in the army in 1914. He said, "When the war broke out you cannot believe it unless you were there. Everyone wanted to be a hero." After joining, Remington was sent to the tent city in Valcartier. At Valcartier, he said, "there was nothing but field and bush and it was cold, it was frost on the ground, and they said 'We'll blow fall in' and I said 'C-C-can't blow anything.' I was so cold I couldn't talk."

There was no doubt that Bugler Remington's troubles were just beginning, because as a bugler he was required to play reveille, the soldier's wake-up call. E. C. Russel, in his book, *Customs and Traditions in the Canadian Forces* said, "It is a rare individual who really enjoys getting up in the morning, particularly when he is being coerced into getting out of bed by some insistent jarring noise." This, says Russel, led Irving Berlin to

12th Mounted Rifles Brass Band, Calgary, Alberta, 1915. (Public Archives of Canada NA 2881-5)

59th Battalion Band, June 1917. (Peterborough Museum and Archives)

write a song with the title, "Some Day I'm Going To Murder The Bugler (Oh How I Hate To Get Up In The Morning)."

When war came in August 1914, the colony of Newfoundland undertook to enlist five-hundred men for overseas duty. On August 21, a proclamation was issued and men began volunteering for service with the 1st Newfoundland Regiment. Following their training the contingent departed for England and Salisbury Plain. On arrival, a bugle band was formed. In October 1914, the regiment was dispatched to the Mediterranean and joined the Gallipoli Expeditionary Force. The regiment sustained heavy shelling in their first encounter with the Turks and one of the casualties was the loss of the band's bugles and drums on the beach. The instruments had been piled in a gully, and when the band returned to claim their instruments the next day it was discovered that "an unmusical Turkish shell" had silenced them forever.

In January 1916, the Newfoundland Regiment was urged to form a military band and it was organized under the direction of L. L. Worthington. Mr. Worthington was the former bandmaster of the 1st Battalion King's Regiment of Liverpool. After a long service in the British army he came to Newfoundland and became the director of the Newfoundland Ayr Burgh Band. When he was invited to return to active service, he brought with him a number of musicians from the Ayr Burgh Band. Bandmaster Worthington was awarded the Royal Victorian Order for his contribution as bandmaster to the Newfoundland Regiment. Bandmaster Worthington was also responsible for arranging the folk tune, "The Banks of Newfoundland" as a regimental march, and the effect of this march on the Newfoundland troops was enormous. The troops responded on every occasion that it was performed, and the impact of the song was truly one of the most amazing results of the war.

The Regimental Band was invited to London from France during the summer of 1917 for Newfoundland Week. This occasion was to honour Newfoundland for her war effort. The band, under the direction of Warrant Officer Worthington, appeared in numerous concerts all around London, including one in Hyde Park where ten thousand enthusiastic spectators greeted every one of their selections with a spirited applause. They also appeared in a gala formal concert where they played a variety of both national and patriotic airs as well as many special numbers from their repertoire.

208th Canadian Infantry Battalion, The Irish Canadians. Milford, Surrey WW1. (Scugog Shores Historical Museum, Port Perry, Ontario)

A survey of bands from the Calgary area showed at least nine bands originating from that city during the war. The Calgary Regiment Band was formed by Sergeant Tommy James with a new set of band instruments. These were destroyed, however, when an explosion rocked their headquarters just after their arrival in France. The 12th Canadian Mounted Rifles Band was formed in 1914, mostly of musicians from Calgary and various locations in British Columbia. The bandmaster was Sergeant G. Goodwin.

In the fall of 1918, the RCGA Band and the RCHA Band were the only permanent prewar bands still operational in Canada. It was, therefore, with utter shock and disbelief that Lieutenant-Colonel Jameson, the commanding officer of the depot which regulated the band's activities, received a communication that the RCGA Band had volunteered its services for the Canadian Expeditionary Force to Siberia. His response was to describe to the commanding officer of the Royal Canadian Artillery the state of the band at that time. Most of the men, including Bandmaster Charles O'Neill, were unable to be employed in anything other than limited service due to medical restrictions or other factors. He also mentioned several upcoming engagements for which the band was committed.

The matter appeared to be resolved until a cable arrived at Kingston HQ from the Adjutant General's Office for Military District 5 suggesting that sending the RCGA Band to Russia would be a good move "both as it is a Permanent Force Band and for Propaganda purposes." Perhaps when he responded to the cable, the commanding officer of the RCA had in mind that regular army units had suffered an identity crisis throughout the war because of the practice of distinguishing Canadian regiments and battalions by numbers rather than by name. Also, under the Militia Act regular members of Canada's small standing army did not have to serve overseas unless they volunteered. Many, such as the RCR Band, did agree to serve as a unit and remained with their parent unit overseas. The units that remained in Canada on standby were very often undermanned and had difficulty in maintaining their identity.

The RCA commanding officer's response included the following: "What safeguard do you propose extracting from CEF, Siberia, that band will retain its identity and be known throughout the CEF as the RCA Band."

Colonel Jameson, now armed with some support for his position, began a strong offensive of his own. He said,

> The strength of the band is thirty-one, of whom five are in hospital and three struck off. The band is mostly low category, and there are five who should not go even if their keenness is greater than their physical condition. Therefore should it be considered advisable for the band to go as

Canadian Expeditionary Force Band, Siberia, 1918. (Public Archives of Canada C 91705)

representative of the Permanent Force, I would recommend it going with the Siberian Expeditionary Force, but respectively with the following provisos: That it should not lose its identity, but continue to be known, as at present, the Royal Canadian Garrison Artillery Band. It should be a Headquarters band and not be attached to or form part of any other unit.

It was finally decided to allow individual volunteers from the RCGA Band who were physically fit to join the 259th Battalion Canadian Rifles CEF Sibera, with, however, "no intention of earmarking these men RCGA Band."

Correspondence connected with the volunteers for the 259th Band seems to have petered out, and the file was closed. As a footnote and in retrospect, no individual members of the band volunteered for service in Siberia. The fact that the Adjutant General did not guarantee replacements certainly mitigated against them leaving to join the 259th Band. The future of the band could have been jeopardized and this damaging effect to their numbers would have certainly materialized in 1922 when the Royal 22e Regiment Band was organized from the ranks of the RCGA band.

58

CHAPTER 4

Between the Wars

In between the wars, bands, like the rest of the military service in Canada, were restricted by the shortage of funds. Band grants were denied to bands of the Permanent Active Militia who desired them and who under normal conditions would have been entitled to them. By 1928, there were four authorized bands in the Permanent Force and one hundred and twenty-five militia bands. In the Regular Force it was often necessary for bandsmen to carry out military chores to free as many men for training as possible.

One of the most serious questions facing both the bandmaster and the officers, who administered the band was how to maintain the strength of the band in manpower and instrumentation. Serious efforts had been made prior to the First World War to increase the size of the existing bands with minimum effect. Following the war, various suggestions, such as having bandmasters go to England or placing advertisements in newspapers across Canada, were made, but they were not very successful. When the Prince of Wales visited Canada in late July 1919, the lack of musicians became even more exasperating. The RCHA Band was selected to play for his arrival, and because of the shortage of musicians the ceremonies were in jeopardy. The following angrily-worded letter was forwarded to the Militia Council:

> I beg to enclose herewith a copy of a request formulated by the Officer Commanding RCGA (Quebec) after an interview between that officer and the General Officer Commanding No. 5 Military District, in which it is stated that the RCGA Band must be up to strength on the occasion of HRH The Prince of Wales visit to Quebec. It appears to be quite clear that the difficulties recruiting bandsmen is not understood, and in this connection should you decide that the RCHA Band be drawn upon to reinforce the RCGA Band for that special occasion, I beg to state that the

RCHA Band can only furnish the following players: trombone, euphonium, 1st cornet, 2nd cornet, 1st clarinet, 2nd clarinet.

Despite repeated requests to allow bandmasters to hire musicians in Europe and elsewhere the conditions, described as "deplorable" continued, and the permission to install an interchange of musicians was granted.

Charles O'Neill's efforts to enlist musicians in Toronto and Montreal brought forth three men in 1920, but the RCGA Band languished for nearly two years, unable to appear in public because of a lack of proper instrumentation. The band never returned to its previous excellence and it was only through the transition to the Royal 22e Regiment in 1922 that it was totally revitalized.

When the Royal Canadian Regiment returned from active service in 1919 and took up residence in Halifax, it also discovered that very few musicians were available. Bandmaster Michael Ryan was faced with the same problem as his colleagues in the other bands. He was unable to recruit musicians in the United Kingdom as the government would not pay relocation expenses.

In 1920 the band was transferred to London with a very small remnant of the prewar band totaling only fourteen musicians. Bandmaster Ryan demonstrated his initiative by requesting a grant of $500 from the regiment's canteen committee to bring a few good musicians back with them from England. The terms were simple, the musicians had to stay in the regiment for two years and pay back the cost of transporting themselves from England.

The competition for jobs after the advertisement was circulated in newspapers and trade magazines was astonishing. Over one hundred bandsmen applied, and Mr. Ryan, very shrewdly, selected musicians with staff band experience or well-known line band background. The process employed by Ryan was later to prove to be an important milestone in the progress of the RCR Band, raising the standard of the band immeasurably. He also was able to get a band grant to purchase instruments in England and both instruments and men began arriving in Canada in the spring of 1921.

One of the particular highlights of the Royal Canadian Regiment Band was its attendance at ceremonies dedicating the Cross of Sacrifice at Arlington National Cemetery in Washington, D.C., in November 1927. The Cross was erected by the Canadian government to honour Americans who had served in the Canadian forces during the Great War.

Captain Ryan. (Kopstein Collection)

With the establishment of the peacetime army, the Princess Patricia's Canadian Light Infantry, became one of Canada's most illustrious wartime units. The PPCLI Band was officially approved as a unit of the regiment in March 1919, and Lieutenant Thomas (Tommy) William James was given the responsibility of enlisting bandsmen and training the band. James was qualified for both these undertakings, although there were other applicants. Having been one of the originators of the Calgary Regiment Band during the war, James won the bandmaster's job and immediately became a magnet, attracting a group of very highly qualified musicians. In 1920, the band moved to Winnipeg. In 1924 it appeared at the British Empire Games and gave a series of sold-out concerts at various London theaters and a broadcast from Savoy Hill Radio Station, at the time one of the largest broadcast studios in Europe.

On its return to Canada, the band was honoured by a visit from the distinguished composer Serge Rachmaninoff, who conducted it through a transcription of his "Prelude in C-flat Minor," pronouncing great pleasure at their superb rendition.

The band toured extensively throughout the American Midwest and the Prairie provinces, often playing at the grandstand shows of Class 'A' fairs. This brought about some difficulty with the Saskatoon Musicians Association in 1932. The secretary of that union wrote to his provincial Member of Parliament complaining that local musicians were being eliminated from professional employment by the band. "It is extremely difficult to understand," he said, "why our Department of National Defence will allow bands under its control to offer the unfair competition of which we are complaining."

Princess Patricia's Canadian Light Infantry Band, Winnipeg, Manitoba, 1921. Director of Music is Lieutenant T. W. James. (Kopstein Collection, W. R. Stephens)

Captain Tommy James, PPCLI Band, 1921. (Kopstein Collection, WR Stephens)

Royal 22e Régiment Band, The Citadel, Quebec City, 1924. (Kopstein Collection)

In the end, it was decided that, since the Fair organization had originally approached the band to appear, and the contract had already been
signed, the Department would not permit a breach of the contract. It was
also determined that since no local musicians would have been hired for
the special grandstand performance, no local musicians were, in fact,
deprived of employment.

In the final analysis, the Permanent Force musicians had indeed created
a condition of unfair employment. It must be remembered, of course, that
in 1932 the nation was in depths of the Depression and union militancy
was just beginning to surface. In order to establish a future conduct for
service musicians, a King's Regulation was drafted and approved which,
having stood the test of time, is embodied today in the Canadian Forces
Administration Order 32-1.

The PPCLI Band under Captain James was comprised mainly of sea-
soned British army musicians and a few Canadian bandsmen. The band
reached its pinnacle during the 1930s giving as many as fifty free concerts
per year and playing cross-Canada radio broadcasts. Captain James
retired in 1939 and the band was taken over by another British army
bandmaster, WO1 Len Streeter. His leadership lasted only a few months
with one grand concert in Winnipeg. In September 1939 the war in
Europe began, and fifteen band members signed the pink slip to volunteer
for overseas service.

The Regimental Band of the Royal 22e Regiment was the last Permanent Force band to be formed in between the wars. On April 1, 1920, the R22R had been officially recognized as a unit of the Permanent Force, and one of its immediate concerns was the formation of a band. Unfortunately, several requests to the Military District brought the answer that the budget did not permit the formation of a band. The only concession was permission to employ the RCGA Band on certain occasions — if it was available.

The Commanding Officer, Lieutenant Colonel Chasse, was resolute in his desire to have his own military band, and stated his views in a tersely worded note to No. 5 Military District:

> I am in command of 229 soldiers and I consider it to be essential for esprit de corps and the fellowship of soldiering that permission be granted to form a band. The men need the diversion from the monotony of the every day rigours of the soldier's life. They are able now only to go to the library, the canteen and the gymnasium and they desperately need the inspiration that only the music of a military band can provide.

Lieutenant Colonel Chasse finally realized his dream in the summer of 1922, when the defence department agreed that the new regiment should have a band. It was created by the fact that the Royal Canadian Garrison Artillery, which had been stationed in Quebec since 1871, would join the

The Coronation Band, 1937, Captain O'Neill, Conductor. Selected musicians are from RCR, PPCLI, R22R, RCHA. (Kopstein Collection)

Canadian Expeditionary Band with troops from the Dominions parading through London, May 3, 1919. (Public Archives of Canada PA 6194)

Battery in Kingston. This opened the way for the RCGA Band to be transferred to the R22R. Authority was granted to raise the band establishment to thirty men, and Captain Charles O'Neill was appointed as Director of Music. The R22R Band absorbed all of the RCGA Band's equipment, music, and most of its personnel.

From the moment of its inception, the R22R Band attained a popularity that continued for over six decades. It appeared frequently in Quebec City and Montreal, and in November 1923, played a concert at the Orpheum Theatre which was broadcast on CKAC, an early radio station. This concert was picked up as far away as California and Texas. It was an unqualified success, and Captain O'Neill received many complimentary letters and telegrams. The band appeared at the CNE in Toronto in 1927 and in a tattoo with the RCR and RCHA in 1930. In 1931, the band inaugurated the CPR Radio System from the Chateau Frontenac in Quebec City.

The band maintained a fully balanced instrumentation which included thirty-five musicians: a leader, one flute, one oboe, one E-flat clarinet, ten B-flat clarinets, two saxophones, three horns, one bassoon, three cornets, two trumpets, three trombones, two euphoniums, two tubas, one string bass and two percussionists.

Regina Regimental Band, October 4th, 1919.

In the summer of 1936, the band performed throughout the arrival of President Franklin Roosevelt, and in 1937, Captain O'Neill was given the task of selecting and training a composite band of Permanent Force musicians for the coronation of King George VI in London, England. He visited all Permanent Force bands to select the best possible musicians, as well as to have representation from all the regular units in Canada. Rehearsals began in April with twelve musicians from the RCR, nine from the PPCLI, one from the RCHA and twelve from the R22R. Prior to their departure, the band gave a charity concert at the Capitol Theatre. On May 18, 1937, the band led the Canadian contingent through the streets of London to a deafening applause. It received many plaudits from the British press, who were often stingy in their praise of foreign bands. In later years, Captain O'Neill would remark that the composite band was the most professional musical ensemble that he had had the privilege of conducting. He also noted that he was amazed at how easily the musicians developed a fondness for one another and how well they worked together as a team.

The patriotism felt by many Canadians lingered long after the Great War, particularly in war veterans, who maintained a watchdog image.

In September, 1921, the Department of Militia received a letter from a Mr. A. Hewson of Hamilton, describing having seen the 13th Regiment Band on the streets of Hamilton advertising a sale of goods. He characterized the situation as "absurd and humiliating" and went on to say, "not only were they riding on a truck in the King's uniform, but they were play-

10th Battalion Brass Band, Calgary Highlanders, 1920s. (Public Archives of Canada NA 3311-14)

ing Jazz. I am disgusted to say the least and their conduct in my opinion is prejudicial to the good order and conduct of the Army."

The letter caused a great deal of consternation. The minister's private secretary passed his comments to the Chief of Staff, and the letter, with minuted personal observations, wended its way through Defence Headquarters. Almost coincidentally, a very similar incident took place right under the noses of department officials. The Governor General's Foot Guards were spotted on the main streets of Ottawa in full dress on a truck advertising a Mary Pickford movie. As a result, the Adjutant General circulated a letter reminding all concerned that "close supervision must be kept over band engagements with a view to preventing episodes such as the above described which only tend to belittle and injure the Canadian Militia."

Canadian Militia units had been reorganizing as early as 1919. The Royal Regiment of Canada reactivated its band in 1921 under Bandmaster, Warrant Officer Harold Bromby, who had recalled former band members and begun rebuilding the band to its prewar strength. He left in 1926, and Lieutenant Walter M. Murdock was appointed Director of Music. Under Lieutenant Murdock's guidance the band numbers and efficiency improved rapidly and that same year the unit won the Dominion Championship for Class A Bands at the CNE. The 1926 triumph was duplicated every year from 1926 to 1931 until the contest was abandoned for want of competitors. In the decade that followed, many honours were bestowed upon the sixty-member Royal Regiment Band. The band performed a gala concert in Massey Hall in Toronto that was the dawn of a new era as the Royals were the first band to perform in this Canadian institution.

The band played for the opening of Maple Leaf Gardens on November 12th, 1931, ushering in an association between the Gardens and Toronto militia bands that lasted well on into the 1950s. On the one hundredth anniversary of the incorporation of the City of Toronto in 1933, a memorial was held in the Coliseum, and a chorus of over two thousand five hundred voices joined the band for the event. The program ended triumphantly with the performance of the "Hallelujah Chorus" by Handel.

Following the war, the Queen's Own Rifles Band continued to earn a unique reputation as one of Canada's finest military concert bands. In 1921, Captain R. B. Hayward was appointed Director of Music. A hero of the Great War, he had been an outstanding bandmaster in England. He was in charge of instruction in wind instruments at the Toronto Conservatory of Music for several years and under Captain Hayward's direction the Queen's Own regained their prewar eminence. In 1922 and 1923 the band won the CNE Class A Band Contest, and one of its greatest achievements occurred in 1924, when it provided the background for a massive choir at the CNE showcasing a new and ambitious work by Captain Hayward, entitled "Pageant." The entire performance received rave reviews and undoubtedly raised the band to a high level of public esteem. The instrumentation was listed in the 1924 catalogue of Boosey and Hawkes, the largest supplier of musical instruments in Canada, with

Massed bands (pipers and buglers) at the dedication of the Vimy memorial, 1936. (Ed Hall, Ottawa)

Royal Canadian Horse Artillery Band with massed buglers. Note the different uniforms present with band: Dragoons, PPCLI, RCHA, and RCR. Regimental buglers are positioned in front of Major F. Coleman. (Ed Hall)

a photograph which showed one flute, ten clarinets, two saxophones, one bass clarinet, four horns, four cornets, four trombones, two euphoniums, four tubas and three percussionists. Captain Hayward was succeeded as bandmaster by James J. Buckle, who had been a bandmaster in England with the West Surrey Regiment.

In 1922, the Governor General's Foot Guards Band in Ottawa, under Captain Joseph Miller Brown, began to resume its activities. The music critic for the Ottawa *Citizen* commented, after attending a concert by the band that year, that, "it was the first time the band had been at full strength for some years and I was surprised that Ottawa had such a fine band."

Captain Brown passed away the next year and was succeeded by his son Joseph T. Brown. In December, 1925, the GGFG Band went to New York City's Madison Square Garden to play when the National Hockey League was introduced to that city. "Great Ovation is Given GGFG Band in New York," read the headline in the Ottawa *Citizen*. The band marched up Broadway to the New York City Hall where they were officially welcomed by Mayor-elect Jimmy Walker. The West Point Military Academy Band joined them for the national anthems of Canada and the United States.

In 1937, the GGFG Band performed for the opening of the International Peace Bridge before a distinguished audience which

The Elgin Regiment Band, St. Thomas, Ontario, 1936. Captain R. W. Pearson is the Band President and Adjutant. (Pearson Collection)

included President Franklin Roosevelt and Prime Minister Mackenzie King.

Captain Joseph T. Brown resigned from the army in 1938 to become the Director of the RCMP Band. His successor was Sergeant Edwin Stelles, who had served with the band since 1928 as a clarinetist. He had come from Britain where he had been a member of the Royal Artillery Band. The new bandmaster's first task was to prepare the band for the many ceremonial activities to be held in May 1939 in connection with the visit of King George VI and Queen Elizabeth. The first event was the dedication of the National War Memorial, at which the GGFG Band played together with the RCOC Band and the Canadian Grenadier Guards Band. The massed bands were under the direction of Captain J. J. Gangier.

The RCHA Band continued its practice of attending summer camps in Petawawa during the 1920s. The Nova Scotia Brigade, also at camp at the completion of training, marched out with a Nova Scotia flag at their head while the RCHA Band played Scottish marches. In 1926, the unit decided to bring along several pipers as gunners since only a limited number of pipers were authorized in training camp. The group achieved short-term fame, however, when, at the Protestant Church Parade, they skirled "The McKenzie Highlanders" march-past. The RCHA stood poised and ready to play the march-past for the whole parade and were not amused when a piper from a Nova Scotia regiment sounded before the down beat. The next issue of Camp Orders dealt with the matter, "The RCHA Band will be the only band to play at Church Parade."

The RCHA Band, however, was not able to do much playing in Petawawa after June 26, 1926. During a night-time exercise a flare struck the Mars-Aleum that housed the band's rehearsal hall and instrument storage. This included their very valuable library of music. Ironically, an audit had taken place in March to determine the value of non-public property held by the band. The non-public property was insured and was replaced immediately. The next year, a special grant of $750 compensated the band for public musical instruments destroyed in the fire.

St. Catharines is the home of the Lincoln and Welland Regiment and their regimental band traces its history back to the formation of the Lincoln Militia in 1863. At the turn of the century, the band was under the direction of Lieutenant William Peel and was known as the 19th St. Catharines Regiment. The band served overseas during the Great War, and in 1924, Lieutenant Frank Egener became the director. Lieutenant Egener was a very talented organist and was selected for the position because of his ability as a teacher.

During his tenure, Lieutenant Egener became embroiled in a court case with the Musicians' Union of St. Catharines. Several incidents had taken place that led to open warfare between the union and the Lincoln and

The Ontario Regiment Band, Niagara-on-the-Lake, 1929. (Town of Whitby Archives 29-001-107)

Royal Canadian Horse Artillery Band at the opening of the Silver Dart Aerodrome, Petawawa, Ontario, June 17th, 1936. (Public Archives of Canada PA 63240)

Welland Regiment Band. One incident concerned a transfer member from Niagara Falls who was denied permission to play with the Lincoln and Welland Band for a public performance because the union claimed he had not fulfilled the residency rule. However, he soon afterwards appeared with the St. Catharines Concert Band.

The substance of the main problem, which led to the court case, came as a result of some band members not having sufficient cash to forward applications for membership, which was required for all band members to perform public concerts in a City of St. Catharines concert series. Another member, who was a spare member, had allowed his union membership to lapse.

On July 11, 1929, the band was to play a concert in the park. Prior to the concert Lieutenant Egener received notification that he was not to permit the three non-union members to perform and was advised to provide a list of all his musicians. Lieutenant Egener advised the union that they had no jurisdiction over him, and that King's Regulations stated that a man is at all times subject to military law when in uniform, and he cannot be subject to any law of an organization whose by-laws are contrary to military law or the Statutes of Canada.

The concert proceeded, and Lieutenant Egener and twenty-six band members were fined and suspended by the Musicians' Union. Lieutenant Colonel Gander, the Commanding Officer of the Lincoln and Welland, considered this action an affront to the military and the band, and he

73

Canadian Scottish Regiment Brass Band at the coronation of King George VI, 1937. Director of Music is Lt. James Miller. (Pearson Collection, Gibson Photo)

retained legal council, laying information before the Police Magistrate charging that members of the Musicians' Union were in violation of the Militia Act. The Magistrate tried to bring the parties together to resolve the case amicably to no avail. He found the union executive members guilty as charged and fined them $50 each. He also ordered that the fines assessed against band members by the union were to be returned and that all members were to be reinstated. The union appealed to the Supreme Court, but the decision was upheld. The incident left scars for many years and created an element of distrust that took a war to cure.

Lieutenant Egener quit his post with the band in 1930 and went on to become one of Canada's most respected organists and composers.

In August 1934, over ten thousand First World War veterans gathered for the Canadian Corps Reunion in Toronto. It was one of the most ambitious and well-organized military reunions in Canadian history. Captain John Slatter, with his vast experience in organizing large groups of bands, was selected to be the musical coordinator, and twenty-five bands appeared in both a drum head service and a tattoo.

The grand tattoo took place on the sloping hills of Riverdale Park in the Don Valley. Three hundred thousand people gathered to view the performance, the largest mass of people ever assembled to watch a single event in Canada. There were marches and selections by each of the bands as they took their position on the field, and the finale began with a fanfare. Next came a powerful array of flares and fireworks. A calcium light spelled out the name of General Sir Arthur Currie, the military's beloved leader, and as the word Currie lit up the night sky, the bands began to play

Queen's Own Rifles of Canada Band July 1, 1924. Director of Music is Captain W. Atkins. The photo was used to advertise the band's appearance at Canadian National Exhibition. (Fred Ashton, Toronto)

the requiem "Nightfall in Camp." bringing to a close one of the most memorable spectacles in Canadian military history.

The national anthem of Canada became a concern of the defence department during the twenties and thirties. Following the Great War, "O Canada" became very popular in Quebec in preference to "God Save the King." In 1934, Members of Parliament from Quebec raised the issue with the department; why was "God Save the King" played as the national anthem, and not "O Canada," which had been written by native Quebec son Calixa Lavallée? The response, quoted in its entirety, defines the department's position in the matter.

1. The National Anthem in so far as custom of the service, is that Anthem which is commonly known as "God Save the King."
2. This is the Anthem referred to and intended to be played by Military Bands in Canada, Great Britain and the Colonies.
3. The Canadian Militia follows the customs and precedents of the British Army, hence "God Save the King" is the National Anthem for the purposes of the Defence Forces of Canada.
4. There may be a Royal Warrant by His Majesty the King designating a certain hymn, or anthem set to a score of music, as the National Anthem.

The "certain hymn" referred to in the memorandum was "O Canada" which remained the national hymn for the next forty-six years, until legislation was finally passed in 1980 making it the national anthem.

Nationalist fervour was again censured in June 1936 when Major General Constantine wrote to all military district commanders outlining another problem that had come to his attention regarding the national anthem.

> I am directed to inform you it has come to my notice that in some instance military bands are playing marches consisting of medleys of the "National Anthem" and "The Maple Leaf Forever." It is considered that the National Anthem should be preserved for one purpose only and should at all times be accorded the greatest respect, which is impossible when played in this manner.

By 1937, the recruitment of musicians for most of the Permanent Force bands was becoming a severe problem and a survey was conducted giving the bandmasters and musicians an opportunity to voice their opinions regarding the difficulties.

The RCR Band complained that the lack of musicians was due to slow promotion, no remuneration from private engagements, and that bandsmen were being employed on fatigue duties. The RCHA claimed the difficulty in maintaining their strength resulted from the lack of qualified musicians in Canada. They also resented being employed in outside-band duties. The PPCLI indicated that they were five under strength and they had begun enlisting on probation partially trained musicians.

The survey also requested information on securing replacements for the bands. There were numerous responses to this question including the fact that pay was very low and that young married men could not be placed on the married establishment list, which would allow access to housing and married allowances. Many of the qualified players that applied for the R22R Band were rejected owing to physical disability. In the winter of 1936-37, the PPCLI placed an advertisement for bandsmen and they received one hundred and six applications of which sixty were rejected as unsuitable, another five were medically unfit, three withdrew their application, thirty failed to reply to further correspondence and four were married. The remaining four were enlisted. Another reason for the failure to recruit musicians was that the service offered little attraction for professional musicians. Promotion was very slow, and there was no opportunity to perform outside the band. Regular musicians were no longer permitted by regulation to join the union.

In 1938, the Adjutant General circulated a letter on behalf of the RCR Band hoping to attract active militia musicians to the regular force. The results were not very encouraging, as photographs from the era indicate. The 1938 RCR Band photograph taken in Wolseley Barracks shows a band of eighteen on parade. Similarly, the RCHA Band photograph, taken in Kingston in 1939, also illustrates a meager number of musicians.

Army Service Corps Brass Band, Calgary, Alberta, 1934. (Public Archives of Canada NA3164-1)

The high point of the decades between the wars certainly was the royal visit in 1939. The bands made valiant efforts to create a royal spirit during the reigning monarchs' triumphal swing through Canada. Ike Eberts, a member of the prewar RCR Band, said in an interview:

> There were twenty-one of us who marched down from Wolseley Barracks to the train station on York Street in London, we were in full dress and there was no question that what we lacked in numbers we made up for with every bit of power we could muster.

The ominous gathering clouds of war overshadowed the warmth accorded the royal couple. In September 1939, the Canadian government declared war on Germany. It would be several months before the bands and musicians would become a necessary ingredient for troops in the mobilization of the fighting forces.

CHAPTER 5

The War Years
1939–1945

I am delighted at the action you have taken about bands, but when are we going to hear them playing about the streets? Even quite small parade marches are highly beneficial... In fact, wherever there are troops and leisure for it there should be an attempt at military display.

Winston Churchill, Note to Secretary of State for War, 12 July, 1940

The Army Bands

At the outbreak of war in 1939 many of the bandsmen were swallowed up into fighting units. However, the necessity of maintaining the morale of the troops brought about the authorization of wartime bands.

The Permanent Force bands remained at their regimental depots and continued to function as both regimental and depot bands. None of the reserve militia units that mobilized for the war were authorized to enlist their bands for overseas service, although Highland regiments were permitted to take six pipers.

In September 1940, Lieutenant General A. G. L. McNaughton, Chief of General Staff, proposed that the various holding units should organize bands. This involved the organization of nine bands for units of the Canadian infantry divisions. The Minister of Defence, Colonel J. L. Ralston, approved the formation of the bands effective February 1, 1941. Lieutenant A. L. Streeter, Director of Music for the Princess Patricia's Canadian Light Infantry, was promoted to Captain and appointed the Co-ordinator and Director of Music for Canadian-based units.

Streeter experienced some difficulty in organizing bands because of the lack of suitable Canadian bandsmen. Many units were reluctant to send in the names of musicians on their rosters, preferring to maintain unofficial

79

Royal Canadian Horse Artillery Band, Fort Frontenac, Kingston, 1939. (Ed Hall, Ottawa)

bands and orchestras. Another problem was obtaining enough trained bandmasters. This situation was corrected when arrangements were made to obtain, on loan, the services of some British bandmasters.

Captain Streeter had been able to organize three bands to go overseas in 1941. The main band, called the No. 1 Canadian Infantry Band, was able to function independently of the other two bands. The Royal Canadian Artillery (Overseas) Band and the Royal Canadian Army Service Corps Band combined whenever a second band was required for an official occasion. The composite band marched in London, England, in the Lord Mayor's Procession on November 10, 1941, and, according to the London News Chronicle, "They put up the best performance of the lot, beating even the Grenadier Guards."

In 1941, all units and training centres in Canada were authorized to have bands, and Captain Frank Coleman, the former director of the Royal Canadian Horse Artillery Band in Kingston, was promoted to major and installed as Inspector of Bands for Canada. Major Coleman helped to develop and standardize the musical requirements for the trade and to introduce a special bandsman's badge. This was the traditional cloth badge with a lyre on a khaki background.

The enlistments for the nine overseas bands began to increase substantially by 1942. The bandmasters who had been requested were approved for service with the Canadian bands. There were now four overseas bands and four bandmasters: WO1 Donald Keeling and WO1 Reg Newman from Great Britain joined Canadians, WO1 S. A. Garnet and WO1 Philip

Royal Canadian Engineer Concert Band, England, 1945. (Kopstein Collection)

Murphy. With the assistance of the British bandmasters considerable progress was made in organizing and training the new bands. Garnet headed the No. 1 Infantry Band, Murphy the Armoured Corps Band, Keeling was the Director of the No. 3 Infantry Corps Band and Newman was leader of the Royal Canadian Artillery (Overseas) Band.

Many of the musicians who sought service in the bands had good professional backgrounds and were capable on several different instruments. As a result, many of the military bands provided dance bands of varying sizes, which became immensely popular. The band report for late 1941 was very positive, stating that "all bands are heavily engaged and for the first time some requests for bands could not be filled."

In July 1942, two more bands were authorized and two more bandmasters were obtained on loan from the British War Office. They were Alfred Hollick, who took over the RCASC Band and Harold Hicks, who became the Director of the Royal Canadian Ordnance Corps Band.

By 1942 there were 136 authorized active-service bands in Canada and 69 overseas. The total number of musicians was a whopping 5,535. Not all bands were operational, but many bands were well over their manning level.

Overseas, in the fall of 1944, there were ten full-time bands, which were identified as staff bands. These were: The Canadian Armoured Corps Band, The Royal Canadian Artillery Band, The Royal Canadian Engineers Band, The Royal Canadian Corps of Signals Band, The Royal Canadian

Army Service Corps Band, The Royal Canadian Ordnance Corps Band, The Number 1 Canadian Infantry Corps Band, The Number 2 Canadian Infantry Corps Band, The Number 3 Canadian Infantry Corps Band, and The Number 4 Canadian Infantry Corps Band.

In Canada there were thirty-three full-time bands plus a nucleus of permanent volunteer bands. The training centres such as Camp Borden, Shilo, and Petawawa maintained full-time military bands. Operational units who were on standby for overseas service had volunteer bands.

When Canada began mobilizing for war in the fall of 1939, the Royal Canadian Air Force and Royal Canadian Navy had already developed plans for bands, thus creating handicaps for the army in recruiting personnel, not the least of which was the pay; the musicians in the air force and navy were better paid than those in the army. Bandsmen were paid $1.85 per day in the navy, $1.55 in the air force and $1.30 in the army. In order to equalize the pay, in 1942, full-time army bandsmen were awarded an additional twenty-five cents per day, an amount later granted to bandsmen in volunteer bands. The Adjutant General's office stated that this additional $500,000 per year "was money well spent."

The ten staff bands reached very high standards, compable to those of the British and American bands. The RCA Band, for example, under Bandmaster Reg Newman, was in constant demand. In addition to being a military band, it had within its personnel a dance band, an old-time band, a salon orchestra, a choir, and instrumental and vocal soloists.

11th Army Reserve (Tank) Band, Camp Niagara, Ontario, 1945. (Oshawa Community Archives A985.41.58)

82

Midland Regiment Band, Prince Rupert, BC, 1943. (Len Collins, Oshawa, ON 26961)

The Royal Canadian Regiment Corp of Drums, IJmuiden, Holland, 1945. (Len Collins, Oshawa)

This band also spawned future Canadian Army Band Supervisor of Music, Major Melville Scott. Major Scott had been Band Sergeant of the R22R Band before the war, was selected for Kneller Hall to take the bandmaster training in 1944 and was later commissioned in the Canadian army.

No. 3 Canadian Infantry Band, WO1 Donald Keeling, Bandmaster. (Fred Ashton, Toronto)

When Canadian troops went into action, the corps staff bands did not all remain in England; they were allocated to several theatres of war on a rotation system. Judging by the bandmasters' reports, corps bands were kept busy, and their work was very much appreciated. The following extract is from a 1945 report from Bandmaster Philip Murphy of the Armoured Corps Band:

> Throughout the tour, the Band was very much appreciated by the troops in the units and the hospitals. They never seemed to hear enough of the Band. We played as many as six church services on a Sunday and five concerts a day. British and American units were eager to hear the Band. Records were made for transmission to Canada.

But not all was sweetness and light. Many bandmasters commented unfavourably on arrangements made for them while on tour. Criticism covered almost every aspect of administration, quarters, rations, transportation, mail, schedule, communications and reinforcements. It seems that although the units wanted the bands and liked the music, they did not want to "pay the piper."

On the Canadian side of the Atlantic, the Lincoln and Welland Regiment Band had been reorganized under Bandmaster W. P. Kiddell. The unit was integrated into the Canadian Active Service Force, and the musicians of the prewar band were taken on strength. A highlight of the war years for the band was its regular appearances during the winter of

Lake Superior Scottish Regiment Band, Current River Barracks, Port Arthur, Ontario 1940. (Thunder Bay Military Museum)

1940 at Maple Leaf Gardens in Toronto by invitation from Conn Smythe, the Gardens' owner, who had a penchant for brass and pipe bands.

In 1941, the Lincoln and Welland Band saw service at both ends of the country. In August, it moved to British Columbia where it served as the District Band at Vancouver Barracks, as well as being stationed in Nanaimo. In September, it moved to Newfoundland, taking up duties in Gander. The band came into its own during this period. The Concert Band, under the direction of Warrant Officer Kiddell, was in constant demand, as was the Regimental Dance Orchestra, led by Sergeant Fred Willett. The National War Services of the YMCA benefitted regularly from the band's presence and showed their appreciation in 1942 when they wrote, "The entertainment given last Monday by your regiment's brass band orchestra and concert party was without question the finest ever presented on the stage. I wish to express to you our sincere thanks."

With the onset of the war, the army bands lost many musicians who exercised their option and signed up for overseas duty. The R22R Band was decimated, operating for some time with less than fifteen members. In the fall of 1941, the band was boosted by the addition of musicians from various other units. A photograph taken in 1941 at the Quebec training camp known as Monument des Braves illustrates how the band reached nearly its pre-war level. It shows the bandmaster, Captain Belanger, one piccolo, four clarinets, two saxophones, two horns, four trumpets, three trombones, one euphonium, a tuba, and three percussionists.

Royal Canadian Armoured Corps Band, Amsterdam, The Netherlands, 1945. Bandmaster is Phil Murphy. (Kopstein Collection)

In 1942, the R22R Band moved to Camp Valcartier and played for various camp functions as well as touring Quebec on recruiting tours. It provided dance bands and played on radio station CHRC in support of recruiting drives. As the war progressed the band increased in size, and, by 1944 had over forty members, including some of Quebec's finest instrumentalists.

The RCHA moved from Kingston to Petawawa, where it was attached to the A-11 Canadian Artillery Training Centre. Like the other band, its size had decreased when many of its musicians left to go overseas. A draft of musicians from two disbanded groups helped to bring the band up to strength. With the departure of recently promoted Major Coleman, Warrant Officer Horrace Tidman was appointed bandmaster. He was able to nurse the band through some difficult years until 1945.

When newly promoted Captain Streeter of the PPCLI Band was appointed Supervisor of the Overseas Bands, Warrant Officer G. W. Butler, who had been a band sergeant under Captain Streeter, replaced him. Butler was able to increase the band's strength to twenty-five before it was posted to Camp Shilo. The band became very popular in the Prairie provinces during the war years. An article in the base newspaper, describes the extent of their activities: "The band has recently returned from a tour in which they covered over seven hundred miles of southern Manitoba. Sponsored by the Victory Loan Committee with the object of creating enthusiasm for the sixth loan drive, the trip appeared to be a bang-up success. There were four concerts per day."

86

Royal Canadian Ordnance Corps Band. (Kopstein Collection)

The RCR Band had accompanied the regiment to Camp Valcartier in November 1939, however, in 1940, it was ordered to return to its home station, and it took up residence in London's Wolseley Barracks. Warrant Officer John Proderick was appointed bandmaster and later was promoted to Lieutenant, Director of Music. In the fall of 1940 the band moved again, this time to Camp Borden, where it was kept busy with the usual round of engagements. At this time the band had twenty-two members: Lieutenant Proderick, one flute, five clarinets, two saxophones and two horns, four cornets, two trombones, one euphonium, two tubas, and two percussionists, but by 1942, when the band returned to London to begin touring for bond drives and recruiting, its strength had grown to twenty-nine. The band travelled extensively in 1943 and on several occasions journeyed to Windsor and Detroit to play for recruiting and bond drives. The highlight of the band's wartime service was a cross Canada radio program which featured the band in concert.

Despite a heavy turnover of personnel, the Governor General's Foot Guards Band in Ottawa managed to keep functioning under the direction of Bandmaster Warrant Officer Harry Gossage. The band accompanied the troops from the Ottawa area to training camps and gave numerous concerts for War Bond drives.

Throughout the duration of the Second World War, the Royal Rifles of Canada maintained its band for training purposes at Fort York Armoury in Toronto. In July 1940, Canadian troops went to Iceland to reinforce the British garrison against a possible Nazi invasion. In the same year, the Active Service Force of the Royal Regiment of Canada arrived in Iceland from Canada. The original band remained in Toronto while a second overseas band was organized to accompany the unit to Iceland. The band was organized by Major Brian S. McCool. Instruments were purchased and bandsmen recruited from the different battalion companies.

The patriotic fervour in Canada reached it peak in 1943, and full-dress parades were held frequently in order to boost civilian morale. The very popular Royal Canadian Army Service Corps Trumpet Band in Toronto had long had a reputation for excellence, and the efforts made by this band during the war were quite remarkable. Its appearances in full-dress blue uniforms, enhanced with a marching display, were real crowd pleasers. The band's instrumentation included ten side drums, four tenor drums, two bass drums and thirty trumpets with no valves, making it unique among Canadian military bands.

At the outbreak of the war the Grenadier Guards Band remained in their home station of Montreal and continued to be part of the Second Reserve Battalion. When the First Battalion was mobilized for active duty in 1940, a band was recruited for this unit under the leadership of Bill Finlayson of Ottawa. Most of the personnel came from the Ottawa Valley. The thirty-member band was posted overseas in 1944 and became known as the Second Canadian Infantry Corps Band.

The beginning of the Second World War produced some major changes for bandsmen in Calgary. Some of the groups such as the Royal Canadian Army Service Corps Military Band were dispatched overseas and formed the original RCASC Overseas Band. Calgary was the military training centre for southern Alberta and many bandsmen were posted to the bands and attached to various units across the city. Harry Kirk led the A16 Canadian Training Band, which was in operation from September 1940 to the fall of 1945, participating in Loan Drives and in the Calgary Stampede parades. Many of the musicians were from Fernie, BC, including some who had been members of the 191st Battalion Band in the Great War.

The 1939 army list provides an insight into why there were so few bandmasters available for overseas duty. Most of the prewar bandmasters were over-age. For instance, Oliver Bertrand of the Voltiguers de Quebec was sixty-eight and had become the leader of the band in 1911. Mr L. Collie of the Cameron Highlanders Brass Band was sixty-nine. P. H. Marsh of the Regina Rifles was the youngest at twenty-eight, and the average age of the thirty-eight bandmasters on the list was fifty-five.

Canadian Women's Army Corps Band marching to Amsterdam's City Theatre, 1945. (National Archives of Canada PA 17433)

The Canadian Women's Army Corps Band was formed in 1943 under bandmaster Nadia Svarich of Vegreville, Alberta, a very accomplished pianist and musician. The band trained in Currie Barracks in Calgary. In October 1943, it began a four-month tour across Canada visiting every camp in the nation. The band settled down in the Kitchener Basic Training Centre in February 1944. The forty-three musicians had a very well-balanced brass band instrumentation, with the addition of two saxophones. The band contained ten cornets, six horns (mellophones), six trombones, three euphoniums, three baritones, six tubas, one alto sax, one tenor sax, and six percussionists.

Colonel Margaret Eaton, the Director General of the Canadian Women's Army Corps, visited Kitchener and the band provided music for an inspection parade. Colonel Eaton later informed the band in a note, "How proud I am of having a band of such fine musicians in the Corps."

In April 1945 the band, which now included reed instruments, was posted overseas and played numerous concerts in Holland and Belgium.

Canadian Women's Army Corps Band on parade at the Kitchener Training Base. (Kopstein Collection)

They often massed with the overseas staff bands in open-air concerts. Art Bergin, a Canadian army bandmaster during the war, said, "They were really excellent musicians. The Women's Band certainly measured up to any of the overseas bands." Certainly, the CWAC Band's contribution as performers and good ambassadors certainly helped in later years to break down the barriers of a male-dominated Canadian Forces Music Branch.

Camp Aldershot, Nova Scotia, the counterpart of the camp by the same name in England, produced the twenty-seven-piece Aldershot Military Band. Many of the musicians in the band had been in the armed forces in the First World War, in fact, the band was originally the Pictou Highlanders Brass Band that had been part of the 85th Battalion.

Defence Minister J. L. Ralston, who knew many of the Pictou Highlanders members personally, went to his old comrades and asked the band to serve at Camp Aldershot for the duration of the war. His request was met with keen enthusiasm. Major Dan Mooney, a native of Nova Scotia who had played in circus bands, was selected to lead the band in 1939. He had eventually become the Assistant Director of the Barnum and Bailey Circus Band. One of the trademarks of the Aldershot Band was their renditions of circus marches and novelty numbers.

In 1943 the band spawned a twelve-piece dance orchestra, which became an overnight sensation. Praise for the dance orchestra continued long after the war, and Nova Scotians still call it the best wartime dance group in Canada.

The musicians of the various staff corps bands generally mirrored the nationalistic fibre of the wartime Canadian Armed Forces; the Armoured Corps Band, for example, had musicians from across the country. However, the Number 3 Canadian Infantry Corps Band under Bandmaster Donald Keeling was essentially made up of musicians from Toronto. This band took part in a concert in November 1944 at the Royal Opera House in Ghent, Belgium, featuring the 2nd and 3rd Canadian Infantry Corps Bands as well as the Ordnance Corps Band.

The bandmaster of the RCASC Band, A. W. Hollick, compiled an unofficial diary of everyday life in a Canadian band serving overseas. Mr. Hollick's documentation of daily events reveals the quintessential nature of military banding and gives an intimate first-person account of a well-organized, finely tuned musical organization.

May 1944. Band attached to 7th Battalion, Italy:
Wednesday 17:
Our heavy luggage not having arrived spent the day sorting out kit and washing our clothing. Instruments and stores arrive late afternoon.

Canadian Women's Army Corps Pipe Band. (Kopstein Collection)

Friday 19:
Gave our first concert to the troops in the town of Avellino in a nice little spot "The Maple Leaf Gardens." The best spot in town probably. A good audience and we passed a very pleasant hour and a half.

July 1944:
Saturday 9:
Pesaro, waiting for word as to duties in this district so turned out and played for troops while they had their noon meal. Men very warmly received this and it gave us quite a fill up to see our playing give so much pleasure. In the evening a small band gave a "jam session" in the men's lines, a session that is always popular.

Tuesday 12:
Was at practice in the morning when message came in which was our program of work up to the 23rd of the month. Went to 32nd Company and found the Commanding Officer and the Officers very "band minded" much to my pleasure. Everyone here very hospitable and it was a real pleasure for us to play for the company. We set up and played "music while you work."

In 1944 the band went to France for a ceremony at the Vimy Memorial.

November 1944:
Saturday 7:
Final rehearsal on the ground at Vimy. Everything went well and we were back in Arras by lunch time. Remainder of the day spent cleaning up.

The Royal Canadian Regiment Band, Camp Borden, Ontario, 1941. (RCR Museum GN 77 1831)

Sunday 8:
We went to do a church parade and service for an English REME Regiment. Marched the troops through the streets of Arras creating quite a stir on the Sunday morning in the town.... gave a concert for the civilian population. Found we had an enormous crowd to play to and received a wonderful reception. Altogether a very good morning. The OC of the REME was very profuse in his thanks.

Monday 9:
This was the day of the Ceremonial at Vimy. Everything went off well. Very colourful by veterans carrying large flags. Followed by us playing a good march "The Sons of the Brave."

The band returned to England in May 1945 and was posted to the transit camp in Nijmegen, Holland. They played for a broadcast over the Hilversum Radio and were finally demobilized on May 22, 1945. Hollick revealed his genuine affection for his experience with the RCASC Band when he said "it has been a job well done by the men at all times. I shall always look back on a useful three years work with the band and my connection with the Canadian Forces."

After VE Day in May 1945 most units in the Canadian army began to disband, and the Canadian Occupation Forces were withdrawn in early 1946. The last corps band was disbanded on March 28, 1946. The regimental bands returned to Canada and were disbanded with their units.

Many of the hundreds of musicians who served overseas with the Canadian bands look back at their experience with glowing pride. Most said that in retrospect it was indeed a wonderful way to serve their country and to spend the early years of their lives. One musician, Don McDonald of Ottawa, said: "It helped make me a better musician and a better person, I would not trade my experiences for anything and the great friends I made have lasted me through my lifetime."

The Navy Bands

In November 1939, naval headquarters in Ottawa received an offer from Alfred Zeally, a well-known bandmaster, who volunteered to organize and equip a band at no expense to the government. His proposal to help organize a navy band was accepted, however, the navy did fund the band and provided instruments and music. Mr. Zeally also enlisted with the rank of lieutenant and posted to Halifax for service with HMCS *Stadacona*. This proved to be only the opening chapter in Alfred Zeally's role as the Father of Canadian Navy Bands as he subsequently organized and trained fifteen navy bands during the five years of the war. His name became synonymous with personnel development in the Canadian navy during the war because, in addition to helping to structure bands, he was instrumental in creating the Royal Canadian Navy School of Music in Toronto.

In 1942, the Naval Board had recognized the need for the development of a school of music, and, at the urging of Lieutenant Alfred Zeally, it was decided to establish the Royal Canadian Navy School of Music at HMCS *York*. The school had a humble beginning in a tiny cubicle at the York naval complex. Zeally and his staff had a double duty to perform. They were tasked with organizing a band for York and formulating a plan for a school to train musicians to be naval bandsmen. Zeally set to work to assemble musicians from across the country. The trainees were for the most part already professional and semi-professional musicians, so the school was not designed to train them to learn a musical instrument but rather to prepare them for service in a naval band. The idea was to train them to play on parade and to react to the special requirements of naval ceremonial drill. The school offered a varied curriculum which included concert-band rehearsals, parade instruction, and dance-band rehearsals. The staff of the school was taken from the ranks of the finest professional musicians in Canada. The Assistant Director of Music was radio artist Ernest Huggins, and the staff arrangers were Petty Officers Geoff Baker and Johnnie Burt.

The RCN School of Music provided another important skill; it was the proving ground for novice bandmasters.

The school was disbanded in December 1944. Over fifteen hundred bandsmen were trained at the RCN School of Music in the two and half years of its operation. Its creation at HMCS *York* served as a model for the formation of the RCN School of Music in Esquimalt that was established in 1954.

Efforts to establish navy bands in Canada before the war had been a struggle as there was no authority for either bands or bandmasters. During the early 1930s, Commander Brodeur, who was Commanding Officer of HMCS *Naden* in Victoria, helped fund and organize a volunteer ship's company band. In 1939, as a result of the Royal Visit, a volunteer band was formed with funding by the government for their instruments. The official *Naden* Band was formed in September 1940 and was the first official navy band on the west coast.

The *Cornwallis* Band was the largest of all RCN bands. It was drafted to the Naval training establishment in the summer of 1942. The number of men in training at this base at times reached a total of eight thousand and the band played at the numerous parades, dinners, and concerts which were required to train and entertain the personnel. The bandmaster of the *Cornwallis* Band was Technical Commissioned Officer Robert McGall, a professional musician who had come from the *Stadacona* Band. The *Cornwallis* Band developed into an outstanding musical organization whose popularity can be credited to Alfred Zeally's foresight in bringing together a group of musicians who could cope with all aspects of the musical spectrum. The musicians had varied professional backgrounds, and many of them were capable dance musicians as well as good concert players. The plus for the navy was that they also developed into highly proficient parade band performers.

In June 1942, the original *Stadacona* Band was disbanded to form the nucleus of three new bands, the *Cornwallis* Band, the *St. Hyacinthe* Band and the *Avalon* Band. In October 1942, Lieutenant Zeally was called upon to reorganize a band for Stadacona, and a number of the original *Stadacona* personnel were included in this new band. James Downie, former bandmaster of the RCASC Band in Toronto, was appointed bandmaster. The band developed into an exceptional musical ensemble with over fifty performers. It maintained a very high profile during the war, particularly in Halifax, where its performances became almost a daily occurrence.

The town of St. Hyacinthe in Quebec was the home of the RCN Signal School, one of the most difficult and rigorous training establishments in

Royal Canadian Navy Reserve Band, Saskatoon, Saskatchewan, summer 1942. (Public Archives of Canada M72-2456)

95

the Canadian navy. The St. Hyacinthe band under Melville Watson provided a much-needed diversion for the sailors and staff of the school. It made numerous tours outside St. Hyacinthe and became popular in the area.

The band of the HMCS *Protector*, in Sydney, NS, was the first product of the Royal Canadian Navy School of Music. Chief Petty Officer Horace Sainsbury was drafted from the *Stadacona* Band in March 1943 and appointed bandmaster, and, after a month of supervision under Director of Music, Lieutenant Zeally, the band began operation. It performed a variety of engagements throughout the war and developed an exceptionally good dance band.

The HMCS *York* Band, in Toronto, also a product of the RCN School of Music, was very fortunate to have many well-known Toronto professional musicians, including five members of the Toronto Symphony. Lieutenant Zeally gave this band his undivided attention, and, as a result, it received rave reviews for its concerts, placing it on a par with some of the finest bands on the North American continent. The double-handedness of the musicians was quite apparent in their ability to provide an outstanding twenty-two-piece dance orchestra. This jazz group, under Petty Officer T. A. Moore, was also blessed with the writing talents of Johnnie Burt. Burt later became one of Canada's best-known musicians.

HMCS Cornwallis Band, 1942. Lieutenant Robert McGall is the Conductor. (Lt (N) Jim Forde)

Royal Canadian Navy Band, Vancouver, British Columbia, 18th November 1942. (Public Archives of Canada PA-134311)

The Band of HMCS *Chatham*, in Prince Rupert, BC, was formed out of relatively inexperienced musicians, most of whom were drafted from the School of Music in June 1943. The bandmaster, Stanley Sunderland, assisted by Herbert Jeffery, shaped this band into an efficient, well-trained unit. The band progressed extremely well, and was able to make several local and provincial radio broadcasts. In March 1944, when Bandmaster Sunderland was drafted to HMCS *Naden* to take over the newly organized *Naden* Band, Petty Officer Guy Noakes replaced him with Petty Officer Lawrence Frayne as his assistant. Petty Officer Noakes had been a member of the *Stadacona* Band and had been a cornet soloist with the 48th Highlanders Band under Captain John Slatter. This band proved to be one of the finest of the smaller navy bands.

The Band of HMCS *Donnacona*, located in Montreal, had originally been a Boy Scout band whose members were later enrolled in the Royal Canadian Naval Reserve. In December 1943, the band was taken on strength of the Naval Service, and, although several changes in the personnel had to be made, the high calibre of the band was maintained. One of the contributing factors to the success of the band was the leader, Lieutenant L. Blackburn, who had long been associated with bands in Montreal. The *Donnacona* Band enjoyed a widespread popularity throughout the city of Montreal, even receiving a generous donation of instruments and music from the Vickers Aircraft Corporation.

The first bandmaster of the HMCS *Naden* Band was Lieutenant Commander Harry Cuthbert. Cuthbert had joined the Royal Canadian

Band of the HMCS Magnificent on the flight deck. (Ted Franklin, Oshawa)

Naval Volunteer Reserve prior to the war, and enlisted as a pay officer. In August 1940, he accepted the position of bandmaster of the *Naden* Band. The backbone of this band was a number of professional musicians, many of whom had played in Canadian and American bands prior to their enlistment. The *Naden* Band eventually developed into one of the finest in western Canada and there was a great demand for its services. In March 1944, Warrant Officer Stanley Sunderland replaced Cuthbert as bandmaster. Warrant Officer Sunderland, who had come from the *Naden* Band, was an outstanding cornetist whose ability as a musician was known throughout Canada.

Lieutenant Commander Harry Cuthbert was sent to Greenoch, Scotland, to lead the first RCN Overseas Band, the *Niobe* Band. The HMCS *Niobe* Band, was formed from the *Naden* Band and various other RCN bands. It became an instant hit in the United Kingdom, receiving numerous requests for its services and broadcasting on BBC Radio. The band made several recordings which were sent out to entertain the troops. An article in the navy's *Crowsnest* newspaper reveals how quickly the band shot into the limelight in the United Kingdom.

> In Canada you can be proud of the Royal Canadian Navy Band aboard the HMCS *Niobe*. They have proven themselves an instantaneous success with the people of the British Isles. Life in the band is busy and

crowded, with little time for homesickness. The day begins with divisions after which the band adjourns to the drill hall for practice. At noon hour, they play a concert to entertain the men and on Tuesday and Thursday, the dance band swings out to a packed audience of sailors.

In the afternoon, they rehearse for a broadcast or a concert. Tuesday and Friday evenings the dance band gives forth with jive at the nearby YMCA. While all the broadcasting has to be timed to the final second, the boys believe the toughest is the recording sessions.

Later reports in the *Crowsnest* went on to recount the band's unusual success, and a navy writer began calling them the "Niobe Globe Trotters." Their recording sessions were done in London and from pretty exclusive territory; they recorded at the BBC's Maida Vale Studios and at the Fortune Theatre in Covent Gardens. At the BBC's Broadcasting House, the band made recordings of hymns and voluntaries, along with portions of the divine service read by Bishop Wells, principal chaplain of the navy, for use of ships at sea which had no facilities for religious services.

The Second World War also saw the development of another unique style of military music — Canadian naval bands serving afloat. The first, formed in March 1944, was under the direction of Petty Officer Elliot Van Evera, and was aboard the HMCS *Nabob*, a former British aircraft carrier. A second ship's band was formed at the School of Music in 1944 and served aboard the HMCS *Uganda*. These bandsmen, aside from their

Royal Canadian Navy Band, Halifax, 1940. (Kopstein Collection)

duties as musicians, were required to fit into the clock-like precision of the operational functions of the ships. They acted as medics, spotters, manned guns and did a variety of jobs under action conditions. A typical ship's band during the war was utilitarian by design and the musicians selected were very versatile. *Nabob's* fifteen musicians were a leader, three clarinets, two saxes, one horn, two trumpets, one trombone, one euphonium, one tuba, and three percussionists.

The RCN bands were an inspiration to sailors during the war. The musicians were untiring performers and entertainers. They played for thousands of wartime functions and gave many spirited concerts across Canada and overseas. Their contribution in ceremonial parades and precision marching has endured four decades of changes within the Canadian military system.

The Air Force Bands

During the visit of King George VI and Queen Elizabeth to Canada in 1939, a special grant was used to purchase a set of band instruments to equip a brass and reed band for RCAF Station Trenton. Band personnel consisted of tradesmen with musical ability who volunteered their services for this work in their leisure time. The band developed a fair degree of proficiency as a volunteer organization, but numerous difficulties continually detracted from its performance. For instance, the band might be called out for an engagement but the tradesmen were not available during working hours because it interfered with their duties.

With the declaration of war, the part-time bandsmen scheme continued to be impractical as a number of musicians in the band were in strategic wartime occupations. The volunteer band was able to continue until 1940 when it was decided that a different system would have to be inaugurated. In June that year, authority was granted to form five RCAF bands, each consisting of a leader and twenty-nine players. The bands were to be formed in Vancouver, Toronto, Ottawa, Brandon and Dartmouth. The Vancouver location was later changed to Patricia Bay and the Brandon location to Winnipeg. The suggested instrumentation for these bands permitted flexibility; as an example, the original band consisted of one leader, seven clarinets, three saxophones, six cornets, three horns, three trombones, two euphoniums, three basses and two percussionists.

Personnel were remustered from other trades, five bandmasters were selected, and within a few months the bands were functioning successfully. A departure from the usual form of organizing military bands was tried and proved successful. Instead of attempting to organize a complete

Royal Canadian Air Force Band in front of Grace United Church, Winnipeg, 1943-44. (Public Archives of Canada PL 1750)

band from the personnel in the district where the band was situated, all potential players were auditioned, and suitable formations were established from this pooling of resources. In this way, a better balance was obtained throughout all the bands.

In the beginning, bandsmen were to be classified as standard general duties (bandsmen) and were to be employed as such except for two practice periods of two hours per week. The position of bandmaster was for full-time duties on musical work. Personnel for these positions were enlisted as aircraftsmen second-class, their promotion was accelerated and they qualified as acting sergeants after three months' service. Upon enlistment, all bandsmen were required to sign a waiver to the effect that, although classified as a bandsman, they would be required to do other jobs when not employed with the band. Other bands with part-time bandsmen were formed across the country in such centres as Calgary and Regina.

In January 1941 the RCAF Central Band was posted to RCAF Station Rockcliffe near Ottawa and became the first full-time air force band in the summer of that year, under the direction of Flying Officer Martin Boundy. By late that fall, there were sixteen part-time RCAF bands across Canada, including trumpet bands. The sixty-six piece RCAF Central Band provided the headquarters to test and select musicians and bandmasters for all other RCAF bands.

Flying Officer Boundy took the RCAF Overseas Headquarters Band, consisting of forty musicians, to the United Kingdom in 1942. The band was immediately successful and became very heavily committed, playing 373 engagements in their first year overseas. In fact, the band was unable to meet all of the requests for their services, and, as a result, three more military bands and a dance band were sent overseas. The Bournemouth Band, under Bandmaster Flight Sergeant S. V. Vowden, arrived in August 1943; the RCAF No. 6 Group Band under the baton of Warrant Officer Clifford Hunt arrived in April 1944; and the Warrington Band, conducted by Warrant Officer Leroy, reached England in October 1944. In addition to being prepared for all military duties, each thirty-three member band was capable of providing a first-class dance orchestra. In 1944, the RCAF Streamliners dance orchestra and show band, under Corporal Carter became the first separate dance band to be posted to a theatre of war.

The RCAF bands toured the United Kingdom playing various military band and dance engagements. Many RCAF church parades were made more impressive by the use of one of the bands. In June 1943, the RCAF Overseas Headquarters Band took part in one of England's most colourful pageants, the parade at the annual Shakespeare Festival at Stratford-upon-Avon. RCAF bands assisted in Victory Loan parades and other campaigns to raise money for the war effort. During the Wings For

Royal Canadian Air Force Band Church Parade, Lincoln's Inn Field 1943-44. The Mayor of the Borough of Holborne is on the left. (Kopstein Collection)

Royal Canadian Air Force Band, No. 7 I.T.S. Band, Saskatoon, Saskatchewan, July 1943. (Kopstein Collection)

Victory campaign in 1943, the Overseas Headquarters Band played over a hundred engagements in the counties of Sussex, Surrey, and Kent.

The first BBC broadcast by the Headquarters Band was made in December 1942, and it became a regular performer on the Home, General Forces and Overseas Service of the BBC. All of the bands took part in recorded programs that were sent to far-flung theatres of war. RCAF bands were heard at least twice weekly on transcription broadcasts and the Streamliners dance orchestra was a popular feature on the RCAF show that went out on the BBC's entire network of live broadcasts.

RCAF bands overseas performed two thousand seven hundred and seventy-eight engagements during their time in Britain. The Headquarters Band alone performed over eleven hundred times during its three years overseas. The bands played a very important role in the life of RCAF personnel overseas, providing a much-needed diversion.

The official organ of the RCAF overseas was the weekly newspaper *Wings Abroad* and it remarked upon the arrival of the first RCAF band in September 1942, under Flying Officer Boundy. Martin Boundy eventually became the wartime Supervisor of Music for the RCAF. He had a wealth of band experience, having been director of the Tillsonburg Citizens' Band and having helped organize and train the Brantford Boys' Band. Later issues of *Wings Abroad* described the RCAF bands' activities and kept them in the forefront. From the May 15, 1944 issue:

HQ BAND TO PLAY THURSDAY AT NOON

Thursday afternoon at 12:30 the RCAF Overseas HQ Band under the baton of F/O Martin Boundy will begin a series of concerts in Lincoln's Inn Fields. The programs have been prepared for the entertainment of HQ personnel. The program includes Colonel Bogey on Parade, The Two Pigeons, If I Were King, Artists' Life, Three Trumpeters, Three Blind Mice, and Road to Morocco.

Other programs in the same series included the international operatic soprano, Isobel Much of Regina, who had joined the RCAF as a Special Entertainment Officer. She sang, "Brown Bird Singing," "Solveig's Song," and "Alleluia." The band program included "Thunder and Blazes," "Sylvia," "Sleeping Beauty," "Plymouth Hoe," "Murmurs des Fleurs," and "Dancing Years." In Montreal, RCAF Bandmaster Carl Friberg created a most unusual souvenir. He turned the head of the bass drum into an autograph album. Each time the band played before a distinguished or famous personage, the bass drum collected another name. Eventually the list of names inscribed on the drumhead read like a "Who's Who" of wartime Canada, including Princess Juliana of Holland, Jack Benny, Lauritz Melchior, Eugene Ormandy, and Billy Bishop, just to name a few. Canadian highlights for the RCAF bands between the years 1942-45 were the Aid Russia Show in the Montreal Forum with Eleanor Roosevelt as guest speaker and

Royal Canadian Air Force No. 5 EFTS Band, September 1944. (Public Archives of Canada PMR 81-296)

104

Royal Canadian Air Force Overseas Band, England, 1945. Governor General Massey is standing at left. (Kopstein Collection)

a 1944 performance as the stage band for an operatic performance of Tristan and Isolde under the baton of Sir Thomas Beecham.

The RCAF Woman's Division Band, a brass and reed band stationed at Rockcliffe, became official in August 1942. The band was composed of spare-time musicians and a year passed before the unit became operational. The job of enlisting and training went to RCAF Bandmaster Maurice M. Dunmall. In April of 1944, the band was posted to Brantford and was featured in a series of concerts. It followed up with a tour in aid of the fifth Victory Loan Drive.

The Women's Division Band, in the last year of its existence, averaged over thirty engagements per month including both military and off-station performances. It was a worthy record of achievement, particularly as most of the young women who took part were neophyte musicians trained in other fields.

RCAF bands in Canada were particularly effective in providing dance orchestras from the ranks of their military bands. One of the most solid station dance bands was organized in Trenton in the summer of 1939, and through the war years, the band became a sensation in the Trenton area. Its original organizer, Flight Sergeant Stan McGuire led the band, which had a twelve-man aggregation.

Royal Canadian Air Force Central Band. Director is Martin Boundy. (Kopstein Collection)

Many of the bandsmen remained with the air force when the war ended in 1945. Although the overseas bands were disbanded, the RCAF retained three of the wartime bands. Many of the musicians, including Cliff Hunt and Carl Friberg, ultimately became the bandleaders after the war. Martin Boundy went on to become the conductor of the London, Ontario, Symphony Orchestra.

CHAPTER 6

The Modern Era
1946–1968

The Royal Canadian Navy was authorized two bands for postwar service, and musicians were selected from wartime personnel who indicated they were interested in remaining in the navy. The end of the war brought about a reduction of personnel in air force bands, but the RCAF Central Band continued to flourish, and two new bands were formed: in 1946, Flight Lieutenant Hunt organized the RCAF Training Command Band in Toronto, followed in 1947 by the Tactical Air Command Band in Winnipeg. In March 1947, all of Canada's full-time active force bands were reduced to nil strength. At the same time, three prewar army bands, the RCA, RCR and R22R were reconstituted. That summer, the PPCLI band was activated. At the same time there began a reorganization that envisaged a gradual peacetime development for both regular and militia bands in Canada.

With the formation of the Korean and European brigades in 1950 and 1951 came a rapid expansion of Canadian army bands as well as pipe and bugle bands. In the Reserve Force over 350 bands were authorized across Canada, including 106 thirty-piece military bands.

On paper, as of December 6, 1951, the Canadian army had nine Regular Force bands in operation. The reality of the situation was that with the exception of the RCR, RCA, R22R and PPCLI (bands that were short-staffed), the other bands did not exist.

When the Canadian army had reorganized in 1946, authority had been granted for the formation of fourteen regular bands. The result of all this restructuring was the recognition of the value of bands and the effect that they had on troops and the civilian population. The following indicates the name of the unit, date of formation and location of bands that were established post-war.

Royal Canadian Horse Artillery Band	24 October 1952	Winnipeg
Royal Canadian Artillery Band	4 February 1952	Halifax
Lord Strathcona's Horse (Royal Canadians) Band	5 September 1956	Edmonton
Royal Canadian Dragoons Band	2 January 1955	Camp Borden
Royal Canadian Regiment Band	1 October 1946	Brockville
Princess Patricia's Canadian Light Infantry Band	5 July 1946	Wainwright
Royal 22e Regiment Band	1 October 1946	Quebec
Royal Canadian Engineers Band	1 July 1953	Chilliwack
Royal Canadian Corps of Signals Band	4 September 1952	Kingston
Black Watch (Royal Highland Regiment) of Canada Band	22 April 1954	Gagetown
Canadian Guards Band	22 April 1954	Petawawa
Royal Canadian Ordnance Corps Band	4 January 1956	Montreal

Authority was also granted for the formation of a band for the Queen's Own Rifles and the Royal Canadian Army Service Corps. These bands were ordered to remain at nil strength until further orders, however, neither band was ever activated in the regular forces.

The air force experienced little difficulty in recruiting musicians for their bands, probably because some of the wartime musicians became well-known bandleaders. Both Cliff Hunt and Carl Friberg, for instance, opted to return to the air force following the war.

Some musicians were attracted to the navy bands because of the universal fascination with the sea and an affinity for the ceremonial aspects of the navy. The navy also took a giant step in 1954 by establishing the Naval Bandsman Apprentice Plan that will be discussed in a later chapter. Both the air force and the navy began actively to seek musicians in the United Kingdom who, on their own volition, were emigrating to Canada. Royal Marine musicians were drawn to the RCN as they were easily assimilated into the naval tradition.

The outlook for Canadian army bands remained bleak throughout the period following the war and into the early 1950s. Since there was no active recruitment in the United Kingdom and many wartime musicians had opted to try other fields, the Supervisor of Music, Major A. L. Streeter, who had faced a similar task during the war, was unable to enrol enough musicians to meet the existing vacancies for the Canadian Army.

In August 1952, there were thirty-three vacancies for bandsmen to staff at least five bands. This included the instrumentation of five flutes, six E-flat clarinets, six oboes, thirty-three B-flat clarinets, five alto saxes, two tenor saxes, eighteen French horns, six cornets/trumpets, three trombones, six bass trombones, one bass, and two percussionists. That year, however, the problems faced by the army in obtaining competent musicians were completely resolved. An agreement was struck with the government of The Netherlands to allow Dutch musicians to emigrate to Canada. This came about as a result of a handover ceremony of Canadian equipment to Holland. The Dutch defence minister asked Canadian Minister of Defence Brooke Claxton what Canada wanted in return, and Claxton replied "Bandsmen."

The only musicians not permitted to join Canadian army bands were members of Holland's two elite bands. The Dutch musicians who were finally accepted for service in the Canadian army were enrolled as privates and were eventually promoted to the rank of band sergeant, which had become the working rank for bands. In addition, in January 1953, permission was granted to enlist professional musicians in the United Kingdom. In early April 1953, the first musicians were posted to army units in Canada.

Following the original postings, several other Dutch musicians were enrolled, and enlistment ceased in 1967, with two hundred and fifty musicians having joined Canadian military bands. The enlistment of musicians from the United Kingdom brought nearly two hundred musicians.

On the unification of the Canadian Armed Forces in 1968, seventeen military bands were divided up among the three services. There were three navy bands, twelve army bands and two air force bands. Between 1952 and 1960 nearly one thousand musicians had been employed by the bands on a full-time basis and most of them were fully equipped with a balanced instrumentation. This period was the golden era of military music in Canada.

An Overview of Regular Force Bands

Royal Canadian Navy Bands

In 1946, demobilization was in full swing, and all but fifteen musicians were released from the navy. Recruiting was instituted again in 1947, and bands were established at three major training bases, HMCS *Stadacona* in Halifax, HMCS *Naden* in Victoria, and HMCS *Cornwallis* in Cornwallis. The *Stadacona* Band enjoyed an outstanding reputation almost from its rebirth. In 1949, provided music for various RCN shows in the Halifax area, and in 1949, an original show the RCN Review, played to sell-out crowds at Halifax's Citadel Theatre. During 1963 the band played over two hundred and sixty engagements across Canada. The director of the band was Lieutenant Stan Sunderland who had served as bandmaster during the war. Another wartime director, Lieutenant Commander Harry Cuthbert, replaced him in 1956.

During the period 1947-56, the *Stadacona* Band also provided all ships' bands for the aircraft carriers *Warrior, Magnificent,* and *Bonaventure.* In 1965, the *Cornwallis* Band and various naval reserve personnel boosted the *Stadacona* Band's manpower to sixty and it was flown to England to perform at the Liverpool Commonwealth Tattoo. It participated at Chatham for the commissioning of the Canadian submarine *Ojibway* and

The HMCS Naden Band, Victoria, BC, 1953. Drum Major is Gord Brown. (DND Photo 41146)

the launching of the submarine *Onondaga*. By this time, the band was under the direction of Lieutenant William J. Gordon, who expanded the profile of the band with performances at the Prince Edward Island Centennial and as guest band at the Tatamagouche Festival of the Arts.

After the war, the *Cornwallis* Band was reformed with a complement of twelve musicians. This band provided music for naval divisions on a daily basis and performed for a variety of military commitments. As *Cornwallis* was a major training base for naval recruits and later for Canadian Forces recruits, the band was extremely busy. It was used as the nucleus for a much larger group which performed the sunset ceremony in Nova Scotia and which travelled to locations across Canada. Captain John Collins, a graduate of the Royal Marine School of Music, was the director of the band during the 1960s, and through his leadership this band was brought to peak efficiency.

The band of HMCS *Naden* in Victoria was reformed in late 1945 for service at the HMCS *Naden* Training Establishment. This band became very popular during its extensive tours of the western provinces in 1949. In 1950, the thirty-piece band visited twenty-five cities in western Canada under the direction of Lieutenant Commander Harry Cuthbert. In 1950, the band served on HMCS *Ontario* for a cruise to Hawaii and began a concert series at the Pacific National Exhibition in Vancouver. They were

Canadian Forces Stadacona Band. Director of Music is Lt (N) Ben Templars, 1980s. (DND Photo)

heavily involved in the Royal visit of 1952. This year also marked the arrival of Harry Bateman, the first Royal Marine musician in the RCN. Bateman rose to the rank of Chief Warrant Officer and became Assistant Director of Music. He was one of the trio of naval musicians who were the driving force behind the establishment of the Royal Canadian Navy School of Music at Esquimalt in 1953.

In 1954, the band was featured at the British Empire Games in Vancouver, performing for the opening display, an extravaganza which showcased the talent of the Assistant Director of Music, Emile Michaux. The following year, Emile Michaux was instrumental in developing the half-time display given by the *Naden* Band, the Training Command Band and the Engineers Band at the Grey Cup football game held at Exhibition Stadium in Vancouver.

In 1955, the navy issued their first Manual of Drill and Ceremonial, one of the most significant documents ever produced for bands in Canada. It detailed the movements for navy bandsmen and drum majors, and it also provided a scale for navy band instrumentation.

Royal Canadian Navy Bands 1955						
Size of Band	16	22	30	37	40	46
Flute and Piccolo	1	1	2	2	2	3
Oboe and English Horn	-	-	1	1	1	2
E-flat Clarinet	-	-	1	1	1	1
Alto Clarinet	-	-	-	-	1	1
B-flat Clarinet	4	6	8	9	10	12
Bass Clarinet	-	-	-	-	1	1
Bassoon	-	-	-	1	1	-
Saxophones	2	2	2	4	3	4
Cornets	4	4	5	5	3	4
Trumpets	-	-	-	-	2	2
Horns	1	2	2	4	4	4
Tenor Trombone	1	2	2	2	2	2
Bass Trombone	-	1	1	1	1	1
Euphonium	-	-	1	1	1	1
Bass	1	2	3	3	4	4
Percussion	1	1	1	2	2	3
Bandmaster	1	1	1	1	1	1

Occasionally sixteen-piece bands were posted aboard ships, a practice which had started in 1951. The last ship's band appeared in 1958 although Canadian Forces bands have shipped out on special cruises over the years.

The *Naden* Band in 1968 went to Disneyland in California for a special celebration honouring the birthday of Mickey Mouse. While in

California, it appeared in a military tattoo sponsored by the United States Marines that was viewed by an audience said to be in excess of twenty thousand people. This performance marked the final hurrah for the HMCS *Naden* Band, as in 1968 it was integrated into the Canadian Armed Forces retaining the name *Naden* Band.

Canadian Army Bands

In 1945, the Royal Canadian Horse Artillery Band was one of three remaining in Camp Petawawa. By 1946, because of releases, only twenty musicians remained in the band. By 1952, it was down to fourteen musicians but still managed to carry out many engagements, including a tour that stretched from Thunder Bay to the Alberta border. The next year, the band received a much-needed increase in manpower, and by 1955 it had fifty-five musicians. The band had moved to Shilo in 1953, and, after a tour of Germany in 1955, it took up residence in Winnipeg. In 1961 Captain Alec Lee became the Director of Music, and the band became a fixture in the prairie provinces, playing at numerous fairs and in special educational programs. In October 1968, the band sounded Last Post and was disbanded under the integration policy.

In 1952, the Royal Canadian Artillery Band established itself in Halifax with Captain Harry Wragg as its first Director of Music, and, like other

Royal Canadian Regiment Band at the National War Memorial, 1948. Drum Major is Pete Graham. (Kopstein Collection)

Royal Canadian Dragoons Band, 1951. (Public Archives of Canada PMR 82-20)

army bands, a very limited instrumentation. In August of 1953, the band, augmented with musicians from Holland and the United Kingdom, left for Korea to entertain troops of the allied forces. Visiting Japan on their way back to Canada, the band performed a concert in the Ernie Pyle Theatre in Tokyo. In 1955, the band was posted to Germany, but Captain Wragg returned to Canada and was replaced by Captain Kenneth Elloway, a dynamic leader who created a whole new dimension for Canadian military bands. He invited guest performers to appear with the band, and he was also able to arrange radio appearances on the BBC. The RCA Band visited Bermuda in 1957 for the Bermuda Tattoo. Under Captain Elloway the band appeared frequently on the CBC and achieved a tremendous amount of publicity for the army in Halifax. He created a versatile musical ensemble that contained the nucleus of a first-class string orchestra as well as swing and dance orchestras. In 1968, the band, like many others, was "axed," with the musicians being absorbed into the *Stadacona* Band.

The Royal Canadian Dragoons Band began operation in July 1955, with twelve musicians under the baton of Captain E. G. Spooner. Several musicians were posted in from other bands to augment the band and by March 1956 it had a strength of forty-two members. The very colourful full dress was introduced that year on a parade for Major General Allen Worthington. The solo cornetist with the RCD Band was Band Staff Sergeant Guy Noakes of the famed 48th Highlanders, who had been a navy bandmaster during the war. In the fall of 1959, the band was selected

Royal Canadian Regiment Band, Wolseley Barracks, London, Ontario, 1968. (Kopstein Collection)

for a two-year tour of duty with the Fourth Canadian Infantry Brigade in Germany. In May 1960, the band flew to Egypt, where they entertained Canadian troops on the Gaza Strip. While in Germany the band also volunteered its services to perform with the Anglo-Canadian group known as the Hemer Amateur Musical Society, winning acclaim for Gilbert and Sullivan operettas. On their return from Germany in 1961, the band was posted to Camp Gagetown and began making tours of the Maritimes. In 1964, it made a six-week tour of Prince Edward Island in connection with the Island's centennial celebrations, and later that year a tour of Newfoundland. It continued to assist amateur theatrical groups, volunteering its services to groups all over New Brunswick. When the band ceased operation in 1968, another victim of integration, forty-three musicians were dispersed to various other bands. This area did not have another professional band until the RCR Band was posted to Gagetown in 1970.

The band of the Lord Strathcona's Horse was activated in Calgary in the fall of 1956. A nucleus of twenty-six musicians was posted from the PPCLI Band in December, and in March 1957 the band became fully operational. During that summer the band went on a twenty-eight-day tour of British Columbia, ending with a tattoo in Kelowna. It made numerous appearances across Saskatchewan during 1958 for the province's diamond jubilee. The band was among those featured at the Seattle World's Fair in 1962 under Director of Music Captain F. M. McLeod. He was replaced in 1968 by Captain Maurice Ziska 1965-68 and the Strathcona's Band was integrated into the PPCLI Band as part of the policy to reduce the numbers of Canadian army bands.

1st Canadian Rifle Battalion Bugle Band, Hanover, Germany, June 1953. (Rick Cain, Oshawa)

In May 1953, authority was granted for the reactivation of the Royal Canadian Engineers Band with members recruited from Canada, Holland, and the United Kingdom. The band was organized very quickly and stationed at Vedder Crossing in Chilliwack, B.C. A review of the instrumentation reveals the depth of this band almost from its inception. It consisted of two flutes, one E-flat clarinet, two oboes, sixteen B-flat clarinets, two alto and two tenor saxes, one baritone sax, two bassoons, four French horns, eight B-flat cornets, five trombones, two euphoniums, two tubas and three percussionists.

In July 1954, the RCE Band left for a six-month tour of duty with the First Canadian Infantry Brigade in Europe. They performed several military and public engagements in Luxembourg, Antwerp, and Nijmegen, one of them the ceremonies commemorating the Tenth Anniversary of the Liberation of Holland. During its formative years, the band's Director of Music was Captain A. L. Brown, a wartime member of the RCR Band. After its return to Canada, the RCE Band played a very big role in the development of music in British Columbia. It gave concerts throughout the province on behalf of the Canadian Army Recruiting Services and was the featured band in 1961 at the Grey Cup game in Vancouver. That same year, Captain Leonard Camplin, who had emigrated from England, was appointed Director of Music. Under Captain Camplin's direction the band appeared at hundreds of music clinics and concerts across British Columbia. The RCE Band met the same fate as other bands in 1968, when it was disbanded. Many of the musicians, including Captain Camplin, moved to the *Naden* Band in Victoria.

The Royal Canadian Corps of Signals Band, based at Vimy Barracks in Kingston, made its debut in September 1952. It was a participant in the ceremonies honouring Queen Elizabeth's coronation in 1953, and the same year, it played a prominent role in the Fiftieth Anniversary of the Royal Canadian Signal Corps. That November, it was posted to Korea for six months with the Twenty-Fifth Brigade, returning to Kingston in May 1954 after playing a one-week tour of Japan en route.

The band's first director was Captain Bernard Lyons, who guided the fortunes of the band for five years. It began a two-year tour of Germany in 1955. While overseas, the band played at a Commonwealth foreign ministers' reception for Queen Elizabeth at the Palace of Versailles and it did a grand tour of the Netherlands that attracted huge audiences because of the band's large Dutch contingent. In 1957, Captain Lyons was replaced by Captain Charles Adams, and the band returned to Vimy Barracks. Because of their proximity to Ottawa, the Signals Band was often called upon to provide music for state functions; it played for President John F. Kennedy, President Charles DeGaulle, and many members of the royal family.

On integration of the Canadian Forces in 1968, the band was retained and renamed the Air Transport Command Band, later assuming the name the Vimy Band for the Kingston area barracks which had been their home since their inception.

Royal 22e Régiment Band, The Citadel, Quebec City, 1964. (Kopstein Collection)

In January 1956, the Royal Canadian Ordinance Corps Band was formed under Captain Gerald Gagnier. The band was located at Long Pointe Barracks in Montreal. By 1957, its fifty-four musicians were playing for recruiting concerts across Quebec as well as making a tour of central Ontario and playing a mass band concert in Ottawa. It took part in the inaugural ceremonies for the Governor General that year and was seen on CBC television coverage of the event.

In May 1960, Captain Charles Villeneuve replaced Captain Gagnier as Director of Music. Captain Villeneuve had had a distinguished background as an oboist with the R22R Band and had been with the Orchestre Symphonique de Quebec as well as having appeared on many CBC classical and variety shows.

The RCOC Band was the last army band to make an extended tour of duty at the Canadian military establishment in Germany, leaving Canada in 1965 and returning in 1968. The band was disbanded in August 1968, and its members became the nucleus for the RCA Band that was reconstituted in Montreal the same year.

Although authorized in 1954, the Black Watch (Royal Highland Regiment) of Canada Military Band was not activated until 1955. In 1958 it took up residence in Camp Gagetown, New Brunswick, under Director of Music Captain Doug Start. Captain Start retired in 1961 and was replaced by Captain Harvey Eagles, who had enrolled in the RCR Band in 1944 and been selected for bandmaster training in 1957. In 1962, the Black Watch Band was posted to serve with the Fourth Canadian Brigade in Soest, Germany, and in 1965, it moved to Montreal to replace the RCOC Band. In nearly fourteen years of operation from 1954 to 1968, the Black Watch Band had a very minimal turnover of personnel and lost only eighty musicians to attrition or release. The band was thirty-nine strong when it was disbanded in 1968.

Royal Canadian Artillery Band, Halifax, 1960s. (Kopstein Collection)

Royal Canadian Horse Artillery Band. Director of Music is C. A. Holt with the 27th Brigade, Germany. (RCA Museum, Shilo, Manitoba)

The Canadian Guards Band was originally the First Canadian Infantry Battalion Band, formed at Camp Valcartier during the summer of 1951, when fifteen bandsmen began training under Captain Melville Scott and Band Sergeant Norman Heathcote. In October 1951, Captain James Gayfer, who had been Command Inspector, replaced Captain Scott, who went on to become Supervisor of Music of Canadian army bands.

The Band departed for Germany in November with a total strength of only twelve musicians. During its thirteen-month tour this little group acquitted itself miraculously, fulfilling all of its commitments. On its return to Canada it took up residence in Camp Borden and began to feel the effects of the heavy recruitment in the United Kingdom and Holland; the band increased in number to over fifty musicians. Also, Captain Gayfer had attracted a number of very good Canadian musicians. The Band was sent to the Far East in July 1954, where it played numerous engagements, often under difficult conditions, before returning to Camp Borden. In 1957, it was renamed the Canadian Guards Band and posted to Camp Petawawa, where its role became chiefly that of a ceremonial band providing music for guards of honour and for public duties in Ottawa.

The Guards Band was the main band employed for several weeks each summer for the Changing of the Guard ceremonies on Parliament Hill.

In October 1968 the band was phased out as part of integration and the members were dispersed to other bands.

Princess Patricia's Canadian Light Infantry Band, 1969-70. (Kopstein Collection)

The Royal 22e Regiment Band had remained active throughout the war under the direction of Captain Edwin Belanger. In March 1947 the band was reformed with the original number of twenty-two musicians. In 1948, the full-dress scarlet uniform was reintroduced. In the 1950s the band did its part for the Korean War effort first by playing for the arrivals and departures of hundreds of troop ships in Fort Lewis, Washington, and then by actually serving in Korea. In 1953, it was selected to tour Europe, where it broadcast over the BBC and led the Canadian contingent for the coronation of Queen Elizabeth.

Captain Belanger was succeeded by Captain Armand Ferland, a brilliant performer and conductor, who helped to organize the gala music evenings that soon became the trademark of the R22R Band. After twelve years, Captain Ferland became a Command Inspector and was replaced by Belgium-born Captain Jean Pierret. Under the baton of Captain Pierret, the band made frequent tours of Canada, the USA, Cyprus, and Europe, bringing international fame to the unit that it represented. The band was maintained in Quebec despite the integration of the forces in 1968.

When the Canadian army was reorganized in 1947, the Princess Patricia's Canadian Light Infantry were authorized to have a military band. It was activated under Warrant Officer R. Summer in 1949. Although the band was able to function, it was not until 1951 that it became firmly established under Captain A. L. Brown. Captain Brown had inherited a small but efficient group of musicians, and he kept the band spirit alive by finding as many performance venues as he could.

In 1953, the twenty-piece band was selected to tour the Far East and performed in many locations, particularly those where PPCLI troops were stationed. On its return to Canada, the band was augmented by new enlistments from across Canada, Holland, and the United Kingdom until it reached its authorized strength of fifty-five musicians. Captain Brown

Air Command Band, 1959. Director of Music is Carl Frieberg. (Kopstein Collection)

left in 1954 to take over the RCE Band and was replaced by Captain F. M. MacLeod, later to become Director of the Strathcona's Band. In 1957, Captain Herb Jeffrey took over and the band was sent overseas. It had an extremely active schedule, appearing in Holland for Queen Elizabeth's visit there in 1958 and being part of the Tenth NATO Anniversary Parade in Mainz, West Germany. In 1959 it was the first Canadian band to appear at the prestigious Royal Military Tournament. Returning to Canada in 1957, the band took up residence in Edmonton and appeared in a Regimental benefit for veterans of the PPCLI. Although efforts had been made to disband the PPCLI Band in 1967, it was retained as a one of the Canadian Forces Bands after integration.

Sergeant Peter Graham was given the task of organizing the reactivated Royal Canadian Regiment Band in 1946, and his untiring efforts gathered together twenty musicians. Warrant Officer Bill Armstrong, who had been a solo cornetist with the RCR Band before the war, was appointed bandmaster in 1947. In 1950, the band moved to Petawawa and Bill Armstrong was commissioned as the Director of Music in the rank of Captain. Captain Armstrong saw the band through its busy tour of duty in Korea, and in 1953 he became a Command Band Inspector. He was replaced by Captain Joseph Purcell, who had spent twenty-five years in the Imperial Army and was a graduate of Kneller Hall. Under Captain Purcell, the band journeyed to Germany as staff band for the Canadian Brigade. They played on Omaha Beach to commemorate the Tenth Anniversary of D-Day. By the time they returned to Canada, the band's numbers had increased from thirty-eight to fifty-five due to the influx of musicians from Holland and the United Kingdom. Captain Purcell retired in 1963 and was replaced by Captain Derek Stannard.

After integration in 1968, the band stayed in London. Its instrumentation was two flutes, one oboe, one E-flat clarinet, nine B-flat clarinets, one bass clarinet, two bassoons, two saxophones, three French horns, eight trumpets, three trombones, two euphoniums, one cello, one string bass, three tubas and three percussionists.

Royal Canadian Air Force Bands

Flight Lieutenant Clifford Hunt organized the RCAF Training Command Band in 1946. Early recognition for this band came when they were engaged to play ten concerts in the bandshell at the CNE in 1947. By 1957, under Flight Lieutenant Hunt, the band had grown to fifty-five musicians. The band made a triumphal tour of Europe in 1961, with performances in England, France and Luxembourg, playing before an estimated one hundred and eighty thousand people. In 1960, Flight Lieutenant Hunt was promoted to squadron leader and appointed Supervisor of Music for the RCAF. In April 1963, the band, now under Flying Officer Ted Robbins, appeared in concert at Massey Hall in Toronto. Two years later, a lack of funding forced the band to be disbanded. The establishment of the RCAF was cut to two bands, the RCAF Central Band in Ottawa and the RCAF Training Command Band in Winnipeg.

Royal Canadian Air Force Central Band, Trenton Gates, Trenton, Ontario, 1958. (Kopstein Collection)

122

The RCAF Training Command Band was one of the three original bands within the air force. The foundation for this band was laid during the war in Winnipeg. It was reformed in 1947 under the baton of Bandmaster Warrant Officer Carl Friberg. In 1947, the band was transferred to Edmonton and remained there until 1964 under three separate names: the Northwest Air Command Band, the Tactical Air Group Band, and finally the Training Command Band. In 1964 the band was transferred to Winnipeg. During the years they were led by Carl Friberg, they travelled extensively and became well known in almost every community in western Canada, including areas where other bands had not ventured, such as Whitehorse, Yellowknife, and Fort Churchill. In 1951, Carl Friberg was commissioned and posted to the Central Band in Ottawa, to be replaced by Flying Officer Leo Corcoran. In 1955, following the band's extensive tour of Europe, Carl Friberg returned as bandmaster, and for the next six years led the band in a most innovative fashion. He introduced several soloists, including trumpet virtuoso Raphael Mendez and world renown saxophone artist Sigurd Raascher.

The instrumentation of the Training Command Band in 1958 was two flutes, two oboes, two bassoons, seventeen B-flat clarinets, one alto clarinet and one bass clarinet, two alto and two tenor saxes, three cornets, two trumpets, four horns, five trombones, two euphoniums, two tubas, two string bass and three percussionists.

Upon unification of the Canadian Forces in 1968, the Royal Canadian Horse Artillery Band in Winnipeg was incorporated into the Training Command Band under Flight Lieutenant Howard Woods. Captain C. Furey replaced Flight Lieutenant Woods in 1969.

The Central Band of the RCAF was officially formed in 1940 and maintained throughout the war. It was one of the few bands that remained in existence after the war. It was originally under the baton of Flying Officer Martin Boundy, who was replaced by Squadron Leader Edward

Canadian Forces Air Transport Command Band, 1968. Director of Music is Captain K. R. Moore. (DND Photo)

Kirkwood. In late 1951, Squadron Leader Kirkwood was appointed Supervisor of Music for the RCAF, and combined the position with his duties as Director of the Central Band. In 1955 the Central Band was turned over to Flight Lieutenant Leo Corcoran who had been transferred from the Training Command Band. Under Flight Lieutenant Corcoran, the band became a favourite of eastern Canadians and appeared throughout the Maritimes, central Canada, the United States and overseas. In 1963, Warrant Officer Kenneth Moore, who had been the assistant conductor and trumpet soloist, replaced Flight Lieutenant Corcoran.

In 1968 it was renamed the National Band of the Canadian Forces and came under the direction of Lieutenant Commander William Gordon, former Director of the Stadacona Band.

Canadian Forces Tattoo 1967

From the earliest days of Canada's history, the military was very closely associated with our growth and development. Therefore, in 1967, it was fitting that the armed forces were called upon to participate in Canada's one hundredth birthday celebrations to demonstrate this vital link with our past.

The Department of National Defence Centennial Planning Committee began to plan the activities for 1967 in 1965. At a meeting in November of that year, the producer of the Canadian Forces Tattoo, Major Ian Fraser, described the presentation of the tattoo. There was to be a specially designed set consisting of a fort with a martello tower, and in front of this, two hours of entertainment would depict various aspects of the military in Canada from 1655 to 1967. The program was designed to include impressions of early French and British garrison life, spectacular drills, Scottish dancing, mass bands marching and countermarching, First and Second World War scenes, the lighter side of UN peacekeeping operations, and a gymnastic display. Throughout the production, authentic costumes, including weapons and accoutrements appropriate for the period, were to be used, and Reserve bands were given financial assistance to update their full-dress uniforms.

By October 1966, a list of band requirements had been compiled by the Director General of the Centennial and passed to the Director of Bands at the Directorate of Ceremonial in Ottawa. The job of co-ordinating this massive operation fell to Major A. L. Brown, and it wasn't long before he circulated a consolidated list of the instrumental requirements from each Regular Force band. Since it was planned that the bands would continue to operate while tattoo performers were away for rehearsals and cross

CF Air Transport Command Band, 1968. (DND Photo)

country performances, each band was asked to submit a levy of musicians in accordance with a formula.

In addition to the tattoo requirements, a Regular Force band was permanently assigned to Expo 67 in Montreal on a rotational basis. Also, all through the summer, the Canadian Guards Band and the Royal 22e Regiment Band were in constant demand to meet VIPs visiting Canada.

An example of how busy the military bands were in Centennial year is seen in the Naden Band's schedule. This band, already fully employed in the tattoo, the British Columbia provincial program, and the Pacific Naval Assembly, was further committed to other performances in Saskatchewan, a two-week duty period at Expo and a ten-day tour of Newfoundland. To ensure that the bands reached all their performances on schedule, the RCAF provided service airlift. For instance, on completion of the outdoor performance in Vancouver on June 5, a massive airlift of personnel was conducted by Hercules aircraft from Vancouver to Montreal.

In late 1965, Captain Ronald Milne had been selected as the Director of Music for the tattoo. He was required to plan all the music requirements in conjunction with the tattoo producer. He eventually arranged the music for all the tattoo scenes, negotiated copyrights, and had all the music copied and forwarded to the bands. He also wrote a dramatic overture to be used as the opening segment. Pipe Major Archie Cairns, who arranged the tattoo's pipe music, assisted him.

The DND Tattoo was a massive military operation. Two contingents travelled by trains to various locations from April 2 until October 7, 1967. The two trains were dubbed the Red Train and the Blue Train, and they carried seventeen hundred service personnel who were involved in the tattoo. The trains were tagged the *Red* and *Blue* and contained a small twenty-five-piece pit band and a field band of forty-five, as well as pipers. Musicians were required to do additional musician duties such as playing

Canadian Provost Drum and Bugle Band, 1955. (Public Archives, DND)

fanfare trumpets and bugles. The trains became "home" to the musicians and tattoo personnel for the duration of the performances.

The Canadian Forces Tattoo opened in Peterborough, Ontario, on the last night of March, 1967. Every seat was filled, and the show, which had been billed as the most ambitious entertainment ever presented in Canada, was an instant success.

On April 8, the tour began and a jubilant producer Ian Fraser echoed everybody's thoughts when he announced to the news media, "I think we've got a bloody great show."

The two trains carrying the indoor shows stopped at thirty-seven communities across Canada. In every location the tattoo was described as "spectacular," and "a triumph of organization." The Kingston *Whig Standard* declared in a headline, "Tattoo Holds Capacity House Enthralled." And the best was yet to come.

The indoor shows were phase one, and the last performances took place on May 15. The Red Train was in Kelowna and the Blue Train in Prince George, British Columbia. Both trains then met in Victoria, where they joined up with the main body of performers, who had gathered for the rehearsals for the outdoor show. The original plan had allowed for eight or nine hundred musicians; that was conservative. When the final tally was made, the figure had grown to over one thousand. The pit band had been expanded, and the field display bands were gigantic.

The first outdoor show opened in Victoria's Centennial Stadium on May 25. A packed house greeted the tattoo, and the audience response was deafening. The show played to sellout crowds across the country before closing the show in Hamilton Civic Stadium on September 9.

This was followed by phase three — more indoor shows. The first was in Summerside on September 16. A fifty-five-piece band composed of musicians from the tattoo performed a concert in the Oakville Bandshell on September 3rd under the direction of Captain Derek Stannard, assisted by Captain Len Camplin. Lieutenant Colonel Cliff Hunt was a guest conductor.

The appreciation for the work of the bands was echoed in an enormous file of letters from provincial authorities. The following extract from the Provincial Secretary of Alberta illustrates the feeling toward the contribution of the bands:

> We received a great deal of co-operation from all the Armed Forces Bands from all parts of the Province...On many occasions their activity in parades and celebration was the "Highlight" of an event. We called upon them for a number of official events...and our requests were always met with courtesy and excellent co-operation. It is the opinion of the Government that this attitude, together with the friendly, courteous spirit of the members of the Armed Forces, did more for public relations for both the Government and the Services than will be realized.

CHAPTER 7

The Pipes and Drums

General Stewart, having regard to the extraordinary loss and fatigue sustained by them, desired that the 92nd [Gordon Highlanders] should not join in the charge…But this time the pipe-major was not to be denied. He struck up the charging tune of "The Haughs of Cromdale," his comrades, seized with what in the Highlands is called mire chath—the frenzy of battle—without either asking or obtaining permission, not only charged but led the charge.

Lieutenant Colonel C. G. Gardyne, The Life of a Regiment, 1903

The Highland bagpipe, or *Piob Mhor* as it is known in Gaelic, has enthralled listeners from time immemorial. Its wild and exciting skirling has spurred men into battle at least as far back as Roman days, as a historian of the first century informs us, Emperor Nero "knew how to play the pipe and the bag thrust under his arm." Evidence also points to the fact that the Romans brought the instrument to Britain at the time of the conquest. It is possible that Scotsmen knew the bagpipe, in primitive form, about two thousand years ago.

Although it figures prominently at the English courts of Edward II and III, as well as Henry VIII, who established court pipes and collected all sorts of bagpipes, its real popularity grew in the rugged highlands. Ideally suited to the outdoors, it was the perfect instrument with which to record clan victories, histories and laments.

From its early form, a simple bag with a melody pipe, or chanter, the Great Highland Bagpipe with its valved mouthpiece, three drones and a reed chanter with finger stops, evolved. Some are instruments of astonishing beauty, with silver embellishments and carvings. Many pipers have been taught their skills by their forebears and are able to trace the family tradition back to days when their ancestors piped the clans into battle on the wild moors. "To the making of a piper go seven generations of his own learning and seven generations before," wrote the historian Neil Munro

Royal Scots of Canada Pipers, 1895. (*Frank Schryver, Toronto*)

some centuries ago. All of the traditional schools of piping in the high-lands of Scotland are gone. There are, however, two main schools for pipers in the United Kingdom; the Army School of Piping located in Edinburgh Castle, affiliated with the Royal Military School of Music, and the College of Piping located in Glasgow, a civilian organization which began in 1947 and is now known throughout the world. In 1983 the Canadian Forces established a school for pipers and drummers under the auspices of the Canadian Forces School of Music located at Canadian Forces Base, Ottawa.

The role of the bagpipe is more than just that of a musical instrument. It is a national institution, particularly in Scotland, and the Scottish fur traders and adventurers who came to Canada over two hundred years ago brought the pipes with them to overcome the tedium of long months and years in isolated trading posts. The explorers, McKenzie and Fraser, are known to have had pipers as members of their teams of adventurers.

In 1759 the pipes brought inspiration to Wolfe's Highlanders at the capture of Quebec. It is recorded that at one point in the fighting, following the climb to the Heights of Abraham, the invaders began to waver. The pipes, silent till then, were brought into action. Rallying, the Highlanders took fresh heart and pressed on to victory. The extent to which Canada's destiny was influenced here by the bagpipe must remain a matter of conjecture, but it is certain that the sound of the pibroch has since marked the progress of many pioneers and Canadian regiments into battle.

A watercolour in the possession of the Hudson's Bay Company, depicts Sir George Simpson, the company's governor, on a tour of inspection in 1828 accompanied by his piper. The same music cheered the Selkirk settlers on their memorable march from Hudson Bay to the Red River. Meanwhile, successive waves of Scottish settlers in the east contributed to the deep-rooted establishment of the pipes in Canadian life and customs. To the uninitiated ear, the bagpipe seems at first to play but one melody, and that one by no means untuneful. Marches, strathspeys, reels, and pibrochs, with all their subtle shades of musical expression, have, to the lover of the pipes, all the emotions of the human heart. Joy or sorrow, love or hate, admiration or scorn, anger or fear, all are within the range of the instrument in the hands of the master. The bagpipes revel in description, the clash of arms, and the tumult of battle, victory and defeat hanging uncertain in the balance. The ecstasy of triumph and the agony of losing are all inescapably linked to the battle music of the pipes.

In war, the piper is the direct descendant of the ancient bards whose part it was to rouse their clansmen to deeds of heroism by reciting the glorious achievements of old time warriors. So has the piper inherited a storehouse of music handed down from ancient days, music in which famous battles of the past are celebrated for the encouragement of soldiers of the present day. Of these *Cogadh no Sith* "War or Peace" is one of the oldest and best known. All the clans played it for centuries when preparing for battle. It was played at Waterloo when the 79th (Cameron Highlanders) formed in a hollow square awaiting the enemy's attack. The

5th Regiment of Highlanders of Canada. (*Frank Schryver, Toronto*)

131

situation was doubtful, every nerve was tense, and the piper, Kenneth McKay, true to his calling, calmly paraded around the outside of the square playing this appropriate tune. There were no misgivings as to the result after that.

Bagpipe tunes formed a musical record of the battles in which Highland regiments or clans with their pipers took part. A piper, who had been there composed a commemorative piece, and if his tune was received with approval, it was added to the list of the tunes of war.

The first Scottish regiments to see service in Canada were stationed in Quebec and Nova Scotia. The first units known to have pipers were Montgomery's Highlanders and the 42nd Highlanders (or Black Watch) in 1759 and the Fraser Highlanders in 1761. This was before the advent of the first officially recognized pipe bands in 1854, but the Fraser Highlanders had at least thirty pipers and drummers. Highland regiments were organized in Canada in the late eighteenth century; the earliest documented being the Royal Highland Emigrants in 1775, later called the 48th Highlanders. The Argyll or 74th Highlanders were established in 1778. These early indigenous Canadian units are not known to have had pipe bands, but there is no doubt that there were pipers among the ranks. The companies of Highland units raised in Canada, along with the Scottish regiments, helped to keep alive the bagpipe as a solo instrument, as individual pipers maintained the traditional role of the piper — stirring their comrades to battle or entertaining them.

Many of the Canadian reserve volunteer units started pipe bands before the establishment of the Canadian militia and the creation of the Highland pipe band as a musical unit. The very early ensembles were comprised of the pipes of the regimental companies who joined together at various times to provide the martial and dancing tunes when their regiment was in camp.

The Canadian regiments that had bands were mostly affiliated with Highland regiments of Scotland, whose titles they bore and whose traditions they sought to preserve. The oldest known pipe band organized in Canada was the Royal Highlanders of Canada dating from 1816 and affiliated with the Black Watch. Other Highland regiments which were formed and had pipes or pipe bands include the Seaforth Highlanders of Canada at Vancouver, the Pictou Highlanders of Nova Scotia, the Queen's Own Cameron Highlanders of Canada at Winnipeg, the Canadian Scottish Regiment in Victoria, the Argyll and Sutherland Highlanders from Hamilton, the Cameron Highlanders of Ottawa, the Calgary Highlanders and the 48th Highlanders of Canada in Toronto. The 48th were founded in 1891 and were, when at their pinnacle, a world-class musical ensemble.

The addition of a small drum corps consisting of rope-tension side drums, bass drums, and tenor drums to the regimental pipers launched that most distinctive and universal musical organization, the Highland pipe band.

Pipe bands were not only in abundance in Highland units but also in mounted contingents. One of the most fascinating and unusual pipe bands to be formed during the First World War was the Mounted Pipe Band of the 1st Canadian Mounted Rifles. The original marching band was formed in Brandon, Manitoba, in December 1914, where the unit was mobilized and remained for the winter of 1914. Band members were approached in the spring by the battalion officers to have a try at a mounted band. The pipers and drummers were surprised at the manner in which the horses calmly responded to the skirling of the pipes and the rat-tat-tat of the drums. The horses were quite fresh off the range and had been broken by bronco busters, who saddle-broke them and thoroughly trained them within a matter of weeks. All of them were trained to respond to knee guidance for direction and kept perfect step while the band was playing.

The band was nineteen strong when they left Brandon. On their arrival in France they were dismounted and converted to infantry, with jobs that included stretcher-bearing and working with ration parties. There were many casualties in the band, but it was reorganized towards the end of the war and appeared on Dominion Day, 1918, in the Corps Sports and Ceremonial Parade at Tinques. Their performance was described in the history of the 15th Battalion, *No Man's Land*:

> The most unusual thrilling sight of the colourful occasion was the spectacular march past of the 1st Canadian Mounted Rifles, 8th Infantry Brigade, 3rd Division. The mounted pipe band of twelve pipers and eight drummers led the Regiment and their beautiful chargers visibly enjoyed their splendid role to the tune of the regimental march past, "Highland Laddie." They were, at that time, the world's first completely mounted band and they made the most of the honour.

To the bagpipe belongs the distinction of being the only musical instrument during the First World War to actually go "over the top." There were pipers with many Canadian regiments overseas including the Princess Patricia's Canadian Light Infantry and the 107th Pioneers as well as the 1st and 4th Canadian Mounted Rifles.

The Princess Patricia's Canadian Light Infantry had the advantage of getting en masse the pipe band of the City of Edmonton, whose members journeyed to Ottawa in August 1914 and offered to "play the battalion into

Fourth Canadian Mounted Rifles Pipe Band, July/August, 1914. (*Fred Ashton, Toronto*)

France and back." The pipers, many of them emigrant Scots, had volunteered for the Patricias, although a very small percentage of the men in the regiment itself had Scottish backgrounds.

In action, pipers were often employed in secondary duties as stretcher-bearers, runners, ammunition and ration carriers and transport men. Frequently they were found at the hearts of their companies, playing them into action before resuming their other duties. Under these battle conditions many pipers were decorated for valour. The pipers of the PPCLI, two of whom were awarded the Distinguished Conduct Medal, played the leading wave of the battalion up the lip of the crater of Vimy Ridge in April 1917.

The 13th Royal Highlanders of Canada (affiliated with the Black Watch) seemed to have been very badly handicapped at the outset of the war by the lack of pipers, only five having gone out with the original contingent and two of those being lost in battle at Ypres in April, 1915. Matters improved for the band two years later when they received a reinforcement of eight pipers from reserve battalions under Pipe Major A. J. Saunders.

The 16th Canadian Scottish Regiment (Princess Mary's) kept to the old Highland clan tradition of using pipers whenever and wherever possible. No battle appeared to have been fought without the strains of one or more of their pipers resounding in the ears of some of the fighting men. One of the colonels had the pipers walk by his side whenever he went into battle. Only the threatened break-up of regimental pipe bands through heavy casualties finally caused the withdrawal of pipers from front-line trenches.

In spite of this, the instrument continued to figure in the fighting until the end of the war. The statistics on the piper casualties, as well as the numbers of them who were awarded medals, is indicative of the courage displayed by the soldier musicians. The Sixteenth Battalion, for example, set out in 1915 with seventeen pipers, and by November 1918 only three remained. Within this unit, Pipe Major James Groat had his gallantry recognized with the Distinguished Conduct Medal and the Military Medal with Bar. Groat was severely wounded and had to be invalided back to Canada. The other pipers of the Sixteenth were equally gallant; eight were awarded the Military Metal.

The crowning award of the Victoria Cross was given to a piper of the 16th Battalion, James Richardson, a native of Chilliwack, B.C., whose heroic deed on October 8, 1916 is summed up in a document in the Canadian War Museum:

> This piper (Richardson) performed deeds of the most extraordinary valour. He implored his Commanding Officer to allow him to play his company over the top. As the company approached the trench they were held up by very strong wire and came under a most terrific fire. The casualties were appalling, and the company was momentarily demoralised. Realising the situation he strode up and down outside the wire, playing his pipes with unhurried calm. The effect on the company was instantaneous and, inspired by his splendid example, they reformed and sprang at the wire with such fury and determination that they succeeded in cutting their way through and capturing the position which was known as Regina Trench. After entering the trench he asked for some grenades from the Company Sgt. Major, and together they bombed a dugout, capturing two prisoners. He was afterwards detailed to take the prisoners out and to assist the Company Sgt Major who had been wounded. After proceeding about two hundred yards he remembered he had left his pipes behind. Richardson was urged not to turn back for his beloved pipes, but refused and never returned and was presumed killed in action. He was awarded the VC posthumously for his gallantry.

During the First World War, Canada equipped and sent overseas between twenty-five and thirty pipe bands. The pipers of these bands were classified as combatants on active service. Records of the Canadian Corps testify to the zeal with which they carried out their duties, despite the fact that not all of their employment was "above and beyond the call of duty." The pipers of the 19th (Argyll and Sutherland Highlanders) Battalion, for instance, acted as stretcher-bearers until 1916, when they were allowed to play their companies to and from the front lines. The pipers of the 21st Battalion also began the campaign as stretcher-bearers and medical order-

Pipe Richardson VC, 16th Battalion CEF, The Somme, France, October 8th, 1916. (*Public Archives of Canada*)

lies, but as this work became increasingly more dangerous, they were withdrawn in order to provide pipe music behind the lines. The twenty-five pipers of the 25th Battalion did duty as stretcher-bearers, and there Pipe Major J. Carson was awarded the Meritorious Service Metal. The eighteen members of the 26th New Brunswick Regiment Pipe Band, mostly from Saint John with a scattering from Fredericton and Moncton, all escaped sickness and wounds until the attack against Amiens in 1918, when several were severely wounded. The 29th (British Columbia) Regiment Pipe Band suffered a number of losses, and from their original twenty-piece band, eight were killed in action on November 6, 1917. The 46th (Saskatchewan) Battalion pipers found themselves bearing stretchers instead of playing their comrades into action, but three members of the pipe band received awards for valour while acting as stretcher-bearers.

The pipers could not complain of monotony in their duties, for they were at times at the heads of their companies playing them into action, and later, when a restriction was placed on their battle activities, they played their regiments to the front lines. When they were not involved with the piping duties they were out with stretchers bringing in the wounded or were back and forth carrying ammunition for the trenches. However, somehow the competitive spirit, which is consistently in evidence among pipers, was maintained, with several great piping tournaments held behind the lines. In October 1917, at Camblain l'Abbé, Sir Douglas Haig reviewed the massed pipe bands of the Canadian Corps. On Dominion Day, 1918, all available pipe bands in the allied forces met for a Highland gathering. The estimated number of pipers for this "fling" was well over five hundred. The festivity, which included every form of the Highland magic, was highlighted with pipe competitions and marching displays.

As the final cease-fire sounded the end of "the war to end all wars," the skirl of the pipes heralded the entry of Canadian troops into Mons. The pipes were strongly in evidence as the Canadians made their triumphal trek across the Rhine in 1919.

Following the First World War something like a piping renaissance swept through Canada. The Highland gatherings, long a feature of Canadian Scottish community life, took a fresh lease on life and spread like wildflowers into other segments of Canadian society. In the west, new gatherings sprang up almost every year and the old games circuit, once confined to Scottish centres in Quebec, Ontario, and Nova Scotia, widened to include all of Canada. In the early 1930s, there were over sixty pipe bands in Canada. The most prestigious event during this period was the CPR's Banff Highland Gathering, which attracted pipers from across Canada and around the world.

Nearly every city of any size from Sydney on Cape Breton Island to Victoria on Vancouver Island had pipe bands. Some cities boasted two or three, and Toronto and Winnipeg had no less than four bands each. There were so many military pipe bands that the militia department published a list in 1938 of their locations, affiliations, tartans, strengths, and pipe majors.

The years between the wars were highlighted for the Canadian military pipers by two separate events — the Canadian Corps Reunion, held in Toronto in August 1934, and the unveiling of the Vimy Memorial in France, which took place in June 1936. The pipers employed for the 1936 ceremony were selected from various militia units across Canada, while the reunion in Toronto featured four Ontario pipe bands in massed formation.

On the eve of the Second World War, the special list for warrant officers showed that, in 1939, there were sixteen pipe bands and eighteen pipe majors on the militia rolls. Many of the pipe majors had served in the Canadian Expeditionary Force in the First World War.

The history of the pipe bands and pipers during the Second World War is interwoven with the military bands. At the outbreak of the war none of the Non Permanent Active Militia (NPAM) units mobilized for the First and Second Divisions were authorized to enlist bands, although Highland regiments were each permitted to take six pipers overseas. The number of pipers, however, who were unofficially on the rolls during the initial stages was considerably higher, because most of the Highland units configured their company manning list extensively with platoon medical orderlies or clerks who were also pipers.

A damaging carryover from the First World War was the King's Regulations that stated that bandsmen and pipers would be trained as stretcher-bearers and in first aid to the wounded. Under these battle conditions, pipers were subject not only to sniper fire but now also intense machine-gun fire. Highland units experienced many losses from among their cadre of pipers and were fortunate that the casualties were not more serious.

Some historians have considered the raid by the Second Division on the resort town of Dieppe on August 19, 1942, a dismal military failure. Other military strategists declared the raid a partial success because it purchased a valuable experience for later use by the Allies. Nevertheless, there were 851 Canadian lives lost and 1,944 men who were captured spent the next three years in captivity. Five of the nineteen Canadian units who hit the

Ottawa Highlanders Pipe Band, 38th Battalion, CEF. (*Kopstein Collection*)

beach at Dieppe were Highland units. The arrival of the Queen's Own Cameron Highlanders of Canada is described in the Canadian War Museum Historical Publication *Canada at Dieppe* by T. Murray Hunter. It dramatically illustrates the precarious nature of military piping:

> Meanwhile, Lt. Gostling had decided to postpone the Camerons' landing ten minutes in order to give the Saskatchewan's more time to clear the bridgehead through which the battalion was to pass. Navigational errors contributed to the delay when, a full 30 minutes late, the landing craft reached Green Beach led by a piper playing in full view of the enemy. The Commanding Officer, who encouraged his men on the run in, was killed as he leaped out on the shingle.

The Essex Scottish of Windsor and Chatham had the misfortune of losing two pipers at Dieppe despite the fact that pipers of that regiment had been restricted to general duties in the rear. Other Highland units, such as the Black Watch, suffered casualties among their pipers or lost them to incarceration by the Germans for the balance of the war. After this debacle, units that had pipers found it advisable to hold them as much as possible out of forward areas. The Cape Breton Highlanders kept their pipers looking after stores in their 'B' Echelon. The Irish Regiment of Canada had their pipers handling baggage in the rear or used them as general duty personnel. The consensus was that medical orderlies and stretcher-bearers were easier to come by than pipers.

After VE Day, units of the Canadian Army Occupation Force were to have their own pipe bands. However, with the last corps bands being disbanded in March 1945, a new approach to raising pipe bands was necessary.

Many of the units who had served overseas returned to Canada and reactivated their pipe bands for peacetime service. Others, for whom no pipe band existed, sought ways to establish a pipe band for their regimental complement. The following letter regarding the Lorne Scots characterizes the emphasis that Canadian Highland units placed on bearing a distinctive Scottish regimental trademark and the reverence military commanders had for pipe bands.

13 Jun 45

Pipe Band

1. The change of name of 1 Cdn NETD to 1 Cdn Repat Depot which took effect 15 Feb 45 under CMHQ WEL NO 58 para d/7 Mar 45, reaffirmed the Regimental charter of this unit by embodying the name "Lorne Scots" in the Official Unit designation. This was done to ensure this Regt a place on the roll of the Army Overseas.
2. It is now desired to apply for authority to classify this unit as a Scottish Regiment, under the terms of CA ORO 5468 and 5797. Under this authority, the Unit would then be entitled to organize a pipe band and to equip them suitably. Some work has already been done on organizing a band and a certain amount of equipment has already been gathered together.
3. It is considered that a pipe band will not only raise the morale and Regimental spirit of the P.E., but would also be of value as an entertainment factor for the transient personnel. All drafts arriving by train would be met by this band, and all trains dispatching personnel would be piped out of the station. In this regard, the most difficult period during the despatch of a draft is the time spent between completion of loading and departure of the train.
4. To fulfil the requirements of a pipe band, an issue of pipes, drums, and kilts would be required. Sufficient sets of pipes are now in possession of the Unit to start the band, as well as two side drums. The greatest need is for a Pipe Major, would/could be carried as an Sgt Instructor (PT) on the establishment. Trades pay is also requested for the pipers.
5. It is requested, therefore, that favourable consideration be given to this application.

[signed] "Louis" Keene Col
Commanding Officer
No.1 Cdn Repat Depot
(Lorne Scots)

43rd Battalion Band. (*Pearson Collection*)

Canadian Forces Directorate of History records indicate that the Lorne Scots were authorized a pipe band immediately, and in December 1945 the Canadian Army Overseas Formation was withdrawn with the last Corps bands being disbanded on March 28, 1946.

In February 1942, No. 9 SFTS Summerside, PEI, requested authority to substitute pipes for trumpets in the trumpet and drum band authorized for that unit. The minister's approval was granted, and the first pipe band in the RCAF came into being. This band operated on a voluntary basis during the time No. 9 Service Flying Training School was at Summerside and later, after it was located to Centralia, Ontario.

In May 1943, the band establishment was authorized for nineteen men. The RCAF tartan was designed, and the band was outfitted with complete Highland regalia. In July 1943, another pipe band was authorized for RCAF Station Sydney, Nova Scotia, and personnel from other RCAF stations in the vicinity were posted in to provide pipers and drummers for this band.

Following the war there were no full-time pipe bands in the Canadian army. However, when the Korean War broke out, the army authorized a pipe band for the 26th Canadian Infantry Brigade that was known as the 1st Canadian Highland Battalion. This band, which was organized in December 1951, became the forerunner of the Canadian Guards Pipe Band. In the Reserve Force there were twenty-four pipe bands authorized in 1951.

The Canadian Guards, with their headquarters in Camp Petawawa, received authority for the formation of a pipe band within the battalion establishment in February 1954. The area headquarters was requested to provide a pipe major, and in mid March, Pipe Major Archie Cairns reported to the battalion and set about organizing a pipe band. Pipe Major Cairns had enlisted from the reserve pipe band of Hamilton, the Argyll and Sutherland Highlanders. He was eminently qualified for his position, as he was a graduate of the British Army School of Piping, had begun piping at an early age, and had followed in his father's footsteps as pipe major of the Argyll and Sutherland Highlanders.

The new pipe major set off on a recruiting tour of militia pipe bands in the command. As a result, two drummers were enlisted and posted to the battalion. In a matter of weeks, he had the drummers playing for a recruit passing out parade. In the meantime, a dozen volunteers from the recruit company had begun the basic music course and were hard at work learning to read music and count time.

Only six months after Archie Cairns' arrival, six students were playing well enough to perform on parade, and the drum section under Drummer Bob Freeman, were well on the way to understanding rudimentary drumming. In May 1955 the band appeared at its first retreat on the parade ground and played public performances on behalf of the Canadian Legions in both Petawawa and Cobden.

In 1955 the band was outfitted in full-dress uniforms of the Royal Stewart tartan, with feather bonnets and sporrans of the regimental pattern.

The Guards Pipe Band under Pipe Major Cairns rapidly became very well known in Canadian piping circles. Following the Canadian Forces Tattoo in 1967, the Guards were disbanded and the band went through various stages before being completely dismantled in 1979. In 1964, Pipe Major Cairns had been posted to Canadian Forces Base Ottawa Pipe Band and stationed in Rockcliffe. Chief Warrant Officer Cairns, before his retirement in 1981, was instrumental in organizing and developing the Canadian Forces School of Piping at CFB Ottawa.

The Royal Canadian Navy's first pipe band was established in October 1954, and was underwritten by the ship's fund of HMCS *Cape Breton* which bought the original training equipment and paid the instructor's fees. In August 1955, naval headquarters authorized the unit as an official Navy Band.

From the beginning, Pipe Major Thomas Deys, a reservist who had served as a medic during the war, molded and encouraged his fledgling pipers. The band made its first public appearance, fittingly, on Cape

Breton Island on the occasion of the official opening of the Canso Causeway, in August 1955. After its debut the navy's pipe band was in much demand. Several weeks later, to the surprise of many of the fifteen thousand spectators, the RCN paraded its pipe band during the Lunenburg Fisheries Exhibition. That Remembrance Day, the band led the RCN contingent in the Grand Naval Parade to the Cenotaph in Halifax.

Newly joined naval apprentices filled the ranks of this pipe band, and at its peak there were twenty-five pipers and drummers. In 1958, the navy department discontinued shipboard bands and the pipe band was disbanded.

The Air Command Pipes and Drums of CFB Ottawa was among four regular and reserve pipe bands selected to participate in Canada's salute to the United States Bicentennial in Philadelphia in May 1976. The massed Pipes and Drums were headed by Pipe Major Archie Cairns and included bandsmen from the Royal Canadian Regiment, Montreal's Black Watch and the Cameron Highlanders of Ottawa. Along with the military bands of the Governor General's Foot Guards and the Royal Regiment of Canada, the RCMP Musical Ride, and a contingent from Ontario's Fort Henry Guard, the kilted bandsmen performed at various celebratory events, including an hour-long downtown street parade that was seen on US national television. The massed pipes and drums and military bands

Massed pipe bands of Canadian Highland regiments marching through Hyde Park during Warship Week Savings drive, March 1942. (*DND Photo 643-12*)

performed specially arranged concert presentations organized in advance by Pipe Major Cairns.

The integration of the Canadian forces brought a change in the defence department's attitude towards pipers and drummers in the forces. Traditionally, pipers had not been classed as musicians and therefore were paid less than their counterparts in the military bands. A Canadian Press news release in January 1964, outlined the problem:

PIPERS NOT MUSICIANS

It's enough to curdle Scottish blood, especially on the eve of St. Andrew's Day.

The Defence Department after considerable deliberation has refused to class bagpipers as musicians. One might think the six full-time pipers in the armed forces, who form an even more select group than generals, would still welcome this confirmation of their exclusiveness.

Anything but.

The reason is that the some 900 full-time musicians in the armed forces are paid each at least $20 a month more than bagpipers. In the recent integration of the armed forces trades pay, pipers were placed in the lowest pay category along with clerks, drivers and drill instructors. The musicians were classified in the next higher pay group. Even though there are only six full-time pipers, there are many volunteers. The Defence Department declined to integrate them with the musicians. The Department's reasons, officials say, is that musicians in the Armed Forces know more about or should know more about music than bagpipers.

Pipers are required to play only one instrument, albeit nine unforgettable notes. Musicians must be able to play at least three instruments. The Triangle counts as one instrument. Ever hear Scotland The Brave on the Triangle?

By 1968, pipes were absorbed into the music branch of the Canadian Forces and ranked with musicians in all benefits, including pay and promotion.

Some Band Histories

When the 48th Highlanders were established at Toronto's Baily Hall in 1891, pipers were recruited to rouse the enthusiasm of the candidates for membership in the newly formed regiment. On the formal recognition of the 48th, one of the first actions taken was to secure the services of a pipe major. The regiment was indeed fortunate to select the finest piper on the

Pipes and Drums of the Irish Regiment of Canada, 1964. (Don Melhuish, Etobicoke)

Lake Superior Scottish Regiment Band, 1983. (Norm Slongo, Thunder Bay)

Le Régiment de Voltigeurs Band, 2000 (Le Régiment de Voltigeurs Photo)

Band of Her Majesty's Canadian Ship York, 2000. (HMCS York Photo)

Stadacona Band of Maritime Command, 1988. (DND Photo)

Band of the Royal Regiment of Canada, 1980s. (Royal Regiment of Canada Photo)

Princess Patricia's Canadian Light Infantry Band, 1991. (PPCLI Photo)

Central Band of the Canadian Forces, 2000. (DND Photo)

Royal Canadian Artillery Band, 1970s. (DND Photo)

The Band of 1 Canadian Air Division, 2000. (DND Photo)

Royal Canadian Air Force Central Band, Ottawa, 1961. (Kopstein Collection)

Royal Canadian Regiment Band at University of Western Ontario, 1964. (DND Photo)

Band of the Lincoln and Welland Regiment, 1989. (Regimental Photo)

Members of the Lincoln and Welland Regiment Band, St. Catharines. (Regimental Photo)

The Band of the Royal Canadian Ordinance Corps, 1961. (DND Photo)

Canadian Armed Forces Tattoo, 1967. (DND Photo)

48th Highlanders of Canada 1st Battalion Pipes and Drums, Toronto, Ontario 1938. (*48th Highlanders of Canada*)

North American continent, Robert Ireland, who came from New York City to take up his position in Toronto.

Under Robert Ireland, the 48th Band became internationally famous. Pipe Major Norman MacSwayed succeeded Mr. Ireland, and is remembered for his composition "Lieutenant Colonel John I. Davidson March," in 1895. Mr. MacSwayed was well known and respected as a military piper and a thoroughly capable leader.

In 1898, Pipe Major MacSwayed returned to Scotland and was replaced by Farquhar Beaton. As Pipe Major, Mr. Beaton raised the establishment of the band to twenty-three members: sixteen pipers and seven drummers. Mr. Beaton maintained the efficiency of the band through the early years of this century by indefatigable practice. There were four practices each week, two for pipers under training and two for band rehearsals for his advanced pipers. Mr. Beaton introduced part playing into his pipe band, having pipers play four parts, the melody, alto, tenor and bass, a practice that he had borrowed from Scotland and that was unknown in Canada. The idea was developed by Mr. Beaton from an encounter he had with the Earl of Aberdeen, an ardent admirer of bagpipes. The Earl was entertained in Toronto at the Ontario Legislature prior to his departure from Canada on the expiry of his term as governor general in September 1898. The pipe band of the 48th was in attendance at the ceremonies. Pipe Major Beaton and one of his pipers played in concert the first and second parts of the tune "Green Hills of Tyrol." The effect produced was at once noted by the Earl, who complimented the pipe major personally and strongly recommended the cultivation of part playing on the pipes.

The next pipe major of the 48th was James R. Fraser, who assumed the position in 1913 and remained at the helm of the band until 1952. During the entire time Pipe Major Fraser served, he remained in the militia at the University Armoury in Toronto. In both wars, when the pipe band accompanied the regiment to Europe, they were considerably augmented. In the First World War, the 48th raised three battalions for overseas service, each with its own pipe band. Pipe Major Fraser's function in both wars was to train pipers for active service and for the band of the Militia Battalion in Toronto. In the Second World War there are said to have been no less than seven 48th Highlanders pipe bands serving at various locations in Canada, in addition to the bands with the First Battalion overseas and the Second Battalion in Toronto. Canadian war-time records of military establishment indicate that Number Twenty Canadian Infantry Basic Training Centre, Brantford, Ontario, was commanded by a 48th Highlanders officer, and had a 48th Highlanders Pipe Band.

The 48th Band, under Pipe Major Fraser, consistently won honours and awards in performance and competition. In 1949, the People's Journal of Dundee, Scotland, surprised the United Kingdom's piping community when it said that the 48th Highlanders Pipe Band of Canada had "out-piped Scotland." This recognition was echoed at home when, in 1950, the Canadian army reported that the 48th Pipe Band was rated the most efficient of all militia bands in Canada, including military brass, bugle, fifes or pipes. This was applause indeed for this outstanding musical organization and the regiment added its congratulations to both Pipe Major Fraser and his band. Between 1946 and 1950, the 48th Band won thirty-three awards in competition, filling their trophy room to capacity.

Pipe Major Fraser retired after thirty-nine years service to the regiment in 1952 and a special night was staged in his honour with pipers rallying from everywhere. The Toronto *Telegram* reported that, "the massed Pipes put on a breathtaking show to honour Fraser. It was a great night for the Prince of Pipers."

Pipe Major Fraser was replaced by one of his students, Archie Dewar, who retained the position until 1965 and led the band to many victories in competition. Subsequent pipe majors have been Ross Stewart (1965-75) and Reay MacKay, who retired in 1985 to be replaced by Archie Dewar's son, Chief Warrant Officer Alexander (Sandy) Dewar. The band continues to maintain the distinction of being the largest pipe band in the Commonwealth performing a variety of military and civilian functions.

Captain John Slater, 48th Highlanders of Canada. (*Frank Shryver, Toronto*)

147

Since its organization during the First World War, the history of the Cameron Highlanders Pipe Band of Ottawa, has been studded with many memorable occasions and ceremonies. The First Battalion of the Cameron Highlanders was stationed in Iceland during 1940-1941, and its presence, under Pipe Major Peter MacLeod, did much toward cementing friendship with a country not reconciled to the occupation of their shores. The band arrived on July 1, 1940, and marched through Reykjavik from quayside to the staging camp playing the "Skye Boat Song." This was the first Highland pipe band to perform in Iceland and the music brought out throngs of listeners.

The band's departure in 1941 left behind a host of followers among the Icelanders and a legacy of appreciation for pipe bands that still exists there today. The band's next posting was in Scotland, and their march-past "Pibroch of Donald Dhu" will always be associated with the many ceremonial parades and inspections that witnessed the Camerons on parade.

The most stirring and historic moment for the Camerons came when they hit the beaches of Normandy on D-Day, June 6, 1944. The Cameron Highlanders of Ottawa touched down well up in the forefront of the assault. The sounds of the highly spirited "March Cameron Men" could be heard above the sounds of the battle.

The Camerons still continue to be an institution in Canada's capital city and are seen at virtually every important ceremonial occasion.

The pipe bands of Canada's Black Watch (Royal Highland Regiment of Canada) have an enviable reputation for longevity and accomplishment. The first authorized band was organized under Pipe Major Duncan Weir in Montreal, in 1876. He was followed by Pipe Majors J. Duncan, 1879-1880, and J. Matheson, 1881-1897. Some of their early highlights included performances in 1887 and 1897 for Queen Victoria's Jubilee celebrations.

In 1901, the pipe band adopted the Royal Stewart tartan while soldiers of the regiment wore the tartan of the Black Watch. Later the regulation Black Watch uniform was completed with the adoption of the badges and sporran.

With the outbreak of the First World War, the first contingent of Royal Highlanders was raised in Montreal and sailed in February 1915 for St. Nazaire, France. The landing is shown in a contemporary painting by Edgar Bundy, depicting the pipes and drums of the 13th RHC, under Pipe Major Grey, leading the battalion ashore. A pipe band was also organized for the 73rd Battalion under Pipe Major A. J. Saunders, formerly of the Highland Light Infantry of Scotland. The 73rd was recruited to provide an active third battalion for the RHC to go overseas.

Several members of the original pre-war pipe band were killed during the war, and some received medals for gallantry under fire. At the end of the war, the Black Watch was inspected by the Prince of Wales (later King Edward VII).

In January 1928, the pipes and drums left Montreal by train for Baltimore, Maryland, where they were to be guests of the St Andrew's Societies of Baltimore and Washington. They were met at the station by the band of the 12th United States Infantry, and, joining up with this unit, they marched to the City Hall to be welcomed by the mayor of Baltimore. The following day, before a large audience, the Pipes and Drums, in review order, gave a Burn's Night performance.

During the period between the wars, the regimental pipe band of the Black Watch was particularly strong both in numbers and proficiency. Many of the pipers and drummers who had served with the regiment's battalions, rejoined in the militia unit and, as well, a number of younger men were added.

At the outbreak of the Second World War in 1939, pipers serving in the Black Watch of Canada were incorporated into the overseas unit. Arriving in the United Kingdom in September 1940, the pipe band was reformed and remained with the unit throughout the war.

The Princess Patricia's Canadian Light Infantry Pipe Band. France, 1917. (*PPCLI Museum, Calgary, Alberta*)

In May 1951, the Black Watch was authorized to have two active service battalions; the Reserve Force unit was designated the Third Battalion. The Regular Force units were allocated positions for a pipe major and NCO/drummer. This enabled each of the active battalions to have pipe bands. The reserve battalion maintained a pipe band at Regimental Headquarters in Montreal.

Both Regular Force pipe bands were very much in demand during the period 1955 to 1958. They combined on several occasions, and, in 1955, sailed to England where they represented the Canadian army in the Edinburgh Tattoo. The band, comprised of thirty-eight pipers and drummers, also appeared at the British Military Tattoo at Copenhagen, Denmark, a spectacle which played before as many as fourteen thousand spectators on each of its fourteen performances.

In 1956 and 1957, the combined pipe bands flew to Bermuda to take part in the island's military tattoo and they were present in Washington, D.C., for the 1957 state visit of Queen Elizabeth. Both battalion pipe bands were well represented in the 1967 Canadian Forces Tattoo.

The Regular Battalion of the Black Watch was disbanded in 1970, a victim of the defence department's integration of the Canadian Forces. The pipe band was redesignated the Royal Canadian Regiment Pipe Band and is still flourishing in Gagetown, New Brunswick.

The Calgary Regiment, 10th Battalion Calgary Highlanders, known as the Fighting Tenth, was formed in 1914 and served overseas during the First World War. Pipe Major W. Piper formed the first pipe band in 1921. The band was active in all militia-training functions including army training at Banff in 1923, and its popularity grew as it made appearances at civilian engagements, including the Calgary Stampede. The Highlanders joined with the various other pipe bands and military bands including the 50th Battalions Bands in presenting a massed band concert at the exhibition grounds on the evenings of July 1st and 5th, 1932.

In 1931, it was reported that the pipe band, which had twenty-three members, had attained a high general standard due to the efforts of Pipe Major W. Pow and Sergeant Drummer J. Fox. In 1935 for the Twenty-fifth Anniversary of the reign of King George V, the Calgary Highlanders Pipe Band, under Sergeant Major W. R. Herbert of the Fiftieth Battalion, participated in a mass parade of military units.

In May 1939, the Highlanders formed the honour guard for the visit of the King and Queen to Calgary, and were then rushed to Edmonton by train to participate in arrival ceremonies there. Later that year, Prime Minister R. B. Bennett, Honorary Colonel of the Regiment, presented the band with uniforms and twelve sets of bagpipes. The following year, the

25th Battalion Pipes and Drums, 1919. (*Public Archives of Nova Scotia N-9948*)

band was fully equipped with the donation of side drums and sticks by an Alberta commercial laundry firm.

At the outbreak of the Second World War, the militia band folded, and the commanding officer sent the pipe major to Edmonton where he recruited the City of Edmonton Pipe Band. The regiment trained in Shilo, Manitoba, in preparation for posting overseas.After its arrival in England the band presented many public performances at Aldershot, where they were stationed. They appeared also at Bristol, following its near-destruction from Nazi bombing. The pipe major at this time was Sergeant Neil Sutherland, an award-winning piper from Scotland.

Following D-Day, the band accompanied the Calgary Regiment on its drive through Western Europe and returned triumphantly to Calgary in November of 1945, to a civic welcome and a parade from the CPR station to the Mewata Armouries.

Since the war, the Calgary Highlanders Pipe Band has been in constant demand for performances and competitions and continues to be a source of pride to the Calgary Regiment.

The RCAF Rockcliffe Pipe Band was formed and officially approved by the RCAF in 1951. As a volunteer group, its members, apart from three instructors, were tradesmen representing many occupational fields of the RCAF. The majority of the band members had had little or no musical experience before joining the RCAF. The band performed at many military and civil functions and competed at many pipe band competitions in Canada and the United States. The first pipe major of the Rockcliffe Band was Flight Sergeant John MacKenzie. He had an extensive background in the United Kingdom as a military piper and joined the RCAF in 1952. Canadian Guards Pipe Major Archie Cairns replaced MacKenzie in 1968. In 1968, the Rockcliffe Pipe Band was renamed the Canadian Forces Base Ottawa Pipe Band, and the bond of association was widened to permit civil servants and dependants of military personnel to be members.

At present, there are nineteen authorized pipe bands for the Reserve Forces and three pipe bands for the Regular Force units in Canada. The Regular Force pipe bands are voluntary units with small cadres of professional pipers and drummers providing instruction and leadership. The military pipes and drums movement continues to flourish in Canada, with both bands and individual band members being particularly noted for their appearances in piping and drumming competitions across Canada.

CHAPTER 8

The Royal Canadian Mounted Police Band

One of the most enduring characteristics of the Royal Canadian Mounted Police has been the survival of its original semi-military attributes. The training of the RCMP recruits and the performance of ceremonial duties has been maintained with a strong military flavour. The persistence of military values and ideas is considered to be an integral and important part of the heritage and traditions of the force. The ceremonial functions carried out by the police in the territories during the latter part of the last century continued into the turn of the century and modern times. The musical ride and other forms of military activities, such as providing guards of honour, symbolized a reverent social status attached to the police. This helped their standing in the community and their prestige because it became intimately connected with their ability to command public support and co-operation in law enforcement. It was with these ideals of building esprit de corps within the Force and earning public favour, that the early bands of the RCMP were conceived.

These bands were made up of volunteers and were semi-official in status. It appears that no serious effort was made to keep them intact or to put them on a permanent footing. Apparently, whenever a troop could pick a dozen or more willing musicians from its ranks, a collection was taken up, instruments were purchased, and a band was born. Its existence depended largely on the bandsmen's love of music, for they had to devote many of their leisure hours to practice and regular engagements without any expectation of extra remuneration.

In the winter of 1876, Captain W. Parker, stationed at Swan River Barracks, organized a band, acting upon a suggestion from Commissioner George A. French, who knew that the strain of loneliness and isolation was almost as much a threat in those early days as were warring Indians and rum runners.

NWMP "E" Division Band, Banff, Aberta, 1888. (*RCMP Centennial Museum 1937.15.4*)

Commissioner French asked the government for money to purchase instruments in order for the force to have a band similar to those of the Dublin and London metropolitan police forces. The band instruments arrived from Winnipeg one frosty spring morning later that year, piled on a dog sled. The government, however, had not come through with the funds, and the members had to pay for the instruments themselves. The officers had agreed to subsidize the purchase of music.

The band of about twenty musicians made its debut on Queen Victoria's birthday, May 24, 1876, at 5:30 reveille and, at the foot of the flagstaff, played "God Save the Queen."

According to Captain Parker, "We used the band that same summer in our long marches making treaties with the Wood Cree Indians at Fort Carlton and the Plain Crees at Fort Pitt. The Indians had never heard a band before and showed intense surprise—especially the squaws and youngsters, who ran to their tepees in terror. The men liked the big drum and made the offer of a good horse for it." This band was led by Sergeant Major Thomas Horatio Lake.

On September 22, 1877, the Honourable David Laird, Lieutenant Governor of the North-West Territories, and Commissioner J. F. Macleod of the North-West Mounted Police, signed Treaty Number 7 with the

Mounted Police Band, 'D' Division Band, led by Sgt. Fred Bagley (centre with sword) Battleford, 1885. (*RCMP Centennial Museum 1940.24.8*)

Indian tribes of the Blackfoot Confederacy at Blackfoot Crossing on the Bow River near Calgary. There was a great gathering of native peoples. A large escort of mounted police and Sergeant Lake's bandsmen attended Governor Laird. During the treaty negotiations, a large procession of Indians led by Old Sun, a chief of shady reputation, marched from their encampment to the governor's headquarters. They were headed by the Mounted Police Band, lustily blaring out "Hold the Fort, for I am Coming." Commissioner Macleod asked Bandmaster Lake why he played such an inappropriate tune. "Well" replied Lake, aware of Old Sun's for- mer activities, "Isn't there a verse commencing, 'See the Mighty Host advancing, Satan leading on?' "

The first RCMP band is seen formed up for a church parade in a pho- tograph taken in Fort Macleod, circa 1877. The instrumentation is completely brass and percussion with American Civil War-style brass horns consisting of five cornets (including the leader), four alto horns, one baritone, one trombone, two basses, three drums (side bass and cym- bals). The unit is dressed in the scarlet jackets with the Wolseley helmets, the first headdress used by the force.

In the spring of 1878, the headquarters of the NWMP was moved from Fort Macleod to Fort Walsh and the band was reorganized there. The fol- lowing anecdote tells how the Fort Walsh band came to an end in a sudden and rather disastrous way:

The band during a full dress parade at Depot, Regina, 1888. (*RCMP Centennial Museum 1933.10.21A*)

North West Mounted Police Band, Regina, 1890. (*RCMP Centennial Museum 1971.94.13*)

The Mounted Police at Fort Walsh, on the edge of the Battle Creek in the Cypress Hills, had only one means of communicating with the east-west telegram from Fort Benton, Montana. Benton, 200 miles away on the Missouri River, was also the chief source of their supplies. These they took overland by mule and bull train in covered wagons. One day in October, when Commissioner Irvine was at Fort Walsh, the mail brought the news of Lord Roberts' smashing victory over the Afghans and of his extraordinary march from Kabul to Kandahar, in August 1881. In celebration of the victory, Colonel Irvine authorized a special issue of grog to men who were giving a concert on front of the Officer's Mess. Stimulated by this liquid refreshment, the band, in high spirits, decided to turn out on the parade ground that evening and give vent to patriotic British Airs. Apparently they had obtained some liquor in addition to the official issue, for when they took their places they were in no condition to produce harmonious music. Whether the first trombone player objected to having a clarinet wailing in his face or they couldn't decide what piece to play, is not known. But the fact remains that they began to quarrel among themselves. Shortly, a free-for-all ensued. The music-making instruments became weapons in the fight and most were destroyed. As a result the band was disorganized. This was the tragic end of the first and only band at Fort Walsh.

According to Sergeant Major Fred Bagley, a notable bandmaster of the North-West Mounted Police, several members of the Fort Walsh band formed the nucleus of a band that operated at Qu'Appelle until 1902, and that played at Fort Macleod, Lethbridge and Calgary.

North West Mounted Police Band leading the parade May 24, 1902 at Dawson, Yukon. (*RCMP Centennial Museum 1936.17.1*)

157

NWMP Band, Regina Barracks, 1895. (*RCMP Centennial Museum1972.68.27*)

In 1882, Sergeant Major Bagley organized another group at Battleford. In 1885, his band turned out to welcome Inspector Frances Dickens, son of the great novelist Charles Dickens, and his party from the beleaguered Fort Pitt. This group broke up in the fall of that year owing to the deaths in action of two of the bandsmen and Bagley's transfer from Battleford. In the years after 1887, Bagley had an excellent band at E Division in Calgary. It often played on special occasions at the Banff Springs Hotel, which the Canadian Pacific Railway commenced building in 1886. Bagley later led the 15th Light Horse Band in Calgary following his retirement from the RCMP.

Perhaps the best known of all the old-time Mounted Police bandmasters of the early years was Sergeant Harry Walker, long stationed at headquarters in Regina. He had come west with the Wolseley Expedition in 1870 and was for a period bandmaster in Winnipeg. He joined the force in 1878 at Battleford and was transferred from there to Fort Walsh in 1870. The NWMP at Battleford and Regina in 1893 under Sergeant Walker, who himself played clarinet, had a membership of fifteen musicians consisting three clarinets, two cornets, three alto horns, two trombones, two basses and two drums. Walker himself was not only a good musician but a noted composer. In the late nineties, the halcyon days of the force, Regina Barracks was the centre of society and hospitality for a large region. Monthly balls were held during the winter and attracted the youth and beauty not only of Regina but of the whole surrounding coun-

RCMP Band, Regina, 1915. (*RCMP Centennial Museum 1964.28.1*)

RCMP Band, Regina, 1960. (*RCMP Centennial Museum 1970.7.12*)

tryside. The ballroom, on these occasions, would be decorated with flags and trophies. The red tunics of the men and the brilliant mess jackets of the officers, the pretty frocks of the ladies and the black coats of the civilian guests all combined to add colour and gaiety to a shifting, swirling scene, the main feature of which was Walker's band.

At Fort Macleod, police musicians formed an excellent unit that ultimately became a mounted organization. Those interested in the band had subscribed nearly $600 from their pay to purchase instruments, and so proficient did they become, it was requested that a yearly grant be allowed by the government towards upkeep and the purchase of music and other necessities for the band.

The Fort Macleod group was most successful in organizing a mounted band in spite of the fact that many of the horses were broncos from the Alberta ranges. At the first note they snorted with fright and stampeded, throwing their riders and instruments in one direction, while they proceeded, manes and tails streaming, with all speed in the opposite direction.

The gold discoveries in the Yukon in 1898 and the outbreak of the Boer War in 1899 took many of the bandsmen away from Regina. For the next few years the members gradually left and the band finally disappeared, despite the commanding officer's attempts to enlist men into the ever-thinning group. He felt that church parades without a band were rather dull affairs and wanted to add a little glamour to them and thus tone down the hard-boiled and irreverent language the men sometimes indulged in on these occasions. He was able to find musicians for all the instruments with the exception of the bass horn. The division piano player was approached, and even though he denied knowledge of how to

RCMP Band, Parliament Hill, Ottawa. (*RCMP Centennial Museum 1999.23.14*)

play the instrument, he paraded before the non-musical officer and was told that the job was his. He was allowed to miss the next morning's parade so that he could practice for his first engagement.

In 1896, the band stationed at Fort Saskatchewan, near Edmonton, had given a concert in the public square, after which they marched down the main street in honour of a distinguished visitor from England. An election was in progress at the time, and by chance the parading band passed the committee room of one of the candidates. The good intentions of the band were misinterpreted by the opposing government faction, which raised a great clamour. We quote from the Edmonton *Bulletin*, May 26, 1896:

> The NWMP band paraded in front of Cochranes' committee rooms today and serenades the Government candidate. The long suffering party will surly (sic) not object to this, as using a government band is surly no worse than using the people's money for their election purposes.

Several attempts had been made to organize a band in Dawson, but without much success. Up to 1901 the population of Dawson was overwhelmingly American. The Fourth of July was the great public holiday, and it was indeed quite customary at public functions, even territorial elections, for the decorations at the platform to consist of the Stars and Stripes with the Union Jack being conspicuous by its absence. At the end of that

Royal Canadian Mounted Police Band at the New York World's Fair, 1939. (*Pearson Collection*)

Royal Canadian Mounted Police Band. (*Pearson Collection*)

winter, Superintendent S. T. Wood of the NWMP personally took in hand the organization of a band and Staff Sergeant Telford was asked to act as bandmaster. Practices continued daily and nightly until May 24, 1902. On that day, the Queen's birthday, every available man from the Dawson Creek detachment, together with the Dawson Rifles, paraded on the barrack square with the police. The Union Jack was hoisted to the top of the flagpole and the national anthem was played, after which a feu de joie was fired. The men then formed a parade and, headed by the band, marched through the streets of Dawson. It is interesting to note that by the time the band had finished its first march a large crowd of citizens, Canadian and British, all overjoyed at the show of nationalism, were marching behind it. On the First of July, the same year, the band proceeded up Bonanza Creek to the town of Grand Forks, where a Dominion Day Celebration was held. During the summers of 1902 and 1903, concerts were given regularly by the band in the barracks square. Later on, opportunities for individual enterprise in mining petered out and the people drifted away. Police personnel were reduced and the band disbanded.

In the years that followed, bands were organized from time to time at various posts. They were volunteer groups, the men giving of their own time to entertain themselves and the community. During and after the First World War, the RCMP became a federal force within a country of growing international importance. Canada's new prominence drew an

Royal Canadian Mounted Police Band concert, Parliament Building, 1939. (*Pearson Collection*)

increasing number of dignitaries and ambassadors to its borders. State and ceremonial functions increased. In 1938, on his appointment as Commissioner of the RCMP, S. T. Wood recommended that the force set up a band, as a result of a visit he had made to England in 1934 during which time he received inspiration from the band of the London Police. The commissioner chose Inspector J. T. Brown as the band's first director and Regina was selected as its headquarters.

Well-grounded in music and leadership by a distinguished bandsman father, Inspector Brown had directed the GGFG Band for fifteen years, making it one of the outstanding musical organizations in Canada. At the same time he led a band of young people, the Ottawa Boys' Band, to several awards. In 1938 he raised and trained the first RCMP military band, largely from among top members of junior bands across Canada, and this musical body soon became a credit to the force under his quiet, inspired leadership. Many difficulties were encountered but in spite of this, a new band of thirty-five pieces made its debut on April 30, 1939, in Regina. Depot Division swarmed with people for the occasion, and the band was an instant success.

In June 1939, King George VI and Queen Elizabeth visited Regina on their royal visit to Canada. While they were being entertained in the RCMP Officer's Mess, the band played on the lawn outside. A week later the band was transferred to Ottawa, and later in the month was signally honoured to play for the monarch's visit to the Canadian Pavilion at the World's Fair in New York City.

During the war years, the band appeared in numerous charity concerts and Victory Loan drives. On one such occasion the band was on the same program as Gracie Fields and some members were unexpectedly drawn into her act. In the absence of service bands, the RCMP unit continually took part in parades for armed services and literally hundreds of dances for these service groups.

In 1944, the band was duty band at the Quebec Citadel conference attended by Prime Minister Winston Churchill of Britain, President Roosevelt of the United States and Prime Minister Mackenzie King of Canada.

With war's end, the band returned to peacetime activity and major engagements and tours began in earnest again. Since its official formation in 1938, the RCMP Band had played concerts in cities, towns and hamlets all across Canada with great success. It became a versatile musical ensemble with the ability to make a smooth transition from light classics to popular show music. It also began introducing a unique Canadian flavour into its programs with indigenous folk songs, a feature of the band that became a hallmark of its performances.

In the spring of 1949 it was decided to form a second RCMP band, to be based in Regina. In the nine years that followed, this unit performed extensively throughout the vast prairie region where the force had played a major role in the early pioneer days.

In 1949, Sergeant E. J. Lydall replaced retiring Inspector Brown. Lydall was born in Liverpool, England, had studied in Edmonton and Vancouver, and had become a very accomplished cornet soloist, joining the force in 1938. The second band unit, under Corporal C. C. Bryson, continued to flourish in Regina, and the two merged for special occasions. RCMP bands continued to thrive through the 1950s despite the difficulties of being on part-time basis. Finally, in 1958, official approval was granted for a full-time band.

The band, now operating on a full-time basis from their headquarters in Ottawa, began extensive tours of Canada and the territories. In 1961 they covered over seven thousand miles by land transport. The Maritimes and Quebec received the band's service the following year during a month-long tour.

Canada's Centennial Year, 1967, was a big one for the band as it joined with the RCMP Musical Ride and toured all across the country. In September, Superintendent E. J. Lydall retired and W. Bramwell Smith, an outstanding trumpet soloist, became Supervisor of Music. Under Smith's leadership, the band made a highly successful tour of the United States, was featured in an hour-long TV Christmas special on the CBC, and in

Royal Canadian Mounted Police Band concert, Parliament Building, 1939. (*Pearson Collection*)

1970, made a dramatic appearance at the EXPO 70 in Osaka, Japan. In1972, the band performed the first of an annual winter concert series at the National Arts Centre in Ottawa. In 1973, the RCMP's centennial year, the band travelled from coast to coast, appearing in some twenty cities across the country. In 1975, Inspector Smith left the RCMP and was replaced by Kenneth R. Moore, who had had an outstanding career as a trumpet soloist in the RCAF, before becoming director of the Central Band in Ottawa, and, after unification, the Canadian Forces Air Transport Command Band in Kingston. Under Moore's direction the band continued to act as the RCMP's musical ambassadors, performing all across the country and occasionally abroad.

A unique and integral part of the RCMP band was the show band, a small group of musicians who travelled extensively, carrying a message of goodwill from the local RCMP sponsoring units. This versatile unit became a very high-profile ensemble with the ability to entertain both young and old.

The role of the band was to support the force's law-enforcement program. Each performance was an integral part of the force's ongoing efforts to promote a better knowledge and understanding of the police, to express appreciation for past public support and to encourage co-operation and support of the police in maintaining security, peace and order in the community. The band's final director was Inspector Charlie Hendricks, who assumed the position in 1988, with Sergeant Gary Morton as assistant director.

On December 14, 1993, the band appeared on a TV show called "Without a Song," and only two weeks later the Toronto *Sun* reported its demise:

> Appeals to the federal cabinet and a countrywide petition failed to save the RCMP band from the budgetary chopping block.
>
> Solicitor General Herb Gray refused yesterday to grant a reprieve after reviewing the force's decision to cut the band, "The RCMP band has made a considerable contribution to Canadian life," Gray said."But when it comes to a choice between maintaining core police functions or saving the band, the RCMP's priority has to be the maintenance of core police functions."
>
> Supporters of the band gathered more than 30,000 names on a petition. The 23 member band played about 200 shows a year, most for charity.

CHAPTER 9

The Canadian Forces
School of Music

What is it that makes a band into an entity which is not only musically proficient but regimentally so essential in many other ways? Who sets the tone of that band in aspects much broader than the merely technical? It is indeed the Bandmaster, and the possession of a really good one is perhaps one of the greatest assets which a regiment or corps can have.

Field Marshal Sir Gerald Templer in
A Hundred Years of Military Music (P. L. Binns, 1959)

A continual shortage of bandsmen prompted the RCN to make what would prove to be a most significant musical decision. In 1954, while the RCAF and the army were recruiting musicians in Europe, at the urging of some naval musicians the Royal Canadian Navy founded the RCN School of Music in Esquimalt. By establishing such a school, the RCN laid a direct pipeline to the hitherto-untapped reservoir of young Canadian musicians.

Alfred Zeally had introduced the concept of a military school of music during the Second World War. Musicians in Zeally's school, however, enlisted during wartime and were trained professionals and semi-professionals. They had a brief course at the school and were dispatched to a band. The post-war RCN school was envisioned as an environment where the pupils would be recruited at an early age as complete novices and trained on military band instruments.

Ex-marine bandsman Harry Bateman recognized the need for a school almost from the moment of his arrival in the RCN and became the driving force behind its establishment. He was joined in his efforts by Emile Michaux, another west-coast navy musician. At the time, Lieutenant Commander Harry Cuthbert was able to convince naval headquarters that in order to meet the future needs of the bands, both at sea and on shore, a school patterned after the Royal Marine School was essential. On this premise, the Naval Bandsman Apprentice Plan was established in 1954.

The apprentices were regarded as the equivalents of civilian apprentices who learned a trade under the guiding hand of a qualified master craftsman. They were enrolled in the navy for seven years. Training was divided into two phases: the first phase was the initial basic navy training of fifteen weeks, and the second was their music training and study. During the first two years of apprenticeship training, they were students at the School of Music at HMCS *Naden* and were trained under highly qualified instructors. After graduation they were required to spend the balance of their seven-year engagement perfecting their skills as members of a navy band.

The young apprentices were trained under conditions suited to a serious student of music, modern studios with proper acoustics and good professional quality instruments. Instructors were the principal instrumentalists taken from existing navy bands, and worked very closely with the students. The student-teacher ratio was very low, enabling the instructor to monitor the student on a daily basis. The students worked eight hours per day on a variety of musical disciplines. They were provided with soundproof cubicles for individual practice, studied theory and did ensemble performances. They also had a recreation lounge and the base had a well-equipped sports facility. The education given at the RCN school was of a very high standard, emphasizing individual rather than group training. Apprentices were paid a regular salary while learning and were not required to pay any tuition or fees.

The bandsmen apprentices were encouraged to make a career of the RCN and it was not unusual for graduates of the school to attain the rank of chief petty officer. Some of the bandsmen were selected for commissioning and were appointed to conduct and direct RCN bands.

In 1954, the RCN school also began training advanced instrumentalists as bandmasters. Initially the course provided the candidates a basic grounding in conducting, scoring for band, harmony and history. Later, the course content was intensified to include musical and aural training. A service-related curriculum was instituted to give each of the student bandmasters a well-rounded indoctrination.

The next year the RCN school opened its doors to naval reserve bandsmen, who attended the school usually for a two-week period either as a full band unit or on individual training.

Instruction for RCAF and army bandsmen began in 1961. At the same time, the instructors became part of a new tri-service establishment. The change was undertaken under the direction of Lieutenant Commander Standley Sunderland who had become commandant in 1956. During the

Canadian Forces School of Music Band, 1991. Commandant is Major W.T. Wornes. (*Pearson Collection*)

period of transition the musical training officer was Captain James Gayfer. Gayfer was not only in charge of the newly formed Tri-Service Musicians Training Plan, but was also Chief Training Officer for the burgeoning bandmasters' class.

In 1968, the school was integrated into the Canadian Forces system and renamed the Canadian Forces School of Music (CFSMUS). The training system for musicians remained largely unchanged, but some updated methods were introduced. The quality of musicians gaining entrance to the school was improved tremendously. Training students with only basic ability had created a very large rate of attrition. The original auditions did not give an adequate reading of a musician's potential, and as a result, the practice of training neophyte musicians proved to be counterproductive and a good many were released prior to graduation. Beginning in the early 1980s young musicians wishing to enter the school had to have played in a high-school or college program.

Auditions were held under professional conditions with the applicant sitting in with a regular-force band and then being formally auditioned. Later an audio cassette of the audition was forwarded to the Supervisor of Music, with the recommendations of the Director of Music. The supervisor would make a determination of the instrumentalists' performances and their potential. The selection procedure also took into account a list circulated by Canadian Forces Recruiting outlining how many musicians and instruments were needed throughout the bands.

In 1987, the School of Music was moved from its historic location at CFB Esquimalt to Camp Borden. This move was prompted by two basic factors: most Canadian Forces schools are situated in Borden, and, more importantly, Borden's proximity to Toronto allowed students access to both clinicians and teachers as well as a variety of cultural activities.

The bandmasters' program, known as the Trade Qualification 7 Course, provided both directors and assistant directors for the bands. Trainees got a hands-on environment where they were able to learn conducting and other training courses under real-life conditions.

In 1994, in line with cutbacks in the band branch, the school in Camp Borden closed and the entire operation was moved to Ottawa and renamed the Canadian Forces Music Centre.

Commandants of the Canadian Forces School of Music

Lieutenant Commander H. Cuthbert	1954-56
Lieutenant Commander S. Sunderland	1956-66
Lieutenant Colonel C. Hunt	1966-68
Commander E. T. Jones	1967-75
Lieutenant Colonel T. Milner	1975-80
Lieutenant Colonel C. Villeneuve	1980-84
Commander G. Morrison	1984-85
Lieutenant Commander B. Templaars	1985-87
Major J. P. Montminy	1987-90
Major W. T. Wornes	1990-93
Major J. French	1993-94

The Kneller Hall Canadian Affiliation
A Roster of Graduates of the Royal Military School of Music with a Canadian Connection

Warrant Officer Arthur Clappe. Graduated 1873. Band of the Governor General's Foot Guards 1877-84. Founded the U.S. Army School of Music. Editor of numerous magazines.

Captain John Waldron. Graduated 1875. Director of Music of the Royal Regiment of Canada 1888-1904. Responsible for the early development of the band and for developing the band's balanced instrumentation.

Captain Alfred Light. Graduated 1890. Director of the Band of the Royal Canadian Horse Artillery 1908-1929.

Warrant Officer L. L. Worthington. Graduated 1896. Director of the Band of the Newfoundland Regiment. 1916-1919.

Captain Richard Hayward. Graduated 1905. Director of the Band of the Queen's Own Rifles of Canada 1921-28. Teacher of wind instruments at Toronto Conservatory of Music. Outstanding composer and arranger.

Captain Charles O'Neill. Graduated 1909. Royal Canadian Garrison Artillery, Band of the Royal Twenty-Second Regiment. The first Canadian to graduate from Kneller Hall, he wrote and arranged several pieces for military band and later taught music at American universities.

Major James Buckle. Graduated 1914. Director of Music of the Band of the Queen's Own Rifles of Canada 1928-1945.

Captain Lawrence K. Harrison. Graduated 1914. Director of the Band of the Royal Canadian Regiment 1924-1939.

Major Frank Coleman. Graduated 1923. Director of Music of the Band of the Royal Canadian Horse Artillery 1929-1939, Band of the Governor General's Foot Guards 1939-1941. Organized wartime bands in Canada. Became Inspector of Bands for Canada.

Warrant Officer Alexander Hollick. Graduated 1930. Bandmaster of the Band of the Royal Canadian Army Service Corps 1942-1945. Seconded to the Canadian army during the Second World War, Hollick worked under very difficult conditions in Italy and Holland. His diary of the band's activities resides with honour in the Canadian Forces Directorate of History.

Warrant Officer F. Buckmaster. Graduated 1935. Bandmaster of the Band of the First Infantry Corps 1942-1944. Seconded to the Canadian army before returning to the British army.

Captain William Atkins. Graduated 1935. Band of the Queen's Own Rifles of Canada 1947-1968. Taught conducting, woodwinds and composition for Ontario Department of Education.

Major A L Streeter. Graduated 1935. Band of the Princess Patricia's Canadian Light Infantry 1938-1939. Organized ten overseas bands during the Second World War. Following the war he was Inspector of Canadian Army Bands 1945-1954.

Captain George Quick. Graduated 1937. Director of Music of the Band of the Ontario Regiment circa 1965-1970. Staff officer responsible for recruiting in England. Assistant Inspector of Bands in Central Region of Canada.

Warrant Officer Lawrence Hicks. Graduated 1938. Band of the Royal Canadian Ordnance Corps 1942-45. Loaned by the British War Office for the duration of the war.

Warrant Officer A. G. O'Connor. Graduated 1932. Bandmaster of the Band of the Royal Canadian Corps of Signals 1942-1945.

Captain C. A. Holt. Graduated 1939. Bandmaster of the Band of the Royal Canadian Signal Corps 1941-1942. Director of Music of the Royal

Canadian Horse Artillery Band 1951-55. Postwar he became the Command Inspector of Bands, Western Command 1955-1961.

Captain Donald Keeling. Graduated 1939. Band of the Second Canadian Infantry Corps 1942-1945. Military Band of the 48th Highlanders of Canada 1954-1977. Seconded to the Canadian army he later emigrated to Canada and became Director of Music of the Band of the 48th Highlanders.

Warrant Officer Reg Newman. Graduated 1940. The Band of the Royal Canadian Artillery 1942-1945 Became the senior Director of Music for the Australian army.

Warrant Officer J. H. Hempstead. Graduated 1942. Bandmaster of the Band of the Royal Canadian Engineers 1942-1944.

Warrant Officer C. T. (Bobby) Beare. Graduated 1942. Bandmaster of the Band of the Royal Canadian Ordnance Corps 1942-1945. His leadership is noted on several Canadian Army Bands General reports.

Captain Joseph Purcell. Graduated 1942. Director of Music of the Band of the Royal Canadian Regiment 1953-1963.

Captain Doug Start. Graduated 1943. Director of Music of the Military Band of the Black Watch of Canada 1955-1961.

Captain E. G. Spooner. Graduated 1945. Director of Music of the Band of the Royal Canadian Dragoons 1955-1965.

Captain Kenneth Elloway. Graduated 1945. Director of Music of the Band of the Royal Canadian Artillery 1955-1965. Became the conductor of CBS Chamber Orchestra in Halifax in 1959-1965. Associate Conductor of the Halifax Symphony 1967-1968. Taught music at Dalhousie University 1974-1980.

Captain Ernest Wragg. Graduated 1945. Director of Music of the Band of the Royal Canadian Artillery 1952- 1955. Inspector of Bands for the Maritime area of Canada until retirement in 1961.

Major Melville Scott. Graduated 1947. Band of the First Canadian Infantry Battalion (later Band of the Canadian Guards) 1947. The first post war Canadian musician to graduate from Kneller Hall, he later became the Canadian Army Supervisor of Bands 1953-1966. Introduced band inspections and developed a program for musicians to advance within the band trade.

Captain James Gayfer. Graduated 1947. Director of Music Band of the Canadian Guards 1951-1961. Became the Training Officer of the Canadian Forces School of Music. Introduced a training program for the first tri- service bandmaster class in 1961. Has several published works, including "Royal Visit Concert March" and the well-known "Fanfare Toccata and March."

Major Al Brown. Graduated 1951. Director of Music of the Band of the PPCLI 1951-1954. Band of the Royal Canadian Engineers 1954-1961. Director of Bands at the Directorate of Ceremonial in Ottawa, he coordinated all CF bands for the 1967 cross-country Canadian Forces Tattoo. Organized all overseas Canadian Forces band tours.

Captain H. Lepage. Graduated 1951. Inspector of Bands for Quebec Region 1951-1954.

Captain Bernie Lyons. Graduated 1951. Director of Music of the Band of the Royal Canadian Signals 1952-1957.

Captain Gerald Gagnier. Graduated 1954. Director of Music of the Band of the Royal Canadian Ordnance Corps 1956-1960.

Captain Armand Ferland. Graduated 1954. Director of Music of the Band of the Royal Canadian Horse Artillery 1955- 1962. Band of the Royal Twenty-Second Regiment 1962-1965. Major work is "Rhapsodie Espagnole," performed by several orchestras in Canada.

Captain Leonard Camplin. Graduated 1955. Director of Music of the Band of the Royal Canadian Engineers 1961-1968. Canadian Forces *Naden* Band 1968-1970, Band of the Princess Patricia's Canadian Light Infantry 1974-1978. Was the music director of the Kelowna, BC, orchestra.

Captain Herb Jeffery. Graduated 1955. Director of Music of Lord Strathcona's Horse Royal Canadians Band 1956-1965.

Captain Charles Adams. Graduated 1957. Director of Music of the Band of the Royal Canadian Signals 1957-1964. The Canadian Guards Band 1966-68. Appointed the Command Inspector for Eastern Ontario Region in 1964-1966. Director of the Band of the Canadian Guards during the 1967 Canadian Centennial.

Captain Tom Higgins. Graduated 1958. Director of Music of the Band of the Canadian Guards 1961-1963.

Lieutenant E. Currie. Graduated 1959. Associate Director of Music of the Band of the Lord Strathcona's Horse 1959-1961.

Captain Harvey Eagles. Graduated 1960. Director of Music of the Military Band of the Black Watch of Canada 1961-1968.

Lieutenant Colonel Charles Villeneuve. Graduated 1960. Director of Music of the Band of the Royal Canadian Ordnance Corps 1960-1968, Band of the Royal Canadian Artillery 1968-1978. Supervisor of Music and Commandant of the Canadian Forces School of Music 1980. Musical Coordinator for cadet bands in the Quebec Region 1981.

Captain Alec Lee. Graduated 1961. Director of Music of the Band of the Royal Canadian Horse Artillery 1961-1968. Director of Music at Red Deer College, Alberta. Associate Director of Bands at National Defence Headquarters.

Captain Joe Dowell. Graduated 1962. Associate and later Director of Music of the Band of the Princess Patricia's Canadian Light Infantry 1968-1972.

Major Derek Stannard. Graduated 1963. Director of Music of the Band of the Royal Canadian Regiment 1963-1969. Associate Director of Music of the Norad Band (Colorado Springs, USA) 1969-1973. Central Band of the Canadian Forces 1973-1984. Assistant Director of the London, Ontario Symphony. Musical Director of several musicals in Ottawa, Ontario. Wrote and arranged numerous compositions for band and woodwinds. Music Director of the Boca Raton (Florida) Concert Orchestra, circa 1990.

Captain George Naylor. Graduated 1965. Director of Music of the Band of the Princess Patricia's Canadian Light Infantry 1965-1968.

Major Keith Swanwick. Graduated 1965. Director of Music of the Band of the Royal Canadian Signals 1964-1968. Associate Director and Director of Music, Air Command Band 1968-1984. Central Band of the Canadian Forces 1984-1986.

Major Jean Pierret. Graduated 1965. Director of Music of the Band of the Royal 22e Regiment 1965-1972. The Princess Patricia's Canadian Light Infantry Band 1972-1980. Canadian manager of the Vimy Memorial in France.

Major Ben Bogisch. Graduated 1965. Director of Music of the Band of the Royal Canadian Dragoons 1965-1967. Canadian Forces *Naden* Band 1970-1976. *Stadacona* Band 1976-1980. Training Officer at the School of Music 1980-1984.

Royal Marines School of Music Attendees

Commander E.Tudor Jones. Graduated 1954. Director of Music, *Naden* Band. Commandant Canadian Forces School of Music. Canadian Forces Supervisor of Music.

Chief Petty Officer First Class A Walter Delamont. Graduated 1954.

Commander Tom Milner. Graduated 1956. Director of Music *Naden* and *Stadacona* Bands. Commandant Canadian Forces School of Music. Canadian Forces Supervisor of Music.

Chief Petty Officer First Class Bill Stitt. Graduated 1956.

Chief Petty Officer First-Class Ernie Spiers. Graduated 1957. Bandmaster HMCS *Magnificent*.

Lieutenant commander Jack McGuire. Graduated 1957. Director of Music *Stadacona* Band. Principal Director of Music Nova Scotia International Tattoo.

Chief Petty Officer First Class Donald M Mackay. Graduated 1958.

Chief Warrant Officer Bill Brooks. Graduated 1963. Assistant Director *Cornwallis* Band 1965-1968, Assistant Director Band of the Royal Canadian Regiment 1968-1978. Canadian Forces School of Music 1978-1982.

Captain John D Collins. Graduated 1964. Director of Music *Cornwallis* Band. Associate Director and later Director of the Band of the Royal Canadian Regiment. Music Officer at Canadian Forces School of Music.

Other Naval Band Directors
Canadian Forces School of Music/Direct Entries

Lieutenant Commander Harry Cuthbert. 1939-1961. First full-time Director of Music for the Royal Canadian Navy. HMCS *Naden* Band. Director of the Overseas *Niobe* Band. Supervisor of Music of the Band of the Royal Canadian Navy.

Lieutenant Commander Stanley Sunderland. 1943-1968. Bandmaster HMCS *Chatham* Band. Bandmaster *Naden* Band. Director of Music, *Naden* Band. Commandant Royal Canadian Navy School of Music. Commandant Canadian Forces School of Music.

Lieutenant (Navy) Mickey Nold. 1941-1967. An original member of the *Stadacona* Band, he was a classically trained pianist and had performed with the CBC before the war. He was commissioned after the war and became the Director of Reserve Bands.

Lieutenant Commander William J Gordon. 1954-1972. Graduate of the Royal Marines School of Music. Director HMCS *Stadacona* Band and Canadian Forces Central Band.

Lieutenant (Navy) Peter Metcalf. 1952-1969. Graduate of the Canadian Forces School of Music. Attended the Royal Marines School of Music. Director the *Naden* Band and Princess Patricia's Canadian Light Infantry Band.

Naval Band Directors in the Second World War

Technical Commissioned Officer Ernest Ainley. 1942, HMCS *Hyacinthe*. Signal School in St. Hyacinthe, Quebec.

Petty Officer Melville Watson. 1942.

Lieutenant Commander Alfred E Zeally. 1943 Royal Canadian Naval School of Music.

Warrant Officer Ernest Huggins. 1943, Royal Canadian Naval School of Music.

Chief Petty Officer Horace Sainsbury. 1943, HMCS *Protector*.

Petty Officer Edward Curry. 1943, HMCS *Protector*.

Petty Officer Vernon Gooch. 1943, HMCS *York*.

Chief Petty Officer Guy Noakes. 1944, HMCS *Chatham*.

Petty Officer Larry Frayne. 1944, HMCS *Chatham*.

Chief Petty Officer John Cuthbert. 1944, HMCS *Shelburne*. 1943, HMCS *Avalon*.

Warrant Officer JL Broadbent. 1944, HMCS *Avalon*.

Lieutenant (Navy) Leslie Blackburn. 1943, HMCS *Donnacona*, (previously a naval division band taken on strength in 1943).

Petty Officer Edwin Bunn. 1943, HMCS *Donnacona*.

Warrant Officer R. Holroyd. 1944, HMCS *Chippawa*.

Petty Officer J Newton. 1944, HMCS *Chippawa*.

Chief Petty Officer Bert Graham. 1944, HMCS *Peregrine*.

Chief Petty Officer Melville Watson. 1944, HMCS *Discovery*.

Petty Officer Casey Piekarz. 1944, HMCS *Discovery*.

Naval Band Directory, Post War
Directors of Music of the *Stadacona* Band

Lieutenant Commander Alfred E Zeally	1940-1942
Lieutenant James Downey Sr.	1942-1945
Lieutenant Commander Stanley E Sunderland	1946-1956
Lieutenant Commander Henry (Harry) Cuthbert	1956-1960
Commissioned Officer Tom Milner	1957-1960
(Associate Director)	
Lieutenant (Navy) Mickey Nold	1960-1963
Lieutenant Commander William Gordon	1963-1966
Lieutenant Commander Jack McGuire	1966-1968
(Canadian Forces Amalgamation, 1968)	
Lieutenant Commander Jack McGuire	1968-1975
Captain Terrance Barnes	1968-1971
(Associate Director)	
Captain Maurice Ziska	1970-1974
(Associate Director)	
Commander George Morrison	1976-1980
Major Bertus Tempelaars	1980-1983
Major Ron McCallum	1983-1985
Lieutenant (Navy) Hugh McCullough	1986-1988
Lieutenant (Navy) Jim Forde	1988-1993
Lieutenant Commander Peter van der Horden	1993

Bandmasters and Directors of Music of the *Naden* Band

Lieutenant Commander Henry Cuthbert	1940-1944
Warrant Officer Stanley Sunderland	1944-1945
Lieutenant Commander Henry Cuthbert	1946-1956
Petty Officer E Michaux	1946

Lieutenant Commander William Gordon	1958-1960
Chief Petty Officer First Class Harry Bateman	1958
Major Tom Milner	1960-1963
Commander Tudor Jones	1963-1966
Lieutenant (Navy) Peter Medcalfe	1966-1968
Captain (Land) Leonard Camplin	1968-1970
Chief Warrant Officer Stanley Webb	1968-1975
Major Bernard Bogisch	1970-1975
Captain (Land) Albert Furey	1975-1981
Chief Warrant Officer Barry Moncur	1975
Commander Gerald Klaassen	1981-1984
Chief Warrant Officer John Pasmans	1981
Lieutenant Commander John French	1985-1987
Lieutenant Commander Bertus Tempelaars	1987-1988
Chief Petty Officer First-Class Robert Michaux	1987
Lieutenant Commander Rudolph Gazarek	1988-1992
Lieutenant (Navy) Hugh McCullough	1992-1994
Chief Petty Officer First-Class Bob Michaux	1992

Directors of Music and Bandmasters of the *Malahat* Band and Marcom Band

Lieutenant Commander John French	1994-1995
WO Andrew Reljic	1995-1997
Lieutenant (Navy) Camile Bouchard	1997

Bandmasters and Directors of Music of the *Cornwallis* Band and the *Shearwater* Band

Cornwallis Band

Technical Commissioned Officer Robert McGall	1942-1945
Chief Petty Officer Mickey Nold	1947-1950
Chief Petty Officer Arthur Delamont	1950
Chief Petty Officer William Stitt	
Commissioned Officer E Tudor Jones	1954-1957
Commissioned Officer Jack McGuire	1957-1964
Lieutenant (Navy) John Collins	1964-1968

Shearwater Band

Chief Petty Officer Vic Goodridge
Chief Petty Officer William Stitt
Commissioned Officer Peter Medcalfe

Canadian Navy Bands Afloat

Petty Officer Elliot Van Evera	HMCS *Nabob*	1944	Cruiser
Petty Officer Walter Jeffrey	HMCS *Uganda*	1944	Cruiser
Petty Officer Harry Sheppard	HMCS *Ontario*	1945	Cruiser
Chief Petty Officer Harry Bateman	HMCS *Cayuga*	1954-1956	Tribal Class Destroyer
Chief Petty Officer Ernie Spiers	HMCS *Magnificent*	1959-61	Aircraft Carrier
Chief Petty Officer Vic Goodridge	HMCS *Bonaventure*	1957-1958	Aircraft Carrier
Petty Officer First Class Vlaho Miloslavich	HMCS *Quebec*	1955-56	Cruiser
Leading Seaman H. L. Coffil			
Leading Seaman H. L. Jeffery			
Petty Officer Edgar Hemmingway	HMCS *Bonaventure*	1958	Aircraft Carrier

Other Ships Afloat with Band, and Bands Aboard for Transits

HMCS *Uganda*	Cruiser (renamed HMCS *Ontario*)
HMCS *Quebec*	Cruiser
HMCS *Cape Scott*	Fleet Supply Ship

Transits

HMCS *Swansea*	Corvette
HMCS *St. Jean*	Gate Vessel
HMCS *St. Laurent*	Destroyer Escort
HMCS *Provider*	Supply Ship Y Class
HMCS *Preserver*	Supply Ship Y Class
HMCS *Ottawa*	Destroyer Escort
HMCS *Iroquois*	280 Class Destroyer
HMCS *Athabaskan*	280 Class Destroyer
HMCS *Montreal*	Canadian Patrol Frigate

CHAPTER 10

Bands Today
1967–1997

No one, not even the adjutant, can say for certain where the soul of the bat-
talion lives; but the expression of that soul is most often found in the band.

Rudyard Kipling, England, January 1915

The 1967 Centennial celebrations suspended the integration of the bands, however, by 1968, the death knell had been rung, and in addition to the elimination of the three-service concept, the seventeen regular bands had been reduced to nine.

And so, a new and challenging era began in the history of Canadian bands, calling as it did for a somewhat abrupt merging of traditions and musical concepts. Surprisingly, the integration of the bands proceeded with few problems, and, by the summer of 1969, there seemed to be very little evidence of upheaval.

In 1968, the former RCAF Central Band, now the National Band under Lieutenant Commander William Gordon, made a triumphal European tour, appearing at a NATO festival in West Germany and playing concerts in Switzerland.

An interesting aspect of the National Band was the development of a string ensemble within the ranks of the band that worked mostly as a sep-arate entity. The group, dubbed the Serenade of Strings, came under the leadership of Raymond Flowers, a former Royal Marine cellist who had studied at the Guild Hall in London. The eight members are often aug-mented for larger performances. The establishment has remained unchanged and has presently a viola, a cello, a string bass, a piano, and four violins.

In 1970, the RCR band moved to Camp Gagetown from London, Ontario. Some name-swapping went on in 1974, when the National Band went back to being called the Central Band of the Canadian Forces. As well, the Air Transport Command Band was renamed the Vimy Band.

The big issue at this time was that of the green ceremonial uniform introduced after integration. The green uniform also spelled, for the time being, the demise of the government-sponsored ceremonial uniform. Almost from the moment of its first appearance the green uniform was criticized as being absurd. From the moment the musicians first wore it, it was christened the Barnum and Bailey in honour of the circus musician's uniforms.

In a 1971 article, Wayne King, a columnist for the Ottawa *Journal*, called the uniforms Jolly Green Jumpers. An unidentified band member, however, took issue with King's remarks and shot back "Does Mr. King want us to wear British uniforms?"

Despite the carping about the band uniform, it wasn't until the Conservative government reintroduced the three-services concept in 1984 that the uniforms of the navy, army and air force were utilized again.

In 1975, the government of Pierre Trudeau ordered the Department of Defence to trim its expenditures. As a result, Chief of Staff General J. A. Dextraze decided to chop four bands.

The Ottawa *Citizen* announced the news in the following article:

Costly Music Hits Sour Note

A sour note has appeared in the Armed Forces progress toward normalcy. As a cost saving gesture, the regular forces bands at Kingston, Gagetown, NB, Calgary and Montreal appear to be on the way out.

Defence Minister James Richardson doesn't like the idea and he is looking for other ways to save money. But under plans announced by Chief of Defence Staff General J. A. Dextraze at a conference last week, the bands are gradually on the way out at a saving of about two and a half million dollars a year.

The news item recounted that the band establishment would be reduced from 465 to 305. In addition, personnel with over twenty years of service were going to have to take mandatory retirement.

In Calgary, the Royal Canadian Legion undertook to get one hundred thousand signatures in an effort to save the PPCLI band. John Diefenbaker rose up in anger in the House of Commons to condemn the government's action, saying it was another attack on royalty in Canada by dropping four royal bands. Conservative member Flora McDonald also raised her voice against the plan to disband the Vimy Band in Kingston.

Geoff Johnson, writing in Ottawa *Journal* said:

It's No Time to Scrap the Bands

Johnson zeroed in on how the government was going to restore the three services and how happy everyone would be, but that Richardson had failed to mention he was about to get rid of the bands which Johnson described as the "Last Waltz." He finished his piece by saying: "We shouldn't be planning to get rid of our military bands. The way things are shaping up in this world, we are going to need every one of them."

Following the rigorous protests in the press and from every walk of life including Members of Parliament, the bands got a reprieve. The minister made the last-minute stay on March 24th. He spoke directly to two senior band officers, Majors A. L. Brown and Derek Stannard who spoke out strongly against the government action. There was a price to be paid, however, for the retention of the bands. The minister decided to keep the bands operational but reduce their ranks by eighty musicians, leaving an effective total of 319 band members in regular force bands and the school.

Public opinion was decidedly in favour of the government decision. The newspaper and the pro-band movement were jubilant. The headlines in the Calgary *Herald* for 25 March said:

We Did It

Defence Department Revokes Decision to Kill Bands

As a result of a 1971 survey, it was concluded that women should be assimilated into the music branch. Four years later the first woman entered the branch; she was pianist Lynn Hong, who joined the Central Band's Serenade of Strings. Two other women had begun training at the School of Music in 1974 under the musicians training plan.

When the original reduction of bands had occurred in 1968, the Canadian Forces in Europe were left without musical support. In the late spring and fall of 1969 the defence department began sending bands to Europe for short stints of six weeks. This deployment has continued along with the practice of sending groups or small ensembles for special occasions. Bands proceeding to Europe in the fall usually perform at the Vimy Memorial during November. The spring tour that may extend into July is often committed to change-of-command parades and band festivals. As an example, the Vimy Band from Kingston played in four festivals or tattoos in 1987. Other bands have travelled extensively to many foreign lands. The *Stadacona* Band went to the USSR in 1976. Under Commander

George Morrison, it was featured in concerts in Leningrad and was part of a ship's visit to Russia. The PPCLI band under their director, Captain Don Embry, made a six-week tour to Australia for their centennial in 1988.

Although cross-Canada tours of the size of the 1967 tattoo were no longer possible, the navy did celebrate their Seventy-Fifth Anniversary in 1985, with a mini cross-Canada tour. The musical direction was by Lieutenant Commander Jack McGuire. He also wrote a great deal of the material. The band was selected from the reserve naval establishment and performed in the massed band portions of the tattoo as well as the different smaller segments. Different regular-force bands were employed as pit bands and in special guest band shots. It was, therefore, possible to show-case several regular-force bands. The show was a tremendous success and attracted large crowds across Canada.

The most popular static tattoo in North America remains the Halifax Tattoo each year in early summer. The show has long been produced by Ian Fraser of 1967 Centennial Tattoo fame, and the music is under the direction of retired Lieutenant Commander Jack McGuire. The *Stadacona* Band provided the pit band for the show and most of the music is arranged and composed by Earl Fralick. The tattoo attracts bands from as far away as Germany, and each year a regular-force band makes an appearance. It is known for its gigantic finales and the huge choirs that appear make the entire event a great hit with audiences from all over Canada and the United States.

During the 1980s the Central Band of the Canadian Forces made appearances in the Roy Thompson Hall in Toronto, in programs shared with Toronto's Welsh Choir. These concerts were inaugurated under Major James Underwood and the tradition has been carried on under Majors Ron McCallum and John French.

In 1979, the NORAD Band, stationed in Colorado Springs, was disbanded and the Canadian musicians returned to Canada. The band had a contingent of sixty during its heyday, with as many as ten Canadian musicians in its ranks. The band had, however, begun to lose favour, and by the end had been scaled down to a thirty-piece band. The Canadian musicians were spread among the existing bands to raise them to their authorized strength of thirty-five musicians.

In 1989, twenty-five musicians were hired to augment the Central Band for the changing of the guard ceremony on Parliament Hill. The musicians were then assigned to other bands employed on the hill for the summer. The program was very successful, and, as a result, the defence department formulated a plan to hire young musicians from either the reserve or from schools to serve in a summer band consisting of from seventy-five to one hundred musicians. Auditions were held in the winter of 1981 and the musicians began arriving in May 1981. The band, called the Ceremonial Guards Band, has since become a fixture on Parliament Hill.

Military band music had a major setback during the 1977 fall sitting of the House of Commons, when Conservative member for Leeds Tom Cossit rose to announce that he was in receipt of information showing theft of sound equipment and musical instruments as well as large-scale embezzlement.

In November the culprit, a warrant officer recently retired from the Central Band, was named. A full investigation commenced in January 1978, and by April, with all evidence gathered, a court martial was convened at Canadian Forces Rockcliffe. The trial became the longest and most expensive in the history of the Canadian Forces. The warrant officer was sentenced to a jail term, much of the equipment was recovered and several interesting areas of the Canadian Forces supply system were laid bare. The question of theft, it was shown, was only part of the problem as despite the checks and counterchecks, someone had succeeded in breaching the system's security.

The fiasco of 1977-1978 was an embarrassment to the music branch and left unanswered questions. Fortunately, within the reams of material contained in the trial transcript, there was not one word of condemnation regarding the music branch as a whole.

In the spring and summer of 1989 the Toronto Reserve District, in association with the Royal Canadian Military Institute, decided to produce a recording of all the marches of the Canadian Forces. It was a huge task and the musical portion fell to Major Bobby Herriot and Major Leonard Falcone. They gathered musicians from the reserve bands in Toronto and completed the record in four segments. In addition a march contest of world-class proportions was undertaken. The contest was advertised in several publications, including the magazine of the American Federation of Musicians. The combined bands of the Royal Rifles and Queen's Own Rifles gathered on July First at Ontario Place to perform a concert and also to play for three distinguished judges from England, Canada and the USA, the marches of the seven finalists. The winner was David Allen Jacob of Victoria, a former Canadian Forces musician. His march became the march of the Military Institute.

In 1994 the Liberal government of Jean Chrétien came to power and with razor-like swiftness several Canadian Forces bands and the School of Music were shaved out of existence. All of the infantry bands, including the Royal Canadian Regiment and the Princess Patricia's Canadian Light

Infantry bands as well as the famous Royal Twenty-Second band were dissolved. The Vimy Band of Kingston was also axed. In addition the *Naden* Band was reduced to ten personnel and renamed the HMCS *Malahat*. The bands remaining were the *Stadacona* Band in Halifax, the Canadian Forces band in Ottawa, the Royal Canadian Artillery band in Montreal, and the Air Command band in Winnipeg. The artillery band eventually moved to Quebec City.

The School of Music was reorganised, no longer training young musicians for service in Canadian Forces bands. The entire operation moved to Ottawa and the name was changed to the Canadian Forces Music Centre. The centre works in conjunction with the Canadian Forces bands and there is still a provision for the training of bandmasters. The Supervisor of Music has facilities in this location.

The emphasis on the reserve bands has taken on new proportions. Reserve units across Canada function extremely well under the auspices of their parent units. They play an effective role in providing music for all facets of the military and civilian communities.

In 1997, the Canadian government, cognisant of the void left by dissolving the bands in 1994, began to help rebuild the morale of the Canadian Forces by reintroducing the *Naden* Band in Victoria. In addition, a new army band was planned for Edmonton under the direction of Canada's first full-time female director of music, Captain Heather Davis.

The story of military music in Canada is very much related to the elements of patriotism. The musicians and the bands come and go, but the universally meaningful story of ups and downs, struggles and successes, hopes and loyalties continues.

CHAPTER 11

The Nova Scotia
International Tattoo

A Tradition of Excellence

From a two-day event in 1979 to a ten-day entertainment extravaganza in the year 2000, The Nova Scotia International Tattoo has developed into an annual event that attracts capacity audiences from around the world. The Tattoo's unique combination of military and civilian performers, bands, pipes and drums, dance, drama, gymnastics, comedy and military displays has developed a devoted audience. What started as a production that featured local talent has grown to include international acts from around the world. As of the 1999 production, the Tattoo had hosted talented performers from Canada, Australia, Bermuda, Denmark, Estonia, France, Germany, Japan, The Netherlands, New Zealand, Norway, Portugal, Russia, Sweden, Switzerland, the United Kingdom, the United States and the list grows every year.

History of the Tattoo

The Tattoos of today can trace their history to a military tradition that began in 17th century Holland. To recall British soldiers, who were billeted with the townspeople, from the local inns and pubs, a drummer marched through the streets calling out "Doe Den Tap Toe." This call was a signal for the innkeepers to turn off their taps and for the soldiers to return to their billets. This phrase was shortened to "Tap Toe" and eventually anglicized to "Tattoo."

The tradition was carried back to England where it became a daily routine, altered by the addition of other musicians. As Tattoos evolved in Britain, various elements were added; military drill displays, musical rides, simulated battle scenes and historical pageants lent colour and excitement. From a simple drill, a form of local military entertainment was created and eventually garrisons were providing short concerts for the benefit of the townspeople each evening.

Early in the 1900s, the Tattoo developed into a form of high quality entertainment. Tattoos were staged to stimulate interest and recruiting in the peacetime army.

The Canadian Concept

Lieutenant Ian Fraser, under the tutelage of General Robert Moncel, modified the European style Tattoo through an approach to production which came to be called the "Canadian Concept." The first Tattoo produced in this manner was "Soldiers of the Queen," performed in Fredericton, NB in 1959. Elements from various European productions were combined for variety and theatrical elements such as lighting, costumes and proscenium stages were introduced to make the show more spectacular.

Ian Fraser developed his unique style of production with "The Canadian Tattoo" which was presented at the Seattle World Fair in 1962. The outstanding success of this show led to Ian Fraser's appointment as Producer/Director of the Canadian Armed Forces Tattoo produced during Canada's centennial in 1967. Fraser added a creative storyline, professional civilian designers and extensive theatrical lighting, but at the same time, he retained the traditional bands, music, display and competition.

The Nova Scotia International Tattoo

For Nova Scotia's initial Tattoo in 1979, A Gathering of the Clans, which was opened by Her Majesty Queen Elizabeth The Queen Mother, civilian performers were successfully combined with the traditional military performance for the first time. A Gaelic choir, the Men of the Deep, highland dancers, pipes and drums, and numerous dance clubs brought to the Tattoo a presentation of the province's cultural heritage.

Each Tattoo after that has been a new event, a completely different show. Under the direction of Ian Fraser, the Tattoo has expanded and taken on new creative dimensions in order to present a unique and spectacular performance each year. It has evolved into a breathtaking spectacle of pomp, pageantry, energy and spirit. Four full-time staff assist Ian Fraser year-round. At production time, the number of people working on the show, in addition to the hundreds of volunteers, grows to sixty.

The Tattoo now carries an annual theme, Bond of Friendship, which represents the coming together of the military and civilian communities, individuals and nations. In addition to this annual theme, several Tattoos have featured sub-themes including; The Immigrants (1988); The Battle of Britain (1990); Battle of the Atlantic (1993); D Day (1994); VE Day (1995); The Militia Story (1996); The Battle of Vimy Ridge/ Canada and the UN (1997); the 125th Anniversary of the RCMP (1998); and the 250th Anniversary of the Founding of the City of Halifax (1999). The 2000 Tattoo featured a tribute to the Canadian Forces of the past 100 years.

The Tattoo is proud of its international participation. The United States was the first international country to join the show. The Quantico Marine Band played at every NS Tattoo from 1980 to 1996. The Tattoo has also enjoyed the presence of the American All Star Dancers in 1985, the US Army Herald Trumpets and the US Navy Band Country Current in 1994, the US Army Drill Team in 1995, the Old Guard Fife and Drum Corps in 1996, the US Atlantic Fleet Band in 1997 and the US Continental Army Band in 1998.

Germany also enjoys a long-standing relationship with the Tattoo. The Band of the German Air Force, Luftwaffenmusikkorps 2, appeared at the Tattoo in 1983. Since then, there have been appearances by military bands, dancers, the Motorcycle Display Team of the Berlin Police Force, The Flying Grandpas of the Hamburg Police Force, the Flying Saxons, the Gym Wheel Show Group and even the Hamburg Police Dog Team.

In 1993, the Tattoo was delighted that The Song and Dance Ensemble of the Northern Fleet of the Russian Federation joined the production. This amazing group, which featured a band, dancers and a choir, is regarded as one of the finest performing groups in the Russian Armed Forces.

The Tattoo was honoured when, in 1999, the Central Band of the Japan Air Self Defence Force chose the Nova Scotia Tattoo as their first place to perform outside of Japan. In fact, it was the first performance of a Japanese military band outside of Japan since the Second World War.

The Nova Scotia Tattoo is the product of hard work and dedication of civilians, volunteers, professionals, youngsters, office workers, stage crews, designers, drivers, sailors, soldiers, airmen, military brass and government officials. It is at once festive, glorious, meditative, heroic and solemn. It is a traditional form of entertainment which, in a uniquely Nova Scotian way, has become a tradition itself.

Today the show is a world-renowned annual event. Each year many loyal performers return to join with ever increasing numbers of international bands and display groups. The participation of local and international performers, combined with the enthusiasm of hundreds of off-stage workers, has given the Tattoo the international reputation it enjoys today.

CHAPTER 12

History of the
Regimental Marches

Both British and French garrisoned the cities, towns and forts of this country. The old forts and parade grounds have resounded to the tramp of marching feet of the red brilliance of the foot regiments, the thunder of artillery blue, the famous rifle green and the ancient sound of Highland pipes. Many of these regiments have since passed into history, but their legacy remains in Canada's regular and reserve forces.

Many regiments were accompanied by their regimental bands and became quite popular with local residents. One of the most popular and important roles was their performance in public concerts. In some places the local army bands were the only musicians available to accompany civilian dances, and they formed the backbone of cultural activities in Canada.

With the Crimean War looming, the British units were recalled to England. However, many of the musicians remained and it was their influence that helped to nurture the military band movement in Canada. The Canadian militia regiments began to play a more prominent role, forming bands and becoming the mainstay of military music heritage in Canada. Between 1850 and the turn of the century several bands developed excellent reputations. The first known enlisted band in Canada, the Independent Artillery Company, was organized in 1851 at Hamilton. Other bands included the Queen's Own Rifles Band and the Governor General's Foot Guard Band.

Scottish and Irish immigrants formed kilted regiments and, along with the French, had a profound impact on our military heritage. Among early militia bands were the 9th Battalion Band in Quebec, the Royal Regiment of Canada Band, the 19th St. Catharines Regiment (Lincoln and Welland Band) and the Royal Winnipeg Rifles.

General Brock proposed raising volunteer units in Canada with bugles or drums however some units developed their own bands. Two Canadian regiments were the Glengarry Light Infantry (nineteen bugles) and the New Brunswick Regiment of Fencible Infantry.

Both the French and the English influenced much of our adopted music. This is reflected in music used by today's military bands. One march, "Heart of Oak," was used before Canada had a notable militia. This old naval tune, used by the Maritime Command, was written to commemorate the Year of Victories that included the British victory over the French at Quebec in 1759. In one odd case, a French-Canadian unit adopted the march of their allied British unit. This was Les Fusiliers Mont-Royal who adopted the York and Lancaster regimental march "The Jockey of York." But the French have a rich tapestry of music including the well-known *"Sambre et Meuse"* used by Le Régiment de Maisonneuve. This march refers to a make-believe regiment honouring an area in France around the Sambre and Meuse Rivers during the Great War. The Royal Montreal Regiment march, *"Ça Ira,"* is one of the few marches earned in battle — this one at Famars during the French Revolutionary Wars. The 12e Régiment blindé du Canada, one of Canada's regular armoured regiments, uses two old French folk songs, *"Marianne s'en va-t-au moulin* (Marianne is Going to the Mill)" and *"Quand vous mourrez de nos amours* (When You Die From Our Loves)."

The music origins of the highland regiments are very old. Some kilted regiments use a variety of marches along with regimental and battalion tunes. The "Highland Laddie" or "Hielan' Laddie," used by a number Canadian regiments, is one of the most well-known Scottish marches. In 1881 Highland units of the British army were ordered to adopt the march but also retained their old favourites that had been used for years. One famous march "The Campbells are Coming," refers to the Campbell Clan in Scotland and is used by the Lorne Scots of Brampton and the Argyll and Sutherland Highlanders of Canada based in Hamilton. The Canadian Scottish Regiment of Victoria and the Toronto Scottish use another Scottish favorite "Blue Bonnets over the Border," which may be also known as "All the Blue Bonnets Over the Border." The Blue Bonnets are the blue woollen caps worn in Scotland during the seventeenth century.

In adopting marches from our British cousins we find that some have been composed by well-known personalities. In 1836, HRH The Duchess of Kent wrote the "Royal Artillery Slow March" was adopted by many artillery units. The Queen's Own Rifles of Canada use "The Buffs" composed by Handel for the Buffs (Royal East Kent Regiment). The Legal Branch adopted Gilbert and Sullivan's "When I, Good Friends, Was call'd to the Bar" from the opera Trial by Jury. Prior to disbandment, the Canadian Airborne Regiment used the theme music of the movie The Longest Day, composed by the Canadian singer Paul Anka. It was fitting that the regiment adopted this because their predecessors, The First Canadian Parachute Battalion played a key role on D-Day, June 6, 1944.

Some marches in use today are uniquely Canadian. The French folk song "*Vive la Canadienne,*" for instance, used by The Royal 22e Regiment, was first used as a patriotic song as far back as 1840, before "O Canada" was written. "The Maple Leaf Forever" was never really appreciated by French Canadians, partly because although the song mentions the thistle, shamrock and rose, it neglects the fleur-de-lis, but mainly because of its reference to Montcalm's defeat on the Plains of Abraham. The Royal Westminster Regiment currently uses "The Maple Leaf Forever" march. "We Lead, Others Follow," was composed for the Algonquin Regiment by one of its officers while fighting in Holland during the Second World War. The title refers to the regimental motto Ne-Kah-Ne-Tah, which is the Algonquin Indian translation of the phrase.

The major changes that occurred in the Canadian Forces during the 1960s forced some regiments, corps and marches into history. Some that disappeared were "Wait for the Wagon" of the Royal Canadian Army Service Corps, "Here's a Health unto His Majesty" of the Royal Canadian Army Medical Corps, "The Village Blacksmith" used by the Royal Canadian Ordnance Corps, the two marches of the Royal Canadian Army Pay Corps, "Pay Parade" and "Primrose and Blue." In their place new branches were formed and marches composed or arranged for them. Such music includes "The March of the Logistic Branch" of the Logistic Branch while the Security Branch uses "Thunderbird."

The lineage of a regiment had in some cases a great influence on the music chosen. The Royal Regina Rifles was allied with the King's Royal Rifle Corps, now the Royal Green Jackets, and adopted their march "Lutzow's Wild Hunt." Canadian Guards units followed their British counterparts' tradition of adopting the marches "Milanollo," the "March from Figaro" and the ever-popular "British Grenadiers," one of the oldest marches in use today. Other music adopted was influenced by the period and popularity of the tunes at the time. At the beginning of the Boer War, "Soldiers of the Queen" became popular and was adopted by Lord Strathcona's Horse, raised to fight in that war. The Princess Patricia's Canadian Light Infantry adopted a medley of three tunes, "Has Anyone Seen the Colonel?," "It's a Long Way to Tipperary," and "Mademoiselle from Armentieres," all popular during the First World War. The Royal Winnipeg Rifles use a tune that became popular about the time of the Red

River Rebellion, "Old Solomon Levi," also known as "Pork, Beans and Hard Tack."

Military musicians have come from a wide background, and their compositions and arrangements became some of the most famous military music used today. Just after the end of the Great War, Sir Walford Davies wrote "The RAF Marchpast" which the RCAF were allowed to adopt as "The RCAF Marchpast" due to their involvement in the air war over England during the 1940s.

Chief Warrant Officer Brian Gossip began his career in the British army and became one of Canada's best-known march arrangers and composers. His arrangements include "Thunderbird" (Security), "*Semper Intelligere*" (Personnel Selection Branch), "The Farmer's Boy" (Medical Branch), the Legal Branch march "When I, Good Friends, Was Called to the Bar," and the Intelligence Branch's "*E Tenebris Lux*," based on Mozart's "A Little Night Music."

Canadian military bands, regular and reserve, keep alive this music connection to our country's past. Each year throughout the country, Canadian military bands play at county fairs, parades, concerts, Highland gatherings and tattoos. Their colourful uniforms, precision marching and stirring marches that once spurred men onto victory now thrill the masses whenever they are played.

Regimental/Corps/Branch Marches of the Canadian Forces

1st Air Defence Regiment (Lanark and Renfrew Scottish)
"Royal Canadian Artillery Slow March"
"Highland Laddie"

1st Canadian Division Headquarters and Signals Regiment
"Corps March of the Royal Canadian Corps of Signals (Begone Dull Care)"

1st Hussars
"Bonnie Dundee"

2nd Battalion, The Irish Regiment of Canada
"Garry Owen"

4th Battalion, The Royal Canadian Regiment (London and Oxford Fusiliers)
"The Royal Canadian Regiment"
"*Pro Patria*"

4e Bataillon, Royal 22e Régiment (Châteauguay)
"*Vive la canadienne*"
"*Marche Lente du Royal 22e Régiment*"

6e Bataillon, Royal 22e Régiment
"*Vive la canadienne*"
"*Marche Lente du Royal 22e Régiment*"

8th Canadian Hussars (Princess Louise's)
"The Galloping 8th Hussars"
"The 8th Hussars"

12e Régiment blindé du Canada
"*Marianne s'en va-t-au moulin*
(Marianne is Going to the Mill)"
"*Quand vous mourrez de nos amours*
(When You Die From Our Loves)"

48th Highlanders of Canada
"Highland Laddie"

49th (Sault-Ste-Marie) Field Artillery Regiment
"A Hundred Pipers" (for pipe band)
"Royal Artillery Slow March"
"The British Grenadiers"
"Bonnie Dundee"
"Keel Row"

Air Command
"Royal Canadian Air Force Marchpast"

Algonquin Regiment
"We Lead, Others Follow"

Argyll & Sutherland Highlanders of Canada (Princess Louise's)
"The Campbells are Coming"

Black Watch (Royal Highland Regiment) of Canada
"The Highland Laddie"
"The Red Hackle"

British Columbia Dragoons
"Fare Ye Well Inniskilling"
"Scotland the Brave"

British Columbia Regiment (Duke of Connaught's Own)
"I'm Ninety-Five"

Brockville Rifles
"Bonnie Dundee"

Calgary Highlanders
"The Highland Laddie"
"Blue Bonnets Over the Border"

Cameron Highlanders of Ottawa
"The Piobaireachd of Donald Dhu"
"March of the Cameron Men"

Canadian Grenadiers Guards
"The British Grenadiers"
"The Grenadiers March"

Canadian Scottish Regiment (Princess Mary's)
"Blue Bonnets Over the Border"

Chaplain Branch
"Onward Christian Soldiers"

Communications and Electronics Branch
"The Mercury March"

Dental Branch
"Marchpast of the Royal Canadian Dental Corps"
"Greensleeves"

Electrical and Mechanical Engineering Branch
"REME Corps Marchpast"
"The Craftsman"

193

**First Combat Engineer Regiment
(Formerly The Elgins)**
"Wings"
"I'm Ninety-Five"
"Waltzing Matilda" (for trumpet
band)

Essex and Kent Scottish
"The Highland Laddie"
"A Hundred Pipers"

Fort Garry Horse
"El Abanico"
"St. Patrick's Day"
"Red River Valley"

Governor General's Foot Guards
"Milanollo"
"The March from Figaro"

**Governor General's Horse
Guards**
"Men of Harlech"

Grey and Simcoe Foresters
"The 31st Greys"

**Hastings and Prince Edward
Regiment**
"I'm Ninety-Five"

Highland Fusiliers of Canada
"Highland Laddie"
"*Seann Triubhas*"

Intelligence Branch
"*E Tenebris Lux*"

King's Own Calgary Regiment
"Colonel Bogey"

Lake Superior Scottish Regiment
"The Highland Laddie"

Legal Branch
"When I, Good Friends, Was
Call'd to the Bar"

Le Régiment de Hull
"*La Marche de la Victoire*"

Le Regiment de la Chaudière
"*Sambre et Meuse*"
"The Longest Day"

Le Régiment de Maisonneuve
"*Sambre et Meuse*"

Le Régiment du Saguenay
"*Le Régiment du Saguenay*"

Les Fusiliers de Sherbrooke
"*Ville Reine* (Queen City)"

Les Fusiliers du St-Laurent
"*Rêves canadiens*"

Les Fusiliers Mont-Royal
"The Jockey of York"

Les Voltigeurs de Québec
"*Les Voltigeurs de Québec*"

Lincoln and Welland Regiment
"The Lincolnshire Poacher"

Logistics Branch
"March of the Logistics Branch"

**Lord Strathcona's Horse (Royal
Canadians)**
"Soldiers of the Queen"

**Lorne Scots (Peel, Dufferin and
Halton Regiment)**
"The Campbells are Coming" (for
pipe band)
"John Peel"

**Loyal Edmonton Regiment (4th
Battalion Princess Patricia's
Canadian Light Infantry)**
"Bonnie Dundee"

Maritime Command
"Heart of Oak"

Medical Branch
"The Farmer's Boy"

Military Engineering Branch
"Wings"

North Saskatchewan Regiment
"The Jockey of York"
"The Meeting of the Waters" (for pipes and drums)

Nova Scotia Highlanders
"The Sweet Maid of Glendaruel"
"The Atholl Highlanders"
"The Piobaireachd of Donald Dhu (1st Battalion)"
"The Highland Laddie (2nd Battalion)"

Ontario Regiment
"John Peel"

Personnel Selection Branch
"Semper Intelligere"

Prince Edward Island Regiment
"Old Solomon Levi (Pork, Beans and Hard Tack)"

Princess Louise Fusiliers
"The British Grenadiers"

Princess of Wales' Own Regiment
"The Buffs"
"Scotland the Brave (Pipe march)"

Princess Patricia's Canadian Light Infantry
"Princess Patricia's Canadian Light Infantry Regimental March"
"Lili Marlene"

Queen's Own Cameron Highlanders of Canada
"The Piobaireachd of Donald Dhu"
"March of the Cameron Men"

Queen's Own Rifles of Canada
"The Buffs"
"The Maple Leaf Forever"
"Monymusk"

Queen's York Rangers (1st American Regiment)
"Braganza"

Rocky Mountain Rangers
"The Meeting of the Waters"

Royal 22e Régiment
"Vive la canadienne"
"Marche Lente du Royal 22e Régiment"

Royal Canadian Dragoons
"Monsieur Beaucaire"
"Light of Foot"

Royal Canadian Horse Artillery & Royal Regiment of Canadian Artillery
"Royal Artillery Slow March"
"The British Grenadiers"
"Bonnie Dundee"
"Keel Row"

Royal Canadian Hussars (Montreal)
"Men of Harlech"
"St. Patrick's Day"

Royal Canadian Regiment
"The Royal Canadian Regiment (St. Catharines)"
"Pro Patria"

Royal Hamilton Light Infantry
(Wentworth Regiment)
"The Mountain Rose"

Royal Montreal Regiment
"*Ça Ira*"

Royal New Brunswick Regiment
"A Hundred Pipers (1st
Battalion)"
"The Old North Shore (2nd
Battalion)"

Royal Newfoundland Regiment
"The Banks of Newfoundland"

Royal Regiment of Canada
"The British Grenadiers"
followed by "Here's to the
Maiden"

Royal Regina Rifles
"Lutzow's Wild Hunt"
"Keel Row"

Royal Westminster Regiment
"The Maple Leaf Forever"
"The Warwickshire Lads"

Royal Winnipeg Rifles
"Old Solomon Levi (Pork, Beans
and Hard Tack)"
"Keel Row"

Saskatchewan Dragoons
"Punjaub"

Seaforth Highlanders of Canada
"The Piobaireachd of Donald
Dhu"

Security Branch
"Thunderbird"

Sherbrooke Hussars
"Regimental March of the
Sherbrooke Hussars"

South Alberta Light Horse
"A Southerly Wind and a Cloudy
Sky"

Stormont, Dundas, and
Glengarry Highlanders
"Bonnie Dundee"

Toronto Scottish Regiment
"Blue Bonnets Over the Border"

West Nova Scotia Regiment
"God Bless the Prince of Wales"

Windsor Regiment
"My Boy Willie"

Below are marches and their associated branches/units

1st Canadian Brigade Group	"Sons of the Brave"
5th Canadian Brigade Group	"*A l'assaut*" "*Allons-y*"
25 Canadian Forces Supply Depot	"March 25 CFSD"
Academic Staff of Canadian Military Colleges	"March of the Peers from Iolanthe"
Administration Branch (disbanded)	"Old Comrades"
Aerospace Maintenance Development Unit	"Salute to Excellence"

Armoured Branch	"My Boy Willie"
Cadet Instructor List	*"La feuille d'érable"*
Canadian Forces Europe (disbanded)	"Canada"
Canadian Forces Publications Depot	"Great Little Army"
Canadian Forces Recruit School	*"Apprendre a servir"*
Canadian Forces Training System	"Century of Progress"
CFB Gagetown Technical Services	"With Equal Pace"
CFB Ottawa	"My Canada"
CFB Montreal	*"Servir"*
CF Leadership & Language School	"Our Challenge"
CF Officer Candidate School	*"Ut Duces Sint"*
CF Parachute Maintenance Depot	"There's Something About a Soldier"
Collège militaire de Saint-Jean	*"La Gaillarde"*
	"La marche du Richelieu"
Communication Command	"Communications"
Eastern Militia Area	"RSM Wally"
First Special Service Force	"Cavalry of the Clouds"
Infantry Branch	"The Canadian Infantryman"
Infantry School	"The Canadian Infantryman"
Land Forces Command	*"Celer Paratus Callidus"*
Northern Region	"Canada North"
Physical Education Branch (disbanded)	"Allsports March"
Postal Branch	"First Post"
Royal Canadian Air Cadets	"Royal Canadian Air Force Marchpast"
Royal Canadian Army Cadets	"Cadet"
Royal Military College of Canada	"Alexander MacKenzie"
	"Precision"
Royal Roads Military College	"Going Home"
	"Hatley Park"
Service Battalions	"Duty Above All"
Special Service Force	"Muckin' O' Geordie's Byre"
Training Development Branch	*"Salut"*

The 8th Hussars

The title and march are most appropriate for the regimental slow march of The 8th Canadian Hussars (Princess Louise's). It is played to the music of the well-known Scottish tune "Road to the Isles" that was used by their predecessor the 8th Princess Louise's (New Brunswick) Hussars prior to adopting the present day title.

The 31st Greys

This march was written around 1900 by Charles Miller, a bandmaster, of the 31st Greys Battalion of Infantry. The 31st later became the Grey Regiment that amalgamated with the Simcoe Foresters ("Young May Moon") to form the Grey and Simcoe Foresters. The Simcoe's march "Young May Moon" was dropped and "The 31st Greys" was officially adopted as the new regimental march.

The march is short in duration but lively and based on the Regimental Call. It uses the repeated A and B sections and the accents in the opening melodic material provide the essence of rhythmic motion necessary in a 6/8 march.

A Hundred Pipers

The words for this old Scottish tune were written by Lady Naire and describe an event during the 1745 uprising in Scotland. After landing in Scotland, Bonny Prince Charlie rallied the clansmen behind him, raised the Jacobite standard, captured Edinburgh and later the town of Carlisle on the Solway Firth. The legend is that he entered the town with a hundred pipers leading the way.

Essex and Kent Scottish Regiment use the march for their 'C' Company in Chatham, Ontario, as a company march.

The 1st Battalion, the Royal New Brunswick Regiment, continue to use this march passed on to it from the 1st Battalion, the Royal New Brunswick Regiment (Carleton and York), who in turn had inherited it from the Carleton and York Regiment.

The pipes and drums of the 49th (Sault-Ste-Marie) Field Artillery Regiment use this selection, as "The British Grenadier" and "The Royal Artillery Slow March" don't really lend themselves to the bagpipe.

The music is a 6/8-flat tempo beginning with a pick-up into the Royal Kent Regimental Call. The music is tuneful, and the key of E-flat modulating into A-flat provides an easy vehicle to assimilate military band with pipes.

A Southerly Wind and A Cloudy Sky

The song begins "A southerly wind and a cloudy sky is all I need for the bye and bye." The march demonstrates the value of simplicity and the effective use of the 6/8 tempo. The A section provides a good measure of quarter-note figures followed by sixteenth notes that is a good rhythmic feature for stepping out on the march. The march was was adopted by the South Alberta Regiment who passed it on to the present-day regiment, The South Alberta Light Horse.

The Atholl Highlanders

The Nova Scotia Highlanders serve the Canadian Forces in a province steeped in Scottish heritage. The Cumberland Highlanders used the march before its amalgamation with the North Nova Scotia Highlanders. The result of the amalgamation was the 1st Battalion, the Nova Scotia Highlanders. The Highlanders adopted the march and combined it with the old Scottish favourite, "The Piobaireachd of Donald Dhu." The regiment underwent realignment but the medley was retained for the 1st Battalion.

The Banks of Newfoundland

This tune is one of Newfoundland's most well-known folk songs and is still heard throughout the province. Although there are six versions, the most popular one is an Irish ballad that reflects the trials of sailors in the freezing North Atlantic.

The tune has been transformed into a martial air and used by the Royal Newfoundland Regiment as a regimental march.

Blue Bonnets Are Over The Border

Also known as "All the Blue Bonnets are over the Border," the tune, called "Leven's March," was used by the Earl of Leven's Regiment in 1689. Earlier, around 1644, it had been known as "General Leslie's March to Longmarston Moor" but it could be even older. The origin of the music is unknown, however, the words come from Sir Walter Scott's poem "Border Ballad." It appears that the words were written to fit the music, with the line "All the blue bonnets are over the border" appearing at the end of each verse. Blue bonnets refers to the blue woollen cap commonly worn in Scotland in the seventeenth century. The poem reflects the border battles waged by England and Scotland during this time.

In Canada, several regiments use this old Scottish favourite. The Toronto Scottish Regiment inherited it from it predecessor the

199

Mississauga Horse in 1921, the Canadian Scottish Regiment (Princess Mary's) most likely adopted it from the Seaforth connection (16th Battalion CEF), the 82nd Battalion, CEF (Calgary Light Infantry) passed it on to the Calgary Highlanders, who combined it with another famous highland tune "Highland Laddie", and the Seaforth Highlanders of Canada combine this tune with the "Piobaireachd of Donald Dhu."

It has two distinct themes, both of which are repeated. A very interesting facet of this march is that the first repeated section is fortissimo (ff) and the second section repeated is marked piano.

Bonnie Dundee

Scottish settlers introduced this tune into Canada and several Canadian units have adopted it as a regimental march. The Loyal Edmonton Regiment (4th Battalion, Princess Patricia's Canadian Light Infantry) inherited the tune from the Edmonton Regiment when it was designated its present title. The 1st Hussars use the march as do the Stormont, Dundas and Glengarry Highlanders who took it over from their predecessor the Stormont and Glengarry Regiment. The 2nd Battalion, the Royal New Brunswick Regiment inherited the slow march in 1954 from its predecessor the 1st Battalion, The Royal New Brunswick Regiment (Carleton and York). The Brockville Rifles have consistently used this march while retaining their rifle lineage. They were a battery of the RCA between 1946-1959, and the adoption of this march, instead of the traditional rifle march "I'm Ninety-Five," may extend from this period in the RCA. The Royal Canadian Horse Artillery and the Royal Regiment of Canadian Artillery continue its usage through the traditions of the artillery.

The words, written by Sir Walter Scott, refers to John Graham of Clavenhouse, the Viscount of Dundee. The march became one of the original fifty marches chosen as a cavalry regimental gallop by the British War Office in 1883. The tune has sixteen bars in its entirety with no real subdominant chord (A-flat in the key of E-flat), but with a series of four bar phrases. It has the distinction of being usable either with horses, or as a traditional marchpast and is very effective when performed by a military band and pipes and drums. Captain John Slatter, Director of Music of the 48th Highlanders of Canada for over fifty years, is credited with this arrangement for military band.

Braganza

The Queen's (Royal West Surrey Regiment) adopted this Portuguese tune from the Queen's Tangier Regiment, raised in 1661 to garrison Tangier, part of the dowry of Catherine of Braganza on her marriage to Charles II. The first battalion was using "God Save the Queen" until the changes in the British army in 1881 altered the regimental marches. It was ordered that the National Anthem not be used as a regimental march. The regiment selected this march instead.

During the First World War the 20th Battalion, CEF, came in contact with the Queen's Royal Surrey (West Surrey) Regiment. In 1927, now called the Queen's Rangers, they adopted the lanyard, facings and march of the British unit. In 1936, the amalgamation of the York Rangers Regiment and the Queen's Rangers, 1st American Regiment formed the Queen's York Rangers, 1st American Regiment. The regiment retained the march.

The origin of the tune is not known, but it does lend itself very well to a military march. "Braganza" is one of many regimental marches that are in the traditional format of the scherzo, which is an introduction, short A section, B section and trio.

The British Grenadiers

This march, identified with the Grenadier Guards, is one of the most widely recognized marches in the world. William Chappell wrote in 1859, "Next to the National Anthem, there is not any tune of a more spirit-stirring character, nor is any more truly characteristic of English national music."

The origins of the song cannot be exactly dated, though a version dates to 1745. The first printing of the lyrics appeared in a remake of Harlequin Everywhere that opened in January 1780 at Covent Gardens.

Francis Grose wrote in 1786 that the words came from "the old grenadier song" and the reference to "louped clothes," distinctive to grenadiers prior to this time, makes it safe to conclude that the song could reach as far back as the later years of the seventeenth century.

The march had great popularity during the Napoleonic War and appeared in Canada during this time. It was played during the capture of Fort Detroit and Niagara during the War of 1812. Canadian volunteer, Charles Askin, described the American capitulation of Detroit:

> After the Americans had marched out, the Grenadiers and Light Infantry of the 41st Regt., and Volunteers in that Regt...marched into the Fort, with Drum and Fife, to the Tune of British Grenadiers. I must say that I never felt so proud, as I did just then.

On December 18, 1813, the British took Fort Niagara. To signify to British and Canadian troops on the opposite side of the river that the assault had been successful, the drummers of the 100th Regiment mounted the roof of a building and played this tune.

In Canada, the Royal Regiment of Canada combine this tune with "Here's to the Maiden." The march came over from the regiment's predecessor the Royal Regiment of Toronto Grenadiers, who inherited it from the amalgamation of the Royal Grenadiers and the Toronto Regiment. The Canadian Grenadier Guards have always used the same marches as their British counterparts, the Grenadier Guards. The Princess Louise Fusiliers continues its use, first adopted by its 1869 predecessor the Halifax Volunteer Battalion of Infantry. The Royal Regiment of Canadian Artillery continues its use as a dismounted quick march in the traditions of the artillery.

The march has been included in numerous compilations and used with effect in movies and television. The music itself is the epitome of simplicity with two sections of separate melodic content. Its strength lies in the use of the eighth note followed by two sixteenth-note configurations. Although there are several band arrangements, the Royal Military School of Music-approved version remains the most universally performed version. Like the music there are also a number of versions for the words.

The Buffs

George Frederic Handel is believed to have composed this march for the Buffs (Royal East Kent Regiment). The Buffs formed the nucleus of the British force that fought in Holland against the Spanish army. Later some of the troops became known as the Holland Regiment and, having adopted uniforms with buff coloured facings, breeches and stocking, became known as the Buffs.

The association between the Queen's Own Rifles of Canada and the Buffs began in 1882 after Colonel Otter, one of Canada's first professional soldiers, received permission to use the march. The Buffs later became the Queen's Regiment and retained their association with the Queen's Own. Another Canadian regiment, the Princess of Wales' Own Regiment, formed in 1863, has continued to use the march throughout its long and proud history.

The opening pick-up into the first subject of the melody is a three-note sixteenth-note pick-up that is reiterated five bars later. It provides an element of speed as this march is often performed at a very brisk pace. The second subject employs a musical nuance that is used frequently and implies a strong impression of motion while the final phrase provides a dramatic finality to the march.

Ça Ira

The refrain of this song first came into use during the French Revolution, when the French aristocrats were being taken to the guillotine. Street singer Ladre wrote the words and the music was composed by De Bécourt. It was first heard in Paris on October 5th, 1789 and adopted at once. In 1797 it was prohibited, but by then it had inspired a revolution. The most familiar words are:

> *Ah! ça ira, ça ira, ça ira,*
> *Malgre les mutins, tout reussira*
> (It will proceed! It will proceed! It will proceed!
> Despite all mutineers, all will succeed)

The tune is unique as it is the only regimental march earned in battle. Under the command of Lieutenant Colonel W. E. Doyle the 14th Foot assaulted the French camp at Famars in 1793. The camp was defended by revolutionary troops inspired by a band playing *Ça Ira*. In order to take the fort, Colonel Doyle cleverly used the thick fog to manoeuvre his troops into an attack position while his band played this French tune. The French assumed that reinforcements had arrived, and the British quickly overran the French position. In recognition of this, the tune was authorised as the Regimental March. Today the regiment, now the Prince of Wales' Own Regiment of Yorkshire combine it with "The Yorkshire Lass."

The Royal Montreal Regiment use the march in a composition that contains "God Bless the Prince of Wales," "Ça Ira," and "The Yorkshire Lass." The regiment is allied to the Prince of Wales's Own Regiment of Yorkshire once designated the 14th Battalion. In the early 1960s the commanding officer of the RMR, Lieutenant Colonel P. Lloyd-Craig, adopted the two marches of the Allied Regiment. Although still known as "Ça Ira." The marches are played in the following order "God Bless the Prince of Wales", "Ça Ira" and "the Yorkshire Lass".

This march is typical of seventeenth-century walking and marching tunes. The rhythmic meter is almost exclusively eights followed by sixteenths or in a series of sixteenth notes. Although this style did not provide for powerful cadence it allowed for a feeling of motion.

The Campbells are Coming

The tune, of course, refers to the Campbell Clan and has long been associated with the Argylls. The fifth Duke of Argyll led Mary, Queen of Scots' troops after her escape from Loch Leven Castle, and it has been suggested that the tune refers to this historic event. Another view is that both the tune and Burns' words refer to the 1745 rebellion.

The Argyll and Sutherland Highlanders of Canada (Princess Louise's) were formed in 1903 and have maintained this march throughout their history.

The Lorne Scots is one of the oldest infantry regiments in Canada, tracing its history back to 1790. In 1881, the Marquis of Lorne, fourth Governor-General of Canada, gave permission for the regiment to use his crest and family heraldry. The march was adopted in 1881, when he officially associated himself with the regiment. The present day regiment was formed when the Lorne Rifles (Scottish) amalgamated in 1936 with the Peel and Dufferin Regiment and retained this march.

This march is one of the most well-known Highland regimental marches. It combines two important elements, simplicity and brevity.

Colonel Bogey

Major F. J. Ricketts RM, composed this march in 1913 under the pen-name of Kenneth J. Alford. He wrote the march after a visit to the Fort George Golf Course in Scotland, where during play an irate colonel, instead of giving the usual "Fore," whistled the first two notes that became the first bar of the march. The name of the colonel is unknown, but the golf term Bogey was the inspiration for the title. From this odd beginning Ricketts built up the tune into the march that has become world famous and was a great favourite during the First World War.

Ray Sonin wrote a song entitled "Good Luck (and the same to you)" at the outbreak of the Second World War. The trio of the march is used for the verse, while the first statement was adopted for the chorus. The words were:

> Good Luck, and the same to you,
> Good Luck in everything you do,
> Black outs can never blot out
> The silver lining that comes shining through
> (No we're not downhearted)
> Britain is going to smile and grin,
> Britain is going to fight and win,
> Cheer up, the skies will clear up
> And soon our boys will be home once again.

The music became closely associated with the movie *The Bridge on the River Kwai*, in which Alec Guinness leads the rag tag remains of a British regiment into a Japanese prison camp, all of them whistling this tune.

The King's Own Calgary Regiment inherited it as quick march from their predecessor the Calgary Regiment (Tank). The Calgary Regiment was formed just two years after the First World War and may have adopted the tune due to its popularity at the time.

In an international poll conducted between 1976 and 1986 by Norman E. Smith (March Music Notes) with 1,000 respondents, "Colonel Bogey" was fourth on the all-time popular list of marches. Today, it remains a popular tune in the repertoire of bands around the world.

Corps March of the Royal Canadian Corps of Signals (Begone Dull Care)

This tune could date back to 1687 and did enjoy a revival in the ballet William Tell around 1793. Possibly derived from The Queen's Jigg, it appeared in two collections of songs, including the Dancing Master and National English Airs. One popular version comes from the reign of Elizabeth and James II. Another appeared in 1687 in *Playford's Pleasant Musical Companion, Part II*. The verse in this collection is:

> Begone, old care, and I prithee be gone from me,
> For i' faith, old Care, thee and I shall never agree;
> 'Tis long thou hast liv'd with me, and fain thou wouldst me kill,
> But i' faith, old Care, thou never shalt have thy will.

The Royal Canadian Corps of Signals have seen a long and distinguished service in Canada, including both world wars and the Siberian Expeditionary Force of 1918-1919. It is interesting to note that the corps assisted in the opening of many areas of the northern regions of Canada with its North West Territories and Yukon Radio System. During the major changes in the Canadian Forces during the mid 1960s the old corps was lost, but over the years the 1st Canadian Division Headquarters and Signals Regiment has managed to retain this old tune as their march. It was authorized on November 22, 1974, as the "Corps March of the Royal Canadian Corps of Signals (Begone Dull Care)" as arranged by Captain Charles A. W. Adams. Prior to unification, the Corps of Signals had been using the "Royal Signals March" granted in 1929 and based on the airs "Begone Dull Care" and "Newcastle." There are two other marches related to the communication field in the Canadian Forces. Communications

Command use the march "Communications" while the Communications and Electronics Branch adopted "The Mercury March."

There are some harmonic differences between this version and the original march, however, the melodic content has been retained. The march has three defined sections in binary form; A repeated A section beginning in B-flat and moving smoothly into the sub dominant key of E-flat, accomplished with two short transition bars in the form of a trumpet call. The second and third sections are combined to give a distinctive duality to the melody.

The Craftsman

The title is unique because it describes the abilities of the former Royal Canadian Electrical and Mechanical Engineers (RCEME). Throughout the history of the corps, especially during both world wars, Korea and UN duties, they have been called upon to repair just about everything anywhere anytime. In this age of high tech and rapid response forces, the need for these craftsmen remains important. After unification, the corps underwent several changes until the present title Electrical and Mechanical Engineering Branch was adopted. The proud heritage of the old corps was passed on through this slow march, and the title continues to reflect the unique ability of these men and women.

This march is an arrangement by Brian Gossip of the Scottish tune "The Flower of Scotland." It is written in a style that allows it to be performed as a stand-alone brass and reed number or in conjunction with pipes and drums. Mr. Gossip has again demonstrated his ability to take traditional harmonies and give them a modern texture, most pleasing to the ear as well as easily combinable with pipes.

E Tenebris Lux

The Intelligence Branch can trace its origins back as far as the Peninsular War and the Duke of Wellington. At that time, the Guides proved to be a valuable resource, but they disappeared after the war. In Canada, the first formation of Guides can be traced to the 4th Troop of Volunteer Cavalry of Montreal, formed in 1862. These Guides were always present as Canada grew; they served with the different military operations during the Northwest Rebellion and became the forerunner of the Intelligence Branch. The branch selected this well-known and popular classical piece for their march. Taken from Wolfgang Amadeus Mozart's orchestral suite *Eine Kleine Nachtmusik*, the extract lends itself perfectly to the march medium. The unification of the Canadian Forces led to this arrangement by Brian Gossip, which replaced the old Regimental March "Silver and Green," the corps colours.

El Abanico (The Fan)

Composer/bandmaster Alfredo Javaloyes led the 33rd Sevilla Regiment Band of Spain. In the title of this work he refers to a popular café situated near where he was stationed in Cartagena. Inside, at a large fan-shaped table, musicians, artists and poets talked away the hours.

During First World War, the Saskatchewan Light Horse, the 12th Manitoba Dragoons and the 34th Fort Garry Horse combined to form the 6th Battalion Canadian Expeditionary Force. While the troops were crossing the Atlantic on the SS *Lapland*, a ship of the Belgian Red Star Lines, the battalion bandmaster found the sheet music for the march. It was used by the 6th Battalion during training on the Salisbury Plain in England. The Battalion became the Canadian Cavalry Depot in 1915 and then the Fort Garry Horse in early 1916, and the march has been used by the Fort Garry Horse ever since. Words were added later, and a version was recorded by Peter Dawson, the famous Australian tenor. During the Second World War, another version appeared but did not really catch on, and the First World War version is retained by the regiment.

Fare Thee Well Inniskilling

In 1906, a new bandmaster assigned to the band of the Inniskillings (6th Dragoons) heard the men singing song entitled "The Inniskilling Dragoon." Charles Lever had written the song during the eighteenth century, about men sailing off to fight in Spain and hoping to return to Ireland. The new bandmaster quickly recognized the tune's popularity and arranged it as a march. He later lengthened it by adding the tune "Far, Far Away." Later, in 1931, it was presented to the regiment as "Fare Thee Well Inniskilling." In 1952, Bandmaster Norman Richardson rearranged the music and it was adopted for the regimental quick march of the 5th Dragoon Guards, British army. This regiment would become the 5th Royal Inniskilling Dragoon Guards until 1993 when it was amalgamated to form the present-day regiment the Royal Dragoons.

The British Columbia Dragoons' predecessors, the British Columbia Mounted Rifles, used the tune "The Farmer's Boy." In 1929, when the present regiment was formed, the march was changed to this Irish tune. The arrangement incorporates the regimental trumpet call in the nine-bar introduction. The two phrases in the second section contain an Irish jig which illustrate the regiment's Irish connection. The tune is used as a quick march along with the Scottish tune "Scotland The Brave."

Farewell to Nova Scotia

This Canadian maritime favourite was first written in 1930 near Halifax and has sometimes been referred to as "The Nova Scotia Song."

The Princess Louise Fusiliers use the maritime tune unofficially as a slow march. It is an appropriate march as the regiment has seen its share of leaving Canada and its beloved Nova Scotia to fight at home and abroad, as its colours clearly show.

Farmer's Boy

The tune has been played all over the world with little change to the words. It is a Scottish ballad, and there are about six different tunes that have been published in Britain for the song.

Brian Gossip arranged the Canadian version, and it is a masterful approach to a very simple folk song. It was selected at unification by a committee headed by Canada's Surgeon General as the march of the new Medical Branch March.

The trumpeting throughout adds an implicit martial quality to the march. A clever introduction of the theme from the old corps march "Here's a Health Unto His Majesty" gives one a sense of the history of the Royal Canadian Army Medical Corps. Mr. Gossip's use of a solid modern approach to the harmonic framework has made this a very sprightly tune.

Figaro

During his 1764 visit to England Wolfgang Amadeus Mozart witnessed the Changing of the Guard Ceremony at St. James's Palace. Impressed, he showed his appreciation by obtaining permission to write a march for the Coldstream Guards. He later used the music in his most popular operatic "The Marriage of Figaro" produced in England around 1812. Londoners were puzzled by the familiarity of the music until they realised that the bands had played the air during the Changing of the Guard Ceremony for some years. It is believed that the march was introduced in 1805 as the Regimental Slow March of the Coldstream Guards.

The Governor Generals Foot Guards use this tune as a slow march through their alliance with the Coldstream Guards.

The Galloping 8th Hussars

The 8th Canadian Hussars use a regimental trumpet call in the opening flourish of this quick march that was adopted by Kenneth Elloway from the British army march "A Galloping 8th Hussar."

Garry Owen

The Irish Regiment of Canada, formed in 1915, may have adopted this recognizably Irish march in keeping with their Irish traditions. The 2nd Battalion is the only battalion to remain and serves as a Reserve regiment stationed in Sudbury, Ontario.

Garryowen is Gaelic for Owen's Garden, the name of a suburb of Limerick in Ireland. The tune was adopted by the 5th Royal Lancers as a drinking song, and it appeared in print for the first time in 1790, by which time it was already a popular tune.

God Bless The Prince of Wales

Written in 1862 by the Welsh musician Henry Brinley Richards, with words by C. Hughes, this tune became the anthem of the principality of Wales. It holds the unique distinction of an anthem becoming a march. The composer presented it in 1867 to Prince Edward (later Edward VII) who became the Prince of Wales. The British Museum library holds thirty-five versions of the tune, including arrangements for choirs, schools, instruments, ensembles and orchestras.

In Canada the West Nova Scotia Regiment have used the march and Linley's version of the words, since their formation in 1936, through their alignment with the Prince of Wales's Volunteers (South Lancashire Regiment) of the British Army. Their affiliation with the Queen's Lancashire Regiment goes back to a predecessor, the 40th Regiment of Foot (Prince of Wales Volunteers) that was raised as Philip's Regiment at Fort Anne, Annapolis Royal, Nova Scotia in 1717. It is for this reason that they decided to retain the march after the amalgamation of the South Lancashire Regiment.

The Royal Montreal Regiment adopted the march in the early 1960s and is combined with "*Ça Ira*," and "The Yorkshire Lass."

Greensleeves

This 350-year-old song has become one of the most durable melodies in folk music. William Shakespeare made reference to it in his play *The Merry Wives of Windsor*. The melody was first printed in a 1686 edition of *The Dancing Master* under the title of "Greensleeves and Pudding." Although today the ballad is sung slowly, this history indicates that it was originally a vigorous dancing tune.

The Pilgrims first brought it to North America, and after the American Civil War, William Dix wrote new lyrics, entitled it "What Child Is This," and it became a Christmas carol, still popular today.

The Canadian Army Dental Corps, Canadian Expeditionary Force, was formed in 1915, and used a specially written march, "Marchpast of the Royal Canadian Dental Corps." The new Dental Branch was created during the unification of the Canadian Forces and retained the march while deciding to use "Greensleeves" as a slow march.

The Grenadiers' March

The British Army adopted the use of grenadiers from the French, and by 1678 these grenade-armed soldiers were appearing in most regiments. One such unit, the Dumbarton's, were on active service in Tangier around 1680 and their deeds are celebrated in a 1685 ballad, "The Grenadier's Rant" or "Hey, The Brave Grenadiers, Ho!"

Other versions appeared over the next century indicating that the tune had become commonly recognised and firmly established with the public. It became accepted throughout the British Army by the time of Napoleonic Wars. The Grenadier Guards adopted it in 1815 to commemorate their actions at Waterloo, and they still use it today, as do their Canadian counterparts, the Canadian Grenadier Guards.

The Grenadiers Slow March

This traditional tune was also adopted after Waterloo by the Grenadier Guards. It has been used in the Trooping of the Colour, and when played returning to barracks it is affectionately known as "The Grenadiers Return." It is used by the Canadian Grenadier Guards as a slow march.

Heart of Oak

The title and words of this song refer to the wooden hulls of the old ships of the Royal Navy as well as the hearts of the sailors. Dr William Boyce, Master of the King's Music, composed the music, and David Garrick wrote the words. It was first performed in the play Harlequin's Invasions (1759) that celebrated the Year of Victories. One of the victories was at Quiberon Bay, Quebec, where General Wolfe successfully made a surprise landing before the Battle on the Plains of Abraham.

The Royal Navy adopted the march in 1794, and the Royal Canadian Navy followed suit in 1910. When Maritime Command was created to replace the Royal Canadian Navy on the unification of the Canadian Forces, the march was retained.

Here's to the Maiden

This old regimental march of the 8th Foot is taken from Richard Brinsley Sheridan's comedy *The School for Scandal*. Sheridan's father-in-law

Thomas Linley, a noted English composer of his time, composed it. Mr. Linley was the music director at the Drury Lane Theatre where the play was shown for the first time in 1777.

The 8th Foot merged into the King's Regiment, one of the oldest regiments in the British army. At the time of the play the regiment was on duty in Canada and as its popularity grew, the tune was brought to Canada.

The Royal Regiment of Canada combine this march with "The British Grenadiers."

The Peel Regiment used the tune as well, until they became the Peel and Dufferin Regiment when their march was changed to "John Peel."

Highland Laddie or Hielan Laddie

This well-known old tune appeared under several titles, including, especially in English and Canadian ports, "Donkey Riding." Charles Nordhoff gives this version in "Nine Years a Sailor," published in 1857. The first verse goes:

> Were you ever in Quebec
> Bonnie Laddie, Highland Laddie,
> Stowing timber on the deck?
> My Bonnie Highland Laddie.

About a dozen different songs were written for this tune, some predating the Jacobite Rebellion of 1745. One of the most popular was published by George Thompson in the 1790s and republished in Graham's 1851 *Songs of Scotland*. Robert Burns wrote a version with the title "I hae benn at Crookerden," and James Hogg's words described a Highland Laddie fighting against Napoleon. It was even used by Beethoven in his settings of Scottish songs.

In 1965 the newly formed Highland Fusiliers of Canada adopted as their march a combination of "Highland Laddie" and "*Seann Triubhas*." Formed by the amalgamation of two regiments, the Scots Fusiliers of Canada and the Highland Light Infantry of Canada, they incorporated a march from each of them.

Essex and Kent Scottish Regiment at one time used this old Scottish tune as a regimental march for the 2nd Battalion. After the reduction to a single battalion, "Highland Laddie" became the official Regimental March and "A Hundred Pipers" was adopted by their 'C' Company in Chatham, Ontario.

Other highland regiments using the tune include the 48th Highlanders of Canada, the Black Watch of Canada, the Calgary Highlanders and the 2nd Battalion, the Nova Scotia Highlanders. The Lanark and Renfrew Scottish converted to artillery in 1993, becoming the 1st Airfield Defence Regiment RCA, but they retained the march as a link to their Scottish past.

The Lake Superior Scottish Regiment use the tune for a quick march, retaining their old march, "Light of Foot" for use on special occasions. Their unofficial slow march past is the "Skye Boat Song."

I'm Ninety-Five

The Royal Green Jackets in Britain acquired this tune from their forerunner, the 95th (Rifle) Regiment. One member of the brigade, Rifleman Goodhall, is reported to have sung the song while entertaining the troops dressed as an old woman. As the tune's popularity grew within the army, a special order had to be issued preventing other units playing it while in the presence of the Rifle Brigade. It was officially adopted in 1852.

The Hastings and Prince Edward Regiment was formed from the 49th Regiment (Hasting Rifles) and the 16th Prince Edward Regiment. Neither of these two regiments had an official march, but the 49th's background as a rifle regiment is one possible reason for its adoption.

Two armoured regiments in Canada retain the march from their rifle backgrounds. The former Elgin Regiment adopted the march from their predecessor, the First Volunteer Militia Rifle Company of St. Thomas, Ontario. The British Columbia Regiment retain the march through their rifle lineage with the 1st British Columbia Regiment (Duke of Connaught's Own) and their alliance with the Royal Green Jackets of the British Army.

The march consists of two repeated sections containing separate themes. It has numerous grace notes and in the B section a long-held trill. The harmonic content demonstrates a dedication to very high-quality arrangements.

The Jockey of York

In 1934, The York and Lancaster Regiment (2nd Battalion) obtained official permission to have its own quick march and adopted this tune. The regimental bandmaster may have composed it under the title "The 84th of Foot Quick March." Bandmaster Douglas Mining, who served with the regiment from 1907 to 1919, perfected the arrangement.

Les Fusiliers Mont-Royal retained the march from their predecessor Les Carabiniers Mont-Royal, formed in 1869.

The North Saskatchewan Regiment adopted the tune from the Saskatoon Light Infantry, but dropped the other regimental tune from their amalgamation with the Prince Albert and Battleford Volunteers, "One and All." Their regimental pipes and drums band adopted the tune "The Meeting of the Waters."

John Peel

John Peel lived at Caldbeck in the Cumberland Fells. One night in 1829, he and a friend, Woodcock Graves, visited the local inn. At the inn, a girl was singing an old northern tune. Graves, caught up in the music, began to mimic the girl, singing the line "D' ye ken John Peel?" These opening words were quickly followed by other verses and the song was born.

In Canada the march is used by the Ontario Regiment (RCAC) and The Lorne Scots (Peel, Dufferin and Halton Regiment). The Lorne Scots inherited the march from the Peel and Dufferin Regiment in the 1936 amalgamation.

The Keel Row

"The Keel Row" is a Northumbrian folk song referring to small boat oaring. The arrangement evolved from the 1800s folk song that was first employed as a double past by the Light Infantry. Later, artillery units adopted it as a trot past when mounted and pulling gun carriages, a tradition used by British and Canadian units.

The Royal Regina Rifles and the Royal Winnipeg Rifles both kept the march as their quick march throughout their separate amalgamations. The 1st Air Defence Regiment (Lanark and Renfrew Scottish) adopted artillery marches in 1993 when it was redesignated with the new role and title.

"The Keel Row" is a quite simple but effective sixteen-bar phrase that seems to emulate horses trotting in a military fashion. The march time is 2/4, but it is universally performed at one beat to the bar to provide the feeling of motion.

La Marche de la Victoire

This interesting tune is used by Le Régiment de Hull and is commonly associated with J. Beaulieu who is believed to be the composer. The arrangement is credited to Sergeant Richard Riedstra, who served in the Canadian Forces from 1958-1962. This original march shows much imagination and originality and is written in the traditional march format. The arrangement shows an unusually good knowledge of band scoring.

Le Régiment de Sambre et Meuse

Although Jean-Robert Planquette is the original composer he sold the rights to Chef-de-musique Francois Rauski. Rauski's arrangement with bugles formed the tune that is recognised today.

"*La Régiment de Sambre et Meuse*" is also known simply as "*Sambre et Meuse.*" During the Two-Hundredth Anniversary of the French Revolution in 1991, it was played often. Its vigour and vitality and the musical development have made it a masterpiece. The tune refers to a make-believe regiment named in honour of an area in France around the Sambre and Meuse rivers. This area was the site of very hard fighting during the First World War. Canadian troops who fought here came the from the 5th Battalion, Canadian Machine Gun Corps, later to become Le Régiment de la Chaudière. The regiment combines the march with "The Longest Day."

Le Régiment de Maisonneuve dates back to 1880, its name honouring the founder of both Montreal and the first local militia, Paul Chomedy de Maisonneuve. This march is a direct connection with their First World War service and rich French-Canadian roots.

Le Régiment du Saguenay

The regiment's name is the same as the march that was inherited from the original 1900 unit, the 18th Saguenay Battalion of Infantry. When the regiment was reorganised in 1937, the march was retained. The tune is an original composition by R. H. Singfield and contains a long introduction that includes the Regimental Call. The main theme effectively utilises chromatic harmony.

Les Voltigeurs de Québec

Les Voltigeurs de Québec holds the distinction of being the first French-Canadian regiment in the Canadian army. Its origins go back to 1862 when it was formed as the 9th Battalion Volunteer Militia Rifles, Canada. The term voltigeurs is a Napoleonic term for an elite infantry group fighting as skirmishers. In 1812, with war looming, an elite unit of French fighters was formed called the Voltigeurs Canadien. The 1958 name change retained the unique status of Voltigeurs.

The march is the first original march composed for a Canadian militia unit. It was penned by Joseph Vezina, the father of military bands in Canada. The traditional march form is not evident in the Vezina composition. There is a strong French military march influence in the music. The march is written in three repeated sections and the styles of music written for drum and bugle bands.

Light of Foot

The Royal Canadian Dragoons adopted the tune as a regimental dismounted march. The music is a published version of the march "Light of Foot" composed in 1910 by the German, Charles Latann. The distinctive characteristic of this march is the trio and Latann developed it into a very strong martial idiom rather than a flowing type of trio we experience in other marches. There is no doubt that this was the reason the Dragoons selected this march. The trio of the march is also heard in the famous march collection titled "Passing of the Regiments."

Lili Marlene

Before the Second World War this German song was almost unknown although it had been written when the composer, Hans Leip, was a private in the German army during the First World War. Thirty German publishers rejected the music, composed by Norbert Schutzer, until Lila Anderson began singing it. During the Second World War, German radio broadcasted it to their North African army, where British soldiers heard it on intercepted radio transmissions.

It came to the attention of Jimmy Philips, an English music publisher, when soldiers of the English Eighth Army returned home on leave to London. Sitting in a pub, bandleader Billy Cotton heard a room full of soldiers singing the German version known as the "Song of the Young Sentry." Philips and Cotton realised the German version would not be well received so they had a translation made and Cotton recorded it with Anne Shelton. In 1944 in America, Marlene Dietrich made it a hit in her shows.

Princess Patricia's Canadian Light Infantry adopted it as their regimental slow march.

The Lincolnshire Poacher

This tune has long been sung as an unofficial local anthem in the County of Lincoln, England. Several regiments by 1881 were using it for parades. Although the tune appealed to many regiments, when marches were finally authorised the "Poacher" became special property of the Lincolnshire Regiment. The march was discontinued in 1964, when the regiment became part of the Royal Anglian Regiment, and replaced with a combination of "Rule Britannia" and "Speed the Plough." The Lincolnshire's allied unit in Canada, and the only Canadian regiment to use the march, the Lincoln and Welland Regiment, inherited it from an early predecessor, the 19th St. Catharines Regiment, formed in 1866.

The emotional power of the song and of the music in the army, was attested to by Rudyard Kipling in a speech at the Mansion House, reported by *The Times* on 28 January, 1915:

> I remember in India in a cholera camp, where the men were suffering very badly, the band of the 10th Lincolns started a regimental song sing-song and went on with that queer, defiant tune, "The Lincolnshire Poacher". There was nothing in it — nothing except all England, all the East Coast, all the fun and daring and horseplay of young men bucketing about pig pastures in the moonlight. But as it was given very softly at that bad time in that terrible camp of death, it was the one thing in the world that could have restored as it did restore shaken men back to their pride, humour and self-control.

The melody is unquestionably the most tuneful of all marches. Surprisingly the melody is only sixteen bars long with an eight-bar introduction and a six-bar finale.

The Longest Day

The Canadian Airborne Regiment adopted this tune as their regimental march and used it up to the time of their disbandment. It is based on the theme music from the 20th Century-Fox movie, The Longest Day, that depicted the Allied landings—spearheaded by paratroopers—of the Normandy coast in France on D-Day.

Le Régiment de la Chaudière also use the march due to the fact that the regiment landed on beaches of Bernieres-sur-Mer, France, on 6 June 1944 and continued fighting throughout northwest Europe until VE Day.

The Canadian singer Paul Anka composed the theme, and the official Canadian Forces arrangement is by the well-known military musician Shel Richardson.

Lutzow's Wild Hunt

The 60th Regiment of Foot, British army, used the "Grenadiers March" until 1820, when "The Huntsman's Chorus" from Weber's opera Der Freischutz was adopted. The rhythm was found unsuitable and to correct the problem some bars of an original tune by Lutzow were used, along with Von Gehriech's Jagersleben (the Wild Hunt). Further changes were made until the tune became the quickstep. In 1905, some of Lutzow's original bars were reintroduced and played by the bugles. This new arrangement was adopted as the regimental march and is still used by the Royal Green Jackets. Their Canadian allied regiment, formed in 1920, the

Regina Rifle Regiment, retained this "rifles" march in 1982 when they became the Royal Regina Rifles.

The remarkable aspect of this march is that they were able to retain the original theme and then introduce bugles into the military band arrangement with a good effect.

Maple Leaf Forever

The Scottish composer Alexander Muir came to Canada and became a schoolmaster in Toronto. While he walked along the Don River with a friend in October 1867, a maple leaf became lodged on his sleeve. This gave Muir the inspiration for a patriotic poem which he entered at the last minute in a contest held by the Caledonian Society of Montreal. He won second prize and the poem became very popular, especially after he set it to music and published it. French-Canadians did not like the text as it made reference the French defeat on the Plains of Abraham and because it refers to the thistle, shamrock and rose that are the national emblems of Scotland, Ireland, and England, but leaves out the fleur-de-lis of France.

The Royal Westminster Regiment retained the tune in 1966 along with "The Warwickshire Lads" when the Westminster Regiment was redesignated and granted the prefix Royal by Queen Elizabeth.

The 1st Battalion of the Princess Patricia's Canadian Light Infantry uses the tune as their signature march, while the Queen's Own Rifles of Canada use it with "The Buffs."

March of the Cameron Men

Mary Maxwell Campbell composed the music just after the Crimean War, and the words after the Egyptian War of 1882, to honour the Queen's Own Cameron Highlanders, British army. The march was retained when they became the Queen's Own Highlanders (Seaforth and Camerons) but was dropped in 1994 when "Scotland the Brave" and "Cock of the North" were adopted.

From their beginning in 1923 The Queen's Own Cameron Highlanders of Canada have continually used this march along with "The Piobaireachd of Donald Dhu."

The march was retained in 1933 when the Ottawa Highlanders were reorganised and designation to form the present-day regiment the Cameron Highlanders of Ottawa.

March of the Logistic Branch

The Logistic Branch was formed in the mid 1960s when several corps and branches were combined: the Royal Canadian Navy Supply Branch, the

Royal Canadian Ordnance Corps, Royal Canadian Army Service Corps, Royal Canadian Army Pay Corps and the Mobile Support Equipment, Supply, Finance and Food Services from the Royal Canadian Air Force.

This march was written in 1973 by Warrant Officer Ken Irons and arranged by Captain Con Furey, both members of the Canadian Forces Central Band. The sixteen-bar theme recurring throughout the march provides both a forceful marching song and excellent tuneful melody which is easily recognisable.

Marchpast of the Royal Canadian Dental Corps

The Dental Branch retained the march after unification in the mid sixties. This sprightly march has endured the test of time and is one of the few original Canadian marches to have been published.

Marche Lente du Royal 22e Régiment

The regiment uses the original composition by C. Gabois, a former member of their band. The march, composed in the traditional form of slow marches, uses trumpeting to good effect. It is also used by the 4th and 6th Battalions.

Marianne s'en va-t-au moulin
(Marianne Is Going to the Mill)

This folk song, popular in France and Canada, tells of a young girl, Marianne, whose donkey is eaten by a wolf while she is at the mill. The miller offers her another animal and when she gets home she explains to her father that donkeys change their coats on St. Patrick's Day. In 1952, Jean Papineau-Couture wrote the music for the song that was aired as a puppet show on CBC television.

Major J. Pierret, former Director of Music of the Royal 22e Regiment, arranged the music in June 1971. Considered a very good rendition, the introduction and first section of the march are used by the 12e Régiment blindé du Canada as their regimental march.

Meeting of the Waters

The basis of this march is an old folk song. The City of Kamloops in the Rocky Mountains of British Columbia is located where the North and South Thompson River meet. As the Rocky Mountain Rangers are stationed in Kamloops, the selection of a march with this title seems quite appropriate.

The pipes and drums of the North Saskatchewan Regiment have adopted the tune while the brass and reed band selected "The Jockey of York."

Men of Harlech
(*Rhyfelgyrch Gwyr Harlech*)

This very old tune survives as the chief patriotic song of Wales. Harlech Castle is built on a commanding position chosen very carefully for its defensive and offensive possibilities. The history of the castle is reflected throughout Welsh history and tales of heroism and sieges are associated to the many skirmishes and battles fought there over the centuries.

In 1282 an uprising was sparked with the death of popular Welsh nobleman, Prince Llywelyn, at the hands of the English. During the rebellion other castles fell quickly but Harlech withstood the initial assault with only thirty-seven defenders holding off a very large attacking force. The defenders were quickly reinforced and it would be three years before the castle finally surrendered. Over one hundred years later Owain Glydwr and other Welsh nobility attempted another siege and again the castle withstood a siege for over three years. During the fifteenth century running battles between the Lancastrians and Yorkists would become part of the castle's history. The castle was eventually surrendered in 1647, marking the end of its military life. This heroic defence was the inspiration for the poem "The March of Men of Harlech" that was first printed in Edward Jones's 1794 collection Musical and Poetical Relics of the Welsh Bards. During the eighteenth and nineteenth century, the castle was used as a jail. Today it is a major tourist attraction.

The march was retained by the Royal Canadian Hussars (Montreal) on its formation from the amalgamation of the 6th Duke of Connaught's Royal Canadian Hussars and the 17th Duke of York's Royal Canadian Hussars.

The Governor General's Horse Guards trace their use of the march back to one of their predecessors, the Governor General's Body Guards.

Mercury March

The Communications and Electronics Branch adopted this march during the unification of the Canadian Forces when all manpower, skills and resources of the previous services were combined. They maintain the old alliance with their British counterparts, the Royal Corps of Signals. The "Mercury March" has all the elements of an original and stimulating martial air.

Milanollo

This march is taken from the Johann Valentin Hamm's composition originally written for Teresa and Marie Milanollo, the Italian violinists who toured the continent during the 1830s. It was during their visit to England in 1845 that the tune was introduced.

The Governor General's Foot Guards use it because they adopted the same marches as that of their British counterparts, the Coldstream Guards.

Both band musicians and listeners love this march because it provides a musical challenge for the performers, particularly on the march. For listeners there is a compellingly heartrendring phrase that begins halfway through the march. The arrangement by McKenzie-Rogan demonstrates his knowledge of good solid march composition.

Monsieur Beaucaire

This mounted march of the Royal Canadian Dragoons was taken from the second act of a French operetta. The march composition was based on a theme by Andre Messager with the arrangement by Thomas Bidgood. The mounted march has a distinct melodic development containing a con spirito followed by a poco tranquillo. The con spirito provides a dramatic finale.

Monymusk

Named after a small town in Aberdeenshire, this tune is in use with several British army regiments. The Queen's Own Rifles of Canada, one of Canada's oldest regiments, have a direct lineage of Rifles which has resulted in them keeping their Rifle-green uniforms and this march as a double past.

The Mountain Rose

Bandmaster George Robinson chose this tune when he was a member of the 13th Volunteer Militia Infantry of Canada between 1869 and 1917. Robinson thought it an apt march for a regiment that stood guard in the shadow of Hamilton's famous "mountain," part of the Niagara Escarpment. The 13th became the Royal Hamilton Light Infantry in 1927, and finally the Royal Hamilton Light Infantry (Wentworth Regiment) in 1936. The music provides two strong motifs and is a very good example of the strong harmonic use of accompaniment to a very busy melodic line.

My Boy Willie

The tank, although an armoured vehicle, can trace it roots back to the chariots of ancient times through medieval Europe and the mounted knights and cavalry of centuries that followed. During the First World War the forerunner of the modern tank was developed and changed warfare forever. The British tank attack at Cambrai in November 1917 proved very successful against the German defensive lines, and tanks became a new tactical weapon.

The Royal Canadian Armoured Corps adopted this tune as a corps march, however, individual regiments have their own mounted and dismounted marches. The exception to the rule is the Windsor Regiment (RCAC) that inherited the march from the 1949 redesignation of the Essex Regiment (Tank).

My Home

The Nova Scotia Highlanders have served the Canadian Forces in a province steeped in Scottish heritage since 1871. The 1st Battalion, located in Truro, was formed from the amalgamation of three regiments in 1954, and the slow march, "My Home" was adopted at this time. The 2nd Battalion located in Sydney was formed at the same time and did not adopt a slow march. A year later both battalions were amalgamated to form one regiment with two battalions. Each battalion has individual marches, but the regimental quick march became "The Sweet Maid of Glendaruel" and "My Home" was retained as the slow march.

The Old North Shore

The Royal New Brunswick Regiment does not have a regimental march, instead each battalion has its own, an arrangement unique in the Canadian Forces. The 2nd Battalion from the 1956 amalgamation of the North Shore Regiment and the 28th Field Battery, RCA, adopted this tune.

Onward Christian Soldiers

Sir Arthur Sullivan wrote the music for this hymn in 1871 while preparing for a children's parade. Baron Gould wrote the words and the original title was "St. Gertrude." The version used today is not the original but the one most commonly known and accepted. It was introduced as a war cry for the Salvation Army in 1914, and over the years it never failed to stir the soul.

The adoption of the tune as a march by the Canadian Forces Chaplain Branch was appropriate. The two main symbols on the cap badge of the branch, the Maltese Cross and Royal Crown, have inspired Christian soldiers throughout the centuries.

The branch itself was formed at the time of unification when the chaplains' services of the Royal Canadian Air Force, the Royal Canadian Navy and the Royal Canadian Army Chaplains' Corps were combined into one branch. Wherever the airmen, sailors and soldiers have gone throughout

221

the many years and battles these men of God have always been there by their side.

Piobaireachd of Donald Dhu

The pibroch is the classical music of the bagpipes. This tune has long been known as "Lochiel's March" after a poem written by Sir Walter Scott in 1816. The arrangement, by Hummel in 1830, was not put into print until eleven years later. The march was composed in honour of an early Chief of the Clan Cameron, Donald Dhu, or Donald the Black.

Several Canadian Scottish infantry regiments adopted the old tune as their regimental march. These units include the Cameron Highlanders of Ottawa, the Seaforth Highlanders of Canada, the 1st Battalion, The Nova Scotia Highlanders and the Queen's Own Cameron Highlanders of Canada.

Pork, Beans & Hard Tack (Vocal Version)
Old Solomon Levi (Musical Version)

With the westward expansion of the railway and the settlement of their lands, the Métis began to feel isolated in the new Dominion of Canada. They rebelled in 1885 and a military force under General Middleton was sent to put down the uprising. Using the new, partly constructed Canadian Pacific Railway wherever they could, they force marched a considerable distance singing as they went.

They sang "Pork, Beans and Hard Tack" set to the tune of "Old Solomon Levi." The words are descriptive in nature and the melody sets an easy marching stride. It was first published in the University of Toronto songbook of 1887. The first three verses describe the outbound trip along the plains while the last two define the return along the Saskatchewan River to Lake Winnipeg and finally to the Winnipeg area.

The Prince Edward Island Regiment, formed from an amalgamation of the Prince Edward Island Light Horse and the PEI Highlanders in 1946, retained the march. It was also retained in 1935 when in the Winnipeg Rifles were reorganised as the Royal Winnipeg Rifles.

Princess Patricia's Canadian Light Infantry Regimental March
(Medley of "Has Anyone Seen The Colonel?," "Its a Long Way to Tipperary," "Mademoiselle from Armentières")

The Princess Patricia's Canadian Light Infantry were raised in 1914 to fight in the First World War. The regiment chose popular songs of the day arranged into a medley as their march. In a letter to the PPCLI Depot

Commander in 1961, Captain Tommy James, the first director of the PPCLI band, described how the march came into being:

> I reported to the Regiment soon after my appointment as Director of the PPCLI Band on the 20th of January, 1920. I was told that the Regiment was without a regimental march and I discussed the matter with some senior officers.

It was decided that since the regiment was formed and had fought in the Great War, the songs should be from that war and be tuneful enough for troops to sing on the march. The songs selected had been much favoured at the time and an arrangement was undertaken with the march becoming one of the favourite marches in the Canadian Forces. Each battalion also has their own signature march — 1st Battalion uses "The Maple Leaf Forever," 2nd Battalion "March Winnipeg" and the 3rd Battalion "Canada" written by Bobby Gimby. Also the colonel-in-chief of the regiment uses the "Lady Patricia March" composed by an officer of the regiment, Captain H. A. Jeffrey.

Has Anyone Seen the Colonel?

The tune is attributed to the famed Canadian army entertainment group The Dumbells. The enlisted men felt that life at the top carried no burdens, less visible work and certainly less danger. This led to frustration and resentment on their parts. Since no recourse was available to combat this feeling, many turned to drink and song. The words to this song reflect that feeling and offer a tongue-in-cheek look at the top echelon.

It's a Long Way To Tipperary

This song was written by country music hall singer Jack Judge and a disabled musician, Harry Williams. The original title was "A Long Way to Connemara," but it was changed by Judge just prior to its performance to Tipperary, a more common name. Judge thus gained the reputation of being the author. This created friction between the two songwriters, but all was forgiven when the song's popularity took off.

After the troops took up the song during the First World War, the two men received five pounds a week in royalties for life. Williams died in 1924 and Judge thirty years later in 1954.

Mademoiselle From Armentieres

First appearing in the First World War, the Mademoiselle was a folk heroine by the time of the Second World War.

223

Pro Patria

The Royal Canadian Regiment's slow march title means the same as their motto — For Country. The march is an original composition by a former musician in the Sandhurst Military Band, Sergeant Claude Keast, a prolific composer of military marches. It is interesting to note that Keast composed this march on the band bus during a tour with the RCR Band in 1961. The band first performed it during a Trooping of the Colour in 1961.

Punjaub

The cavalry regiments of the British army were very fond of this march in 1893 when it was first published. The composer, Charles Payne, was serving in India when the major uprising in the Punjaub took place, followed by another in the Sutlej area.

The Saskatchewan Dragoons perpetuate the 46th Battalion, Canadian Expeditionary Force, combined with the 128th Battalion, CEF, and later became the King's Own Rifles of Canada. Throughout all these changes, they retained "Punjaub" as their regimental march.

Quand vous Mourrez de nos Amours
(When You Die from Our Loves)

The 12e Régiment blindé du Canada adopted the tune as a slow march. Like their quick march, it is taken from a French folk song.

Red Hackle (The)

The Black Watch has worn the Red Hackle for over two hundred years and several stories have been associated with it. One such is that during the American War of Independence, Colonel Maitland informed General Washington that Highlanders could be recognised by their red feathers, "so that he could not mistake, nor avoid doing justice to their exploits." Afterwards, General Sir William Howe, Commander of the British Forces ordered the Black Watch to wear the Red Hackle. Ever since, the Watch has worn it with the exclusive right to do so being granted in 1882 by the War Office. Today, the Black Watch celebrate this proud award for gallantry each year on Red Hackle Day. Their Canadian cousins, the Black Watch (Royal Highland Regiment) of Canada use the same marches.

Red River Valley

The words of "Red River Valley" tell of men going west during the 1890s, leaving girlfirends behind as they seek a new life on the western plains.

Canadian folk-music specialist Edith Fowke suggests that the Red River Valley in question is the Canadian one that flows into Lake Winnipeg. The Canadian version of the tune is said to reflect the feelings of a Métis girl for a soldier who came during the Rebellions of 1869-70 or 1885 and then returned to his home.

The Fort Garry Horse, stationed in Winnipeg, came to use this slow march naturally. The arrangement is by Captain James Gayfer, former Director of Music of the Canadian Guards. The tune was a favourite of a former commanding officer, Lieutenant Colonel J. C. Gardner, CD. The regiment purchased the rights from Captain Gayfer and permission was requested to use the march as the regimental slow march in February 1961. The transformation to a slow march with the use of various musical idioms has produced a very good effect.

Regimental March of the Sherbrooke Hussars

The Sherbrooke Hussars were formed in 1965 when the Sherbrooke Regiment and the 7th/11th Hussars were amalgamated. The march , "The Sherbrooke Regiment" was adopted at this time, but the title was changed to reflect the new regiment's name.

REME Corps Marchpast

This very old tune became popular during the Second World War as the signature tune of the BBC program "Into Battle" and as an unofficial march of commando units. General Rowcroft, the first director of the Royal Electrical and Mechanical Engineers, selected the march because of its aggressive tune.

The original REME Corps march contained two tunes: "Lillburlero" and "Heigh Ho," the dwarves song from Snow White and the Seven Dwarfs. The change in rhythm from one tune to another caused problems on parade, however, and a new arrangement was created by the corps' first Director of Music, Captain D. J. Plater, which dispensed with the dwarves and used a French-Canadian woodsman's song "*Aupres De Ma Blonde.*"

In 1944, the Corps of Royal Canadian Electrical and Mechanical Engineers were formed but the march was not adopted until six years later. The major changes in the Canadian Forces during the mid sixties saw the creation of a new branch now known as the Electrical and Mechanical Engineering Branch. The branch has retained the customs and music of the old corps.

Rêves Canadiens

This march is based on a French-Canadian folk song by Hector Nadeau. During the late fifties and early sixties "Les Fusiliers du St-Laurent" were the 5e Bataillon, Royal 22e Régiment. In 1986 they dropped the association with the R22R becoming a separate regiment and adopted this tune as their new regimental march.

Royal Artillery Slow March

This very distinctive gunners' melody is sometimes referred to as "The Duchess of Kent" because it was composed by the mother of Queen Victoria, the Duchess of Kent. It was originally used as a walk past for mounted artillery.

The Royal Canadian Artillery trace their roots back to 1871, but the regiment was not authorised until 1895. Their marches were adopted from the alliance with the Royal Artillery and are used for mess dinners, concerts and mounted and dismounted parades. This march is considered a distinctive gunner slow march.

The 1st Air Defence Regiment (Lanark and Renfrew Scottish) adopted all artillery marches upon its designation of an artillery unit. They still use "Highland Laddie" for their pipe band, a tradition from their rich infantry heritage.

Royal Canadian Air Force Marchpast

The Royal Air Force and the Royal Canadian Air Force shared this marchpast, written shortly after the formation of the RAF in April 1918. The first Officer Directing Music for the RAF, Sir Walford Davies, composed the original score and Sir George Dyson added the melody that is found in the middle of the march. The march contains elements of music associated with the disbanded Royal Flying Corps and Royal Naval Air Service, along with the army and the Royal Navy.

The Royal Canadian Air Force was formed on April 1, 1924, but the march was not adopted until 1943, at which time the RCAF was so committed to the air war over Britain and Europe that permission was granted for its use. Canadian airmen fought in British squadrons or beside them in Canadian squadrons taking part in the Dambuster Raids, the Battle of Britain and Pathfinder duties just to name a few. Canadian airmen also fought with great distinction against Japan and in Korea. After unification, the new Air Command retained the march for its official marchpast.

Pipe Major Alex Howie of the Air Transport Command Pipe Band composed the pipe version in the early sixties. The words are:

Through adversities we'll conquer.
Blaze into the stars
A trail of glory
We'll live on land and sea
'till victory is won
Men in blue the skies are winging,
In each heart one thought is ringing.
Fight got the right
God is our might,
We shall be free.

The Royal Canadian Regiment

Late in 1895 a regimental order announced the promotion of Corporal George Offen to Sergeant Bugler. Offen was a bugler who would make regimental history as the composer of the air ultimately adopted by the Royal Canadian Regiment as its regimental march. The story goes that Lieutenant Colonel Maunsell hummed the tune to Offen, who interpreted its spirit through the medium of a piano and later produced a written score.

There was some question as to the tune's originality, and it was submitted to the Commandant of Kneller Hall who ruled that though the tune possessed characteristics common to other marches, the score was an original and should pertain only to the Royal Canadian Regiment. A former Royal Military College graduate, Lieutenant R. J. S. Langford, wrote the words. In 1907, the march had been officially adopted by the regiment and was played by the drum and fife band under the direction of Sergeant A. W. Nanfan at the annual inspection of the London Depot by Major-General W. D. Otter and Lieutenant Colonel R. L. Wadmore.

Scipio

A general belief is that George Frederic Handel wrote this march, then later used it in his opera of the same name. The Canadian Grenadier Guards are allied with their English counterparts The Grenadier Guards, and therefore employ the same marches.

Scotland the Brave

This march remains one of the most easily identifiable Scottish tunes in use today. There are any number of arrangements and it is often performed in the combination of military band and pipes. The British Columbia Dragoons, a Canadian armoured regiment, use the Irish tune "Fare Thee Well Inniskilling" as a quick march and this old Scottish favourite for their pipes and drums.

Seann Triubas (Whistle o'er the lave o't)

This Highland dance is performed to the tune "Whistle o'er the lave o't," and sometimes the title of the dance is incorrectly substituted for the title of the music. The dance title when translated from Gaelic means "kicking off the trews." The Highlanders never did accept the trews in place of the kilt after they were forbidden to wear it following the Battle of Culloden in 1745. The dance demonstrates the shaking of each foot in obvious imitation of removing the trews.

The Highland Fusiliers of Canada retained the march in medley from the Highland Light Infantry of Canada during the amalgamation with the Scots Fusiliers of Canada.

Semper Intelligere

In the late 1930s there were very few psychologists in Canada. As the threat of war approached, those few banded together to form the Canadian Psychological Association (CPA) ready to take part wherever they were needed.

At the start of the Second World War, a Conference on Use of Psychological Methods in Warfare was chaired by Sir Frederick Banting and attended by members of the RCAF, RCN and the army. In September 1941, the Directorate of Personnel Selection was formed and testing was set up for each element of the military. As the war escalated, testing and training proved to be successful and their importance became more apparent. Throughout the war and the Korean War that followed, the testing provided an important role in the selection of Canadian Forces personnel. With the start of unification in 1964, the various Personnel Selection Branches of the army, navy and airforce were combined into one branch. In 1982, the branch received its own cap badge, marking its forty-first year.

Using a French song cycle known as *"Rondo Sentimentale,"* CWO Brian Gossip and the students of the Canadian Forces School of Music, Bandmasters Course, combined talents to arrange this selection. The Canadian Forces Personnel Selection Branch adopted the march in 1984.

Soldiers of the Queen

Originally written in 1881 and used in British music halls, "Soldiers of the Queen" did not attract attention until it was used in the play An Artists Model by Hayden Coffin in 1895. When the Boer War began, the song was used by the British army for recruiting purposes.

When Lord Strathcona's Horse were formed by Lord Strathcona (Donald Alexander Smith) the British were fighting a highly mobile, mounted and well-armed enemy using guerrilla tactics. He recognized this and patterned the regiment to meet this threat. He recruited horsemen from Canada's western provinces and territories because their lifestyle was similar to that of the Boer. The Strathcona's ability to fight as the Boers did would be proven throughout the regiment's involvement in the Boer War. The march may have been adopted due to its popularity of the time.

St. Patrick's Day

Although both the words and music are typically Irish, the tune is English in origin. It was originally a folk melody from sixteenth-century England and first appeared in print about 1650. The words of the song were once printed under the title "The Little Bold Fox."

Just before the War of 1812, Thomas Moore, an Irish poet, wrote the present three verses to the melody for a gala celebration in England honouring the birthday of the Prince of Wales. The tune found its way into Ireland and achieved a modest success. The Irish famine and wholesale evictions drove many to emigrate to the United States. Their songs, such as "St. Patrick's Day," gave them comfort and memories.

Canadian regiments using the march include the Royal Canadian Hussars (Montreal) (gallop) and the Fort Garry Horse. It was the regimental march of the Fort Gary Horse's allied British regiment, the 4/7 Royal Dragoon Guards.

Sweet Maid of Glendaruel (The)

This Scottish favourite is used by the Nova Scotia Highlanders as a regimental march. Although each of the two battalions has their own march, this one was retained from the Pictou Highlanders in the 1954 amalgamation. The 1st Battalion uses a combination of "The Atholl Highlanders" and "The Pibroach of Donald Dhu" while the 2nd Battalion uses "Highland Laddie."

Thunderbird

The Security Branch was formed during the unification and re-organisation of the Canadian Forces in the 1960s. It handles all police and security functions, and its responsibilities include those of the former security elements of the Directorate of Naval Intelligence, Directorate of Military Intelligence and the Directorate of Air Force Security.

The title of this march is taken from the Military Police cap badge: a totem pole in the shape of a Thunderbird, a mythical Indian spirit. The emblem is common to the Northwest Coast Indian tribes and can often be found atop the carved totem pole placed in front of a chief's home. The symbol normally represents supremacy and power in the life of the tribe. The common feature is its role: it is a protecting spirit that gives wise counsel and guards the tribe from evil or misfortune.

The Security Branch adopted Brian Gossip's new composition "Thunderbird" as a replacement for "Through Night to Light" the march that had been used by the Canadian Provost Corps. The arrangement reflects a dedication to solid modern harmony and an excellent knowledge of band scoring.

Ville Reine (Queen City)

This new march composed by Sylvio Lacharité was written in a 6/8 time with a fanfare-style opening. Les Fusiliers de Sherbrooke switched to this tune instead of retaining the march "The Dorsetshire" used by its predecessors, Les Carabiniers de Sherbrooke.

Vive la Canadienne

This tune was first used as a patriotic song before "O Canada" was designated as the national anthem. In 1840 it was arranged for piano and appeared as "The Canadian/a French air." The tune, a popular French-Canadian folk song, takes its title from a 1924 opera written by Omer Létourneau. It was adopted by the Royal 22e Regiment, the famous Van Doos, as arranged by Captain Charles O'Neill, the Director of Music of the Royal 22e Regiment Band. All battalions use the same regimental quick march.

Waltzing Matilda

This song is commonly referred to as Australia's second national anthem. Written by A. B. "Banjo" Paterson over a hundred years ago, the song has significance to all Australians. Paterson and his fiancée, Sarah Riley, were staying with the Macpherson family at Dagworth sheep station in January

1895. He wrote the poem as Christina Macpherson played her version of a Scottish tune "Craigielee."

"Waltzing Matilda" was very popular in England with armoured units and in Canada was used by The Elgin Regiment Trumpet Band. The Elgins became an engineering regiment and adopted the famous Engineers march.

Warwickshire Lads

The words of this tune are believed to have been written by David Garrick and the tune composed in honour of Shakespeare. It was played by the fifes and drums of the Warwickshire Militia and its popularity led to its adoption as the County Tune. In 1782 it was used for recruiting purposes by county regiments and later adopted by the 6th Regiment of Foot as a regimental march. The regiment's name was changed to the Royal Warwickshire Regiment, later Fusiliers, and then to the 2nd Battalion, the Royal Regiment of Fusiliers. In 1927 a revised score took the march back to its original form. The tune had been altered into a stereotypical regimental march that had eight bars in each part. "The Warwickshire Lads" has ten bars in the first and eight in the second but Kneller Hall declined it. About 1890 an eight-bar variation was authorized however whenever possible the original tune was used.

The South Saskatchewan Regiment was formed in 1905 when a regiment of infantry was designated the 95th Regiment in the districts of Assiniboia and Saskatchewan. They marched to this tune until 1968, when the unit was deactivated and placed on the Supplementary Order of Battle list.

We Lead, Others Follow

Paul Mayer, a captain in the Algonquin Regiment during the Second World War, composed this march while fighting in Holland. The title is taken from the regimental motto "Ne-Kah-Ne-Tah" which is Algonkian Indian for "We lead, others follow." This tribe were the pathfinders and navigators for the early explorers of Canada.

When I, Good Friends, Was Call'd to the Bar

This march is taken from Gilbert and Sullivan's operetta *Trial by Jury*, which ran for three hundred performances over a two-year period. The march appealed to members of the Legal Branch of the Canadian Forces and was adopted about 1982.

Wings

In 1861, Ellen Dickson, daughter of an artillery brigadier, using the pen name Dolores, composed this tune, "Wings." William Newstead, the bandmaster of the Royal Engineers, arranged it with a Victorian march "The Path Across the Hills," to form the march we know today.

When General Sir T. Gallwey was appointed commandant of the School of Military Engineering in 1868, he noted that the march used by the corps was that of the Rifle Brigade. He ordered the Band Committee to find a march that the Engineers could call their own. The bandmaster, Mr. Newstead, came up with this arrangement of "Wings."

The Duke of Cambridge, head of the British Army, was concerned about the proper performance and activities of military bands. In 1889, he noted with disapproval that the corps' march was not the one to which the Royal Engineers were entitled by tradition, that tradition being that regiments and corps entitled to wear the flaming cap badge should be using "The British Grenadier." He ordered the Royal Engineers to cease playing "Wings" and return to the original march. This caused an uproar.

General Kitchener was approached by the corps to use his influence to have "Wings" reintroduced as the corps marchpast. He immediately applied to the War Office on behalf of the corps, and the march was restored as the official marchpast in 1903.

After the formation of the Corps of Canadian Engineers they too adopted the march. It was retained after unification along with the "Slow March of the Corps of Royal Canadian Engineers."

Corps of Commissionaires

Captain Sir Edward Walter founded the corps in 1859 with the purpose of finding employment for former servicemen who had effectively been rejected by society after returning from the Crimean War. A barracks was established to house and feed Crimean War veterans, and offices were established in key cities throughout the UK. Today, servicemen and women use their skills and experiences in the service of the corps.

In 1915 the Duke of Connaught, then Governor General of Canada, suggested to the authorities that a corps be formed in Canada. Patterned on the corps in England, it provided a livelihood for unemployed veterans of the First World War. During the Second World War, younger members returned to serve in ranks, but afterwards the ranks of Commissionaires swelled again. Today the Corps have divisions from Newfoundland to Vancouver Island.

The Canadian march was composed by a member of the corps, Ron McAnespie. After obtaining a degree in music he has spent a lifetime composing and playing. During 1967, Canada's Centennial Year, he won first place in the Canadian Forces Band March Competition by composing the Centennial Year march "A Century of Progress."

In 1996 he began composing the music for this march, and it took over a year before the final composition was ready. It was was first played by the 7th Toronto Regiment, RCA, under the direction of Lieutenant G. Brascasin on November 5, 1997.

CHAPTER 13

Vanishing Regiments, Bands and Marches

Be it true or not that old soldiers never die but only fade away, it is absolutely certain that the music connected with soldiering never does in fact. Many famous Regiments in the last few years have passed off the scene, others have been amalgamated. Much of the music of former Regiments is still in use, though the names of the Regiments concerned have vanished, perhaps forever.

LCol C. H. Jaeger OBE, Marches of the Vanishing Regiments,
BBC Records TRC 1033, 1970

1st Battalion CEF
Battalion reported a brass and bugle band
"John Peel"

1st British Columbia Regiment (Duke of Connaught's Own)
"I'm Ninety Five"

1st Canadian Mounted Rifles
Regiment reported a pipe band
"Heilan Laddie"

1st Canadian Parachute Battalion
"Ride of the Valkyries"

2nd Battalion, CEF
"Colonel Bogey"

2nd Dragoons
"Bonnie Dundee" and "Keel Row"

2nd/10th Dragoons
"Annie Laurie"

3rd Battalion CEF
Medley of: "The March of the Buffs," "British Grenadiers" and "Men of Harlech"

4th Battalion CEF
"The Nut Brown Maiden"

4th Hussars of Canada
"God Bless the Prince of Wales"

IV Princess Louise Dragoons
"Men of Harlech"

5th Battalion CEF
"Till the Boys Come Home"

5th British Columbia Light Horse
"The Farmer's Boy"

5th Canadian Mounted Rifles
Battalion reported a brass and bugle band

6th Duke of Connaught's Royal Canadian Hussars
"March of the Scottish Arches"

6th Regiment, Duke of Connaught's Royal Own Rifles
"I'm Ninety-Five"

7th Battalion CEF
Battalion reported a fife, drum and bugle band

7th Regiment, Fusiliers
"British Grenadiers"

7th/11th Hussars
"My Boy Willie"

8th Battalion CEF
"Pork Beans and Hard Tack"

8th Reconnaissance Regiment
"Bonnie Dundee"

10th Battalion CEF
Battalion reported a brass band

10th Brant Dragoons
"Bonnie Dundee" and "Keel Row"

11th Battalion CEF
Battalion reported a fife and drum band

12th Battalion CEF
Battalion reported a brass band

12th Manitoba Dragoons
"Colonel Bogey"

13th Battalion CEF
Battalion reported a pipe band
"Heilan Laddie"

14th Battalion CEF
Battalion reported a brass band

14th Canadian Hussars
"Bonnie Dundee"

14th Canadian Light Horse
"Bonnie Dundee"

15th Battalion CEF
Battalion reported a pipe band
"Hielan Laddie"

15th Alberta Light Horse
Battalion reported a band
"A Southerly Wind and a Cloudy Sky"

15th Canadian Light Horse
"A Southerly Wind and a Cloudy Sky"

16th /22nd Saskatchewan Horse
"One and All"

16th Battalion CEF
Battalion reported a pipe band
(Championship band of the Canadian Corps)
"Blue Bonnets O'er The Border"

17th Battalion CEF
Battalion reported a pipe band

17th Duke of York's Royal Canadian Hussars
"Men of Harlech"

18th Battalion CEF
Battalion reported a brass band

19th (Central Ontario) Battalion CEF
Battalion reported a brass and pipe band
"Bonnie Dundee"

19th Alberta Armoured Car Regiment
"John Peel"

19th Alberta Dragoons
"John Peel"

19th St. Catharines Regiment
"The Lincolnshire Poacher"

20th (Northern and Central Ontario) Battalion CEF
Battalion reported a brass and bugle band

21st Battalion CEF
Battalion reported a pipe and bugle band
"Scotland Forever"

22nd (French Canadian) Battalion CEF
Battalion reported a brass band
"*Sambre et Meuse*"

24th Battalion CEF
Battalion reported a brass band
"The Victoria Rifles March"

25th Battalion CEF
Battalion reported a pipe band
"MacKenzie Highlanders"

26th (New Brunswick) Battalion CEF
Battalion reported a pipe band
"Heilan Laddie"

27th (City of Winnipeg) Battalion CEF
Battalion reported a brass and pipe band
"Hielan Laddie"

28th (North West) Battalion CEF
Battalion reported a brass band

29th Battalion CEF
Battalion reported a brass and pipe band
"Scotland the Brave"

31st (Alberta) Reconnaissance Regiment
"A Southerly Wind and a Cloudy Sky"

31st Battalion CEF
Battalion reported a brass band

31st Grey Battalion
Battalion reported a brass and bugle band

32nd Battalion CEF
Battalion reported a brass band

34th Battalion CEF
Battalion reported a brass and bugle band

35th Battalion CEF
Battalion reported a brass and pipe band
"Heilan Laddie"

36th Battalion CEF
Battalion reported a brass band

37th (Northern Ontario) Battalion CEF
Battalion reported a brass band

38th Battalion CEF
Battalion reported a brass band
Medley: "Will Ye No Come Again" and "Loch Lomond"

39th Battalion CEF
Battalion reported a brass band

42nd Battalion CEF
Battalion reported a pipe band
"Heilan Laddie"

43rd Battalion CEF (Cameron Highlanders of Canada)
Battalion reported a brass and pipe band
"Piobaireachd O'Donald Dhu"

44th Battalion CEF
Battalion reported a brass and pipe band

44th Lincoln and Welland Regiment
"The Lincolnshire Poacher"

46th Battalion CEF
Battalion reported a brass and pipe band

47th Battalion CEF
Battalion reported a brass, bugle and pipe band
"Brigade March of the 56th French Brigade"

49th Battalion CEF
Battalion reported a brass and pipe band
"Bonnie Dundee"

50th (Calgary) Battalion CEF
"Regimental March of the 1st Battalion, Queen's Own Royal West Kent Regiment" and "The Maple Leaf Forever" (one bar), "A Hundred Pipers" (pipe band)

50th Regiment (Gordon Highlanders)
"Blue Bonnets O'er The Border"

51st Battalion CEF
Battalion reported a brass, fife, pipe and bugle band

52nd (New Ontario) Battalion CEF
Battalion reported a brass band

52nd Brome Regiment
"Assault To Arms"

53rd Battalion CEF
Battalion reported a brass band

54th Battalion CEF
Battalion reported a brass band

54th Richmond Regiment
"When Johnny Comes Marching Home"

55th Regiment, Megantic Light Infantry
"Brownie's Quickstep"

56th (Calgary) Battalion CEF
Battalion reported a brass band

57th Battalion CEF
Battalion reported a brass and bugle band

58th Battalion CEF
Battalion reported a brass band

58th Compton Regiment
"The Campbells are Coming"

60th Battalion CEF
Battalion reported a bugle band

61st Battalion CEF
Battalion reported a brass band

62nd Battalion CEF
Battalion reported a brass and band in Canada

63rd Battalion CEF
Battalion reported a brass, bugle and pipe band

65th Battalion CEF
Battalion reported a brass band

66th Battalion CEF
Battalion reported a brass band
and bugle band in Canada

67th Battalion CEF (Western Scots of Canada)
Battalion reported a brass and
pipe band in Canada
"Blue Bonnets O'er The Border"

68th Battalion CEF
Battalion reported a brass and
bugle band

68th King's County Regiment
"The Merry Boys of Kent"

69th Battalion CEF
Battalion reported a brass band in
Canada

70th Champlain Battalion of Infantry
"*Sortons*"

72nd Battalion CEF
Battalion reported a pipe and
brass band
"Scotland the Brave"

73rd Battalion CEF
Battalion reported a brass and
pipe band
"Heilan Laddie"

74th Battalion CEF
Battalion reported a brass band

75th Battalion CEF
Battalion reported a brass and
bugle band
"Colonel Bogey"

77th Battalion, CEF
Battalion reported a brass and
pipe band
"Bonnie Dundee"

78th Battalion CEF
Battalion reported a brass band

79th Battalion CEF
Battalion reported a band brass
and bugle in Canada

80th Battalion CEF
Battalion reported a brass band

80th Nicolet Regiment
"*Pas Au 80th Batallion*"

81st Battalion CEF
Battalion reported a brass band
"The Red Rose"

81st Portneuf Regiment
"*Grande Marche Lauier*"

82nd Battalion CEF (Calgary Light Infantry)
Battalion reported a brass, bugle
and pipe band
"Blue Bonnets O'er the Border"

82nd Queen's County Regiment
"The Gem of the Gulf"

83rd Battalion CEF (Queen's Own Rifles of Canada)
Battalion reported a bugle band

85th Nova Scotia Highlanders Battalion CEF
Battalion reported a silver brass
band and a pipe band
"Cock O' the North"

86th Battalion CEF
Battalion reported a brass and
bugle band

87th Battalion, CEF
Battalion reported a brass and
bugle band

88th Regiment
"Draper Hall"

88th Regiment (Victoria Fusiliers)
"British Grenadiers"

89th (Alberta) Battalion CEF
Battalion reported a brass band

90th Battalion CEF
Battalion reported a brass band

91st Battalion CEF
Battalion reported a brass, bugle
and pipe band

**91st Regiment, Canadian
Highlanders**
"The Campbells are Coming"

92nd Battalion CEF
Battalion reported a brass and
pipe band
"Hielan Laddie"

93rd Battalion CEF
Battalion reported a brass band

94th Battalion CEF
Battalion reported a brass band

95th Battalion CEF
Battalion reported a brass band

96th Battalion CEF
Battalion reported a brass and
pipe band
"Lass O'Gowrie"

**98th Lincoln and Welland
Battalion CEF**
Battalion reported a brass band

**101st Regiment, Edmonton
Fusiliers**
"A Hundred Pipers"

102nd Battalion CEF
Battalion reported a brass and
pipe band
"Blue Bonnets O'er the Border"

103rd Battalion CEF
Battalion reported a brass band

105th Battalion CEF
Battalion reported a brass band

106th Battalion CEF
Battalion reported a brass and
bugle band

107th (Winnipeg) Battalion CEF
Battalion reported a bugle and
pipe band in Canada
"The Campbells are Coming"

108th (Selkirk) Battalion CEF
Battalion reported a brass and
bugle band

109th Battalion CEF
Battalion reported a brass and
bugle band

110th Battalion CEF
Battalion reported a brass and
bugle band in Canada

111th Battalion CEF
Battalion reported a brass and
bugle band in Canada

112th Battalion CEF
Battalion reported a brass band

113th Battalion
Battalion reported a brass/bugle
and pipe band
"All the Blue Bonnets are Over the
Border"

114th Battalion CEF
Battalion reported a brass and
bugle band

115th Battalion CEF
Battalion reported a brass band

116th Battalion CEF
Battalion reported a brass and
bugle band

117th Battalion
Battalion reported a brass band

118th Battalion CEF
Battalion reported a brass and
bugle band

119th Battalion CEF
Battalion reported a brass band

120th Battalion CEF
Battalion reported a brass band

121st Battalion CEF
Battalion reported a brass and
bugle band

123rd Battalion CEF
Battalion reported a brass and
bugle band

124th Battalion CEF
Battalion reported a brass and
bugle band

125th Battalion CEF
Battalion reported a brass band

126th Peel Battalion CEF
Battalion reported a brass band

127th Battalion CEF
Battalion reported a brass and
bugle band

128th Battalion CEF
Battalion reported a brass and
bugle band

129th Battalion CEF
Battalion reported a brass and
bugle band

130th Battalion CEF
Battalion reported a brass band

131st Battalion CEF
Battalion reported a brass and
bugle band

**132nd (North Shore) (NB)
Battalion CEF**
Battalion reported a brass band

133rd Battalion CEF
Battalion reported a brass and
bugle band

134th Battalion CEF
Battalion reported a brass and
pipe band
"Hielan Laddie"

135th Battalion CEF
Battalion reported a brass and
bugle band

136th Battalion CEF
Battalion reported a brass and
bugle band

137th (Calgary) Battalion CEF
Battalion reported a brass band

138th Battalion CEF
Battalion reported a brass band

139th Battalion CEF
Battalion reported a brass, bugle and pipe band

140th Battalion CEF
Battalion reported a brass and bugle band

141st Battalion CEF
Battalion reported a brass and bugle band

142nd Battalion CEF
Battalion reported a brass and bugle band

143rd Battalion CEF
Battalion reported a brass and bugle band

144th Battalion CEF (Winnipeg Rifles)
Battalion reported a brass and bugle band

145th Battalion CEF
Battalion reported a brass and bugle band

146th Battalion CEF
Battalion reported a brass and bugle band

147th Battalion CEF
Battalion reported a brass and bugle band

149th Battalion CEF
Battalion reported a brass and bugle band

150th Battalion CEF
Battalion reported a brass and bugle band

151st Central Alberta Battalion CEF
Battalion reported a brass and bugle band

152nd Battalion CEF
Battalion reported a brass and bugle band

153rd Battalion CEF
Battalion reported a brass and bugle band

154th Battalion CEF
Battalion reported a bugle and pipe band

155th (Quite) Battalion CEF
Battalion reported a brass and bugle band

156th (Leeds, Grenville) Battalion CEF
Battalion reported a brass and bugle band

157th Battalion CEF (Simcoe Foresters)
Battalion reported a brass and bugle band

158th Battalion CEF
Battalion reported a brass band

159th (Algonquin) Battalion CEF
Battalion reported a brass band

160th Battalion CEF
Battalion reported a brass and bugle band in Canada

162nd Battalion CEF
Battalion reported a brass and bugle band in Canada
"Hielan Laddie"

164th (Halton and Dufferin) Battalion CEF
Battalion reported a brass and bugle band

165th Battalion CEF
Battalion reported a brass and bugle band

166th Battalion CEF
Battalion reported a brass and bugle band in Canada

168th Battalion CEF
Battalion reported a brass, bugle and pipe band in Canada

169th Battalion CEF
Battalion reported a brass and bugle band

170th Battalion CEF
Battalion reported a brass and bugle band

172nd Battalion (Rocky Mountain Rangers) CEF
Battalion reported a brass and bugle band

173rd Battalion CEF (Canadian Highlanders)
Battalion reported a brass, bugle and pipe band in Canada
"Bonnie Dundee"

174th Battalion CEF (Cameron Highlanders of Canada)
Battalion reported a pipe band

175th Battalion CEF
Battalion reported a brass and bugle band in Canada

176th Battalion CEF
Battalion reported a brass band

177th Battalion CEF
Battalion reported a brass band

178th Battalion CEF
Battalion reported a bugle band

179th Battalion CEF
Battalion reported a brass and pipe band in Canada
"Piobaireachd O'Donald Dhu"

180th Battalion CEF
Battalion reported a brass and bugle band

181st Battalion CEF
Battalion reported a brass band

182nd Battalion CEF
Battalion reported a brass and bugle band

183rd Battalion CEF
Battalion reported a brass and bugle band in Canada

184th Battalion CEF
Battalion reported a brass band

185th Cape Breton Highlanders Battalion CEF
Battalion reported a brass, bugle and pipe band
"Blue Bonnets O'er the Border"

186th Battalion CEF
Battalion reported a brass and bugle band

187th Battalion CEF
Battalion reported a brass band

188th Battalion CEF
Battalion reported a brass and pipe band in Canada

190th Battalion CEF
Battalion reported a brass band

191st Battalion CEF
Battalion reported a brass band

192nd Battalion CEF
Battalion reported a brass and bugle band

193rd Battalion CEF
Battalion reported a brass and pipe band
"Scotland the Brave"

194th Battalion CEF
Battalion reported a brass and bugle band
"Blue Bonnets O'er the Border"

195th Battalion CEF
Battalion reported a brass band

196th Battalion CEF
Battalion reported a brass band

197th Battalion CEF
Battalion reported a brass and pipe band

198th Battalion CEF
Battalion reported a brass and bugle band

199th Battalion CEF
Battalion reported a brass and bugle band

200th Battalion CEF
Battalion reported a brass band

202nd Battalion CEF (The Sportman's Battalion)
Battalion reported a brass band

203rd Battalion CEF
Battalion reported a brass and bugle band in Canada

204th Battalion CEF
Battalion reported a brass and bugle band

205th Battalion CEF
Battalion reported a brass and bugle band

207th Battalion CEF
Battalion reported a brass and bugle band

208th Battalion CEF
Battalion reported a brass, bugle and pipe band

209th Battalion CEF
Battalion reported a brass and bugle band in Canada

210th Battalion CEF
"Frontiersmen"
Battalion reported a bugle band

211th Battalion CEF (The American Legion)
Battalion reported a brass and bugle band

212th Battalion CEF
Battalion reported a brass and bugle band

214th Battalion CEF
Battalion reported a brass band

215th Battalion CEF
Battalion reported a brass band

216th Battalion CEF
Battalion reported a brass band

217th Battalion CEF
Battalion reported a brass band

218th Battalion CEF
Battalion reported a brass and bugle band

219th Battalion CEF
Battalion reported a brass, bugle and pipe band in Canada

220th Battalion CEF
Battalion had a brass and bugle band

221st Battalion CEF
Battalion reported a brass band

222nd Battalion CEF
Battalion reported a brass and bugle band in Canada

223rd Battalion CEF
Battalion reported a brass and bugle band in Canada

224th Battalion CEF
Battalion reported a pipe band
"Heilan Laddie"

225th Battalion CEF
Battalion reported a brass band

226th Battalion (Men of the North) CEF
Battalion reported a brass and bugle band

227th Battalion CEF
Battalion reported a brass and bugle band

228th Battalion CEF
Battalion reported a brass and pipe band
"Heilan Laddie"

229th Battalion CEF "South Saskatchewan Battalion"
Battalion reported a brass and bugle band in Canada

230th Battalion CEF
Battalion reported a brass band

231st Battalion CEF
Battalion reported a brass and pipe band in Canada

233rd Battalion CEF
Battalion reported a brass and bugle band

234th Battalion CEF
Battalion reported a brass band

235th Battalion CEF
Battalion reported a brass band

236th Battalion CEF
Battalion reported a brass, bugle and pipe band
"MacLean March"

239th Battalion CEF
Battalion reported a brass and pipe band

240th Battalion CEF
Battalion reported a brass band

241st Battalion CEF
Battalion reported a brass and pipe band
"Blue Bonnets are O'er the Border"

242nd Battalion CEF
Battalion reported a pipe band

243rd Battalion CEF
Battalion reported a brass and bugle band

245th Battalion CEF
Battalion reported a brass band
No march

245th Battalion CEF (Quinte's Own)
Battalion reported a brass band

246th Battalion CEF
Battalion reported a brass and pipe band
"Glendaruel Highlanders"

247th Battalion CEF
Battalion reported a brass and bugle band in Canada

249th Battalion CEF
Battalion reported a brass and bugle band

251st Battalion CEF
Battalion reported a brass and bugle band

252nd Battalion CEF
Battalion reported a brass and bugle band

253rd Battalion CEF (Queen's University Highland Battalion)
Battalion reported a pipe band

255th Battalion CEF
Battalion reported a brass and bugle band

Alberta Mounted Rifles
"A Southerly Wind and a Cloudy Sky"

Algonquin Regiment
"We Lead Others Follow"

Annapolis Regiment
"I'm Ninety-Five"

Argyll Light Infantry
"The Campbells are Coming"

Argyll Light Infantry (Tank)
"The Campbells are Coming"

Battleford Light Infantry (16th/22nd Saskatchewan Horse)
"One and All"

British Columbia Hussars (Armoured Car)
"The Farmer's Boy"

British Columbia Mounted Rifles
"The Farmer's Boy"

Bruce Regiment
'The Concentration March"

Calgary Regiment (Tank)
"Colonel Bogey"

Cameron Highlanders of Ottawa
"Pibroch of Donuil Dhu"

Canadian Airborne Regiment
"The Longest Day" and "The Grenadier"

Canadian Armoured Fighting Vehicle Training Centre
"My Boy Willie"

Canadian Forestry Corps
"Heilan Laddie"

Canadian Fusiliers (City of London)
"British Grenadiers"

Canadian Grenadier Guards
"British Grenadiers" and "Grenadier Slow March"

Canadian Guards
"The Standard of St. George"

Canadian Intelligence Corps (The)
"Silver and Green"

Canadian Provost Corps
"Through Night to Light"

Canadian Women's Army Corps
"Athene"

Cape Breton Highlanders
"Heilan Laddie"

Carleton and York Regiment
"A Hundred Pipers"

Carleton Light Infantry (The)
"The Campbells are Coming"

Corps of Royal Canadian Electrical and Mechanical Engineers
REME Corps March Past

Cumberland Highlanders
"Athol Highlanders"

Cumberland Regiment
"To the Ladies' Eyes," "A Round Boys"

Dufferin and Haldimand Rifles of Canada
"Dufferin Rifles of Canada"

Dufferin Rifles of Canada
"Dufferin Rifles of Canada"

Durham Regiment
"The Leopold March"

Edmonton Fusiliers
"A Hundred Pipers"

Edmonton Regiment
"Bonnie Dundee"

Essex Scottish Regiment
"Heilan Laddie"

Essex Fusiliers
"British Grenadiers"

Essex Regiment (Tank)
"My Boy Willie"

Frontenac Regiment (The)
"Hoboken March"

Governor General's Body Guards
"Men of Harlech"

Grenville Regiment (Lisgar Rifles)
"The Royal March"

Grey Regiment (The)
"The 31st Greys"

Haldimand Rifles
"The Kynegad Slashers"

Halifax Rifles (RCAC) (The)
"Lutzow's Wild Hunt"

Halton Rifles
"The Campbells are Coming"

Highland Light Infantry of Canada
"Seann Triubhas" and "Whistle O'er The Lave"

Huron Regiment (The)
"The Maple Leaf Forever"

Irish Fusiliers of Canada
"Garry Owen"

Irish Fusiliers of Canada (Vancouver Regiment)
"Garry Owen" and "St. Patrick's Day"

Kent Regiment
"A Hundred Pipers"

King's Own Rifles of Canada
"Punjaub" and "The Buffs"

Lake Superior Regiment (Motor)
"Bugle Horn" and "Light of Foot"

Lambton Regiment (The)
"The Forward March"

Lanark and Renfrew Regiment
"Heilan Laddie"

Le Régiment de Chateauguay
"*Semper Paratus*"

Le Régiment de Dorchester et Beauce
"The Cottage March"

Le Régiment de Joliette
"*Le Régiment de Joliette*"

Le Régiment de Lévis
"*O Carillon*"

Le Régiment de Montmagny
"*Baccaccio*"

Le Régiment de Quebec (Mitrailleuses)
"*Le Régiment de Quebec*"

Le Régiment de St Hyacinthe
"The Manchester"

Le Régiment de Trois Rivières (RCAC)
"My Boy Willie"

Les Carabiniers de Sherbrooke
"The Dorsetshire"

Les Carabiniers Mont-Royal
"The Jockey of York"

Les Franc-Tireurs du Saguenay
"*Le Régiment du Saguenay*"

Lincoln and Welland Regiment (The)
"St. Catharines"

Lorne Rifles (Scottish) (The)
"The Campbells are Coming"

Lunenburg Regiment
"The Lincolnshire Poacher"

Manitoba Mounted Rifles
"Bonnie Dundee" and "Keel Row"

Middlesex and Huron Regiment
"I'm Ninety-Five"

Middlesex Light Infantry
"I'm Ninety-Five"

Midland Regiment (The)
"The Standard of St. George"

New Brunswick Rangers (The)
"Defiance March"

New Brunswick Regiment (Tank) (The)
"The Invasion March"

New Brunswick Scottish Regiment
"Blue Bonnets O'er The Border" and "A Hundred Pipers"

Norfolk Regiment of Canada (The)
"The Mountain Rose"

Norfolk Rifles
"Parade Quickstep" and "The Mountain Rose"

North Nova Scotia Highlanders
"Atholl Highlanders"

North Shore (New Brunswick) Regiment
"The Old North Shore"

Northumberland Regiment
"L'Etoile March"

Ottawa Highlanders (The)
"Piobaireachd O'Donald Dhu"
and "March of the Cameron Men"

Oxford Rifles
"The Buffs"

Peel Regiment
"Here's To A Maiden of Bashful
Fifteen"

Peel and Dufferin Regiment
"John Peel"

Perth Regiment
"John Peel" and "Kenamure On
A'wa"

Peterborough Rangers
"Lass O'Gowrie"

Pictou Highlanders
"Sweet Maid of Gendarue" and
"Piobaireachd O'Donald Dhu"

**Prince Albert and Battleford
Volunteers (MG)**
"One and All"

Prince Albert Volunteers
"The Lower Castle"

**Prince Edward Island Light
Horse**
"Old Solomon Levi"

**Prince Edward Island
Highlanders**
"Heilan Laddie"

**Prince of Wales Rangers
(Peterborough Regiment)**
"Lass O'Gowrie"

**Princess Louise's Argyll and
Sutherland Highanders of
Canada**
"The Campbells are Coming"

Princess Louise Dragoon Guards
"Men of Harlech"

**Princess Patricia's Canadian
Light Infantry CEF**
(Pipe Band — Edmonton City
Police)
"All the Blue Bonnets are Over the
Border"

**Queen's York Rangers, 1st
American Regiment**
"Braganza"

Regina Rifles Regiment (The)
"Lutzow's Wild Hunt" and "Keel
Row" (Double March)

**Royal Canadian Army Chaplain
Corps**
"Onward Christian Soldiers"

**Royal Canadian Army Dental
Corps**
"Marchpast of the Canadian
Dental Corps"

**Royal Canadian Army Medical
Corps**
"Here's a Health Unto His
Majesty"

Royal Canadian Army Pay Corps
"Pay Parade" and "Primrose and
Blue"

**Royal Canadian Army Service
Corps**
"Wait for the Wagon"/Boer Trek
Song

Royal Canadian Veterinary Corps
"The Village Blacksmith"

Royal Canadian Corps of Signals
"Begone Dull Care"

Royal Canadian Ordnance Corps
"The Village Blacksmith"

Royal Canadian Postal Corps
"Post Horn March"

Royal Canadian Veterinary Corps
"The Village Blacksmith"

Royal Grenadiers
"British Grenadiers"

Royal Hamilton Light Infantry
"The Mountain Rose"

Royal Hamilton Regiment
"The Mountain Rose"

Royal Canadian Infantry Corps
"The Standard of St. George"

Royal Military Colleges
"The Standard of St. George"
(RRMC)
"Hatley Park" (RRMC)
"Goin' Home" (RRMC)

Royal Regiment of Toronto Grenadiers
"British Grenadiers"

Royal Rifles of Canada (The)
"I'm Ninety-Five"

Saint John Fusiliers (MG) (The)
"British Grenadiers"

Saskatoon Light Infantry (MG)
"With Jockey to the Fair"

Sault Ste Marie and Sudbury Regiment
"Regimental March of the Sault Ste Marie Regiment"

Sault Ste Marie Regiment
"Regimental March of the Sault Ste Marie Regiment"

Scottish Fusiliers of Canada
"Heilan Laddie" and "British Grenadiers"

Sherbrooke Fusiliers Regiment CASF
"British Grenadiers" (The)

Sherbrooke Regiment (RCAC)
"The Sherbrooke Regiment"

Simcoe Foresters
"Young May Moon"

South Alberta Horse
"A Southerly Wind and a Cloudy Sky"

South Alberta Regiment
"A Southerly Wind and a Cloudy Sky," and "Lass O'Gowrie "

South Saskatchwan Regiment (The)
"The Warwickshire Lads"

Stormont and Glengarry Regiment
"Bonnie Dundee" and "Heilan Laddie"

Toronto Regiment
"British Grenadiers"

Vancouver Regiment (The)
"Scotland the Brave" and "Colonel Bogey"

Veteran's Guard of Canada
"Ghanadh Baiteach" ("Muckin' O'
Geordie's Bryne")

**Victoria and Haliburton
Regiment**
"Bonnie Dundee"

Victoria Rifles of Canada
"Huntsmen's Chorus" and
"Lutzow's Wild Hunt"

Wellington Regiment
"I'm Ninety-Five"

Wellington Rifles
"I'm Ninety-Five"

Wentworth Regiment (The)
"Lass O'Gowrie"

West Toronto Regiment
"British Grenadier"

Western Ontario Regiment
"British Grenadiers"

Westminster Regiment
"The Maple Leaf Forever" and
"The Warwickshire Lads"

Winnipeg Grenadiers (The)
"British Grenadiers"

Winnipeg Light Infantry
"Soldiers of the Queen"

Winnipeg Rifles
"Old Solomon Levi" and "Keel
Row"

York Rangers Regiment
"I'm Ninety-Five"

York Regiment
"I'm Ninety-Five"

Yukon Regiment
"Marchpast of the Yukon
Regiment"

CHAPTER 14

The Song Book

The hymns and songs that soldiers, sailors, and airmen sang on the march and in battle were in some cases pieces that had been sung at home. Through the years they have been heard over and over again which is a testament to their everlasting popularity.

"Operation Sing-Song" was the competition to name the most popular songs of both world wars and was sponsored by The Hon. Brooke Claxton PC, DCM, QC, LLD, Chairman of the Canada Council. The $100 award went to D. W. Reeves, past president of Canadian Legion Branch No. 23 in North Bay, Ontario.

Mr. Reeves's letter to the Canada Council was quite interesting:

> I am enclosing lists of songs in the order I feel they were popular. Having been a member of the Legion since its inception, I have had an opportunity through the years to take part in many veteran activities and, as the years pass, the old songs have been fewer. Most of the branches have record players and it would give our meetings a lift to hear the wartime favourites once again.
>
> I would like to suggest that a record also be made of popular marches such as Col. Bogey, Cock o' the North, Under the Double Eagle, My Bonnie Lass (with bag pipes), many of the Sousa favourites some with the sound of marching feet in the background. Many of the battalions had their own regimental march which could be incorporated into a stirring record of marches.
>
> At the present time there are many retired First World War veterans, in homes and hospitals, who would enjoy listening to this type of entertainment. It would act as a tonic to them, bringing back many memories, some happy, some sad.
>
> They would also be used at Legion social functions and branch meetings across Canada, and I am sure would be a welcome change from the so-called "hit parades" of today.

It is being said that the Legion is getting to be the same as any other service club. I resent the implications as we are unique in our membership. It is programs such as I have intimated that have made comrades of us all. To the older veterans it may not be a ticket to Heaven but will help make the waiting room more pleasant.

The ten most popular songs selected by consensus were:

First World War
1. It's a Long Way to Tipperary
2. Mademoiselle from Armentieres
3. Keep the Home Fires Burning
4. The Long Trail
5. If You Were the Only Girl in the World
6. Oh, Oh, Oh, It's a Lovely War
7. All the Nice Girls Love a Sailor
8. Roses are Blooming in Picardy
9. Good Bye-ee
10. Roamin' in the Gloamin'

Second World War
1. There'll Always Be an England
2. Bless Them All
3. Beer Barrel Polka
4. Wish Me Luck as You Wave Me Goodbye
5. Lili Marlene
6. I've Got Sixpence
7. The White Cliffs of Dover
8. Waltzing Matilda
9. Praise the Lord and Past the Ammunition
10. Now is the Hour

There were some songs that, although not chosen, were very popular both at home and abroad. These include songs of the First World War such as:

Pack Up Your Troubles in Your Old Kit Bag
Carry Me Back to Dear Old Blighty
Oh, How I Hate to Get Up in the Morning
When You Wore a Tulip
For Me and My Gal
Madelon
Dear Old Pal of Mine

Below is the complete list of all songs that were submitted to the Canada Council.

First World War

Absent
After the Ball
All the Nice Girls Love a Sailor
All the World Will be Jealous of me
Alouette
Always
Annie Laurie
Another Little Drink
Are You From Dixie
Around the Marble Arch
Baby Doll
Believe Me If All Those Endearing Young Charms
Bicycle Built for Two
Carry Me Back to Dear Old Blighty
Carry Me Back to Old Virginny
Cockle & Mussels
Coming through the Rye
Comrades, Comrades Ever Since We Were Boys
Daisy
Danny Boy
Dark Is My Doug-Out, Cold Are My Feet
Dear Old Pal of Mine
Don't Forget You Belong to Me
Don't Let the Old Flag Fall
Don't Let the Stars Get in Your Eyes
Down at the Old Bull and Bush
Down by the Old Mill Stream
Drink to Me Only with Thine Eyes
For Me and My Gal
For My Daddy Over There

Genevieve
Give Yourself a Pat on the Back
Glow Worm
God Send You back to Me
Good Bye-ee
Goodbye Broadway, Hello France
Goodbye Morning Mr. Zip
Goodbye Mr. Bluebell
Hail, Hail the Gang's All Here
Hello My Dearie
Henry the Eighth I am
Here Comes the 42nd
Home on the Range
How We Love Our Sergeant-Major
How You Gonna Keep 'Em Down at the Farm
I Don't Want to Get Well
I Dreamed I Dwelt in Marble Halls
I Lost the Sunshine and the Roses
I Love a Lassie
I Passed by Your Window
I Want a Girl Just Like the Girl that Married Dear Old Dad.
I Want to Go Home
I Was Seeing Nellie Home
I'll Murder the Bugler Yet (oh how I hate…)
I'll Take You Home Again Kathleen
I'm Sorry I Made You Cry
I've Been a WAAC, I've Been a Wren
If You were the Only Girl in the World
In Flanders Fields

255

In the Evening by the Moonlight
In the Twi-Twi-Twilight
It Was the Navy that Brought
  Them Over
It's A Long Way to Tipperary
John Brown's Body Lies a
  Mould'ring
John Peel
Johnny Dough-Boy
Juanita
Just a Baby's Prayer at Twilight
Just a Wearying for You
Just a Wee Doch and Doris
Just Before the Battle, Mother
Keep Right on the End of the
  Road
Keep the Home Fires Burning
Keep Your Head Down, Fritzie
  Boy
Kin Folk
Kiss Me Goodnight, Sergeant-
  Major
K-K-K-Katy
Let Me Call You Sweetheart
Let the Great Big World Keep
  Turning
Let the Rest of the World Go By
Let's All Go Down to the Strand
Little Annie Rooney
Little Brown Jug
Little Grey Home in the West
Loch Lomond
Love Me and the World is Mine
Love Will Find a Way
Madelon
Mademoiselle from Armentières
Mandalay
Mary Doesn't Live Here Any More
Melancholy Baby
Memories
Mickey

Miss You
Mother Macree
My Belgian Rose
My Bonnie Lies Over the Ocean
My Buddy
My Irish Molly-O
My Kin Folk
My Sweetheart's the Man in the
  Moon
My Wild Irish Rose
Now the Day is Over
O Susanna
Oh Frenchy
Oh How I Hate to Get Up in the
  Morning
Oh, Oh, Oh, It's Lovely War
Old Black Joe
Old Folks at Home
Old Grey Mare
Old Soldiers Never Die
Over There
Pack Up Your Troubles
Polly Wolly Doodle
Put Your Arms Around Me Honey
Ramona
Roamin' in the Gloamin'
Rose of Tralee
Roses Are Blooming in Picardy
She's My Lily of Lagoona
She's Got Rings on her Fingers
Silver Threads Among the Gold
Sister Susie's Sewing Shirts for
  Soldiers
Smile Awhile
Somewhere a Voice is Calling
Strike Up the Band
Sure A Little Bit of Heaven Fell
Sweet Adeline
Sweet Genevieve
Sweet Sixteen
Sweethearts Forever

Sympathy
That Old Gang of Mine
The Band Played On
The Bells of St. Mary's
The Boys of the Old Brigade
The Broken Doll
The End of a Perfect Day
The Girl I Left Behind Me
The Long Trail
The Man of the Flying Trapeze
The Man Who Broke the Bank at
  Monte Carlo
The Miner's Dream of Home
The Minstrel Boy
The Old Oaken Bucket
The Quartermaster's Stores
The Rose of No Man's Land
The Soldiers of the King
The Sunshine of Your Smile
There's a Tavern in the Town
There are Smiles that Make You
  Happy
They Wouldn't Believe Me
Till the Boys Come Marching
Till We Meet Again
Two Little Girls in Blue
Two Lovely Black Eyes, Oh What a
  Surprise

Waltzing Matilda
We Will Never Let the Old Flag
  Fall
When Irish Eyes are Smiling
When Johnny Comes Marching
  Home Again
When the Great Red Dawn is
  Shining
When the Lights of London Shine
  Again
When the Red, Red Robin Come
  Bo, Bob Bobbin Along
When You and I Were Young
  Again Maggie
When You are a Long Way From
  Home
When You Wore a Tulip
When Your Hair Turned to Silver
Where Do We Go from Here,
  Boys
Won't You Waltz Home Sweet
  Home With Me
You are Here and I am Here
You are my Sunshine
You Have to Get Up
You Made Me Love You
You're in the Army Now
Your King and Country Need You

Second World War

A Dear John Letter
A Sleepy Lagoon
Adolf, You've Bitten Much More Than You Can Chew
All the World is Waiting for the Sunrise
Aloha
Anchors Aweigh
Anniversary Waltz
Army Air Corps Song
Around the Corner
As Time Goes By
Auf Wiedersehn
Auld Lang Syne
Beautiful, Beautiful Brown Eyes
Beer Barrel Polka
Bell Bottom Trousers
Berkeley Square
Beyond the Blue Horizons
Bless Them All
Blue Bird
Bridge on the River Kwai
Bring Back Sweet Caporals To Me
By the Light of the Silvery Moon
Captains of the Clouds
Carry on Canada
Carry On, Carry On, Carry On
Charmaine
Chatanooga Choo Choo
Coming in on a Wing and a Prayer
Dear Hearts and Gentle People
Deep in the Heart of Texas
Deep River
Desert Song
Don't Fence Me In
Don't Sit Under the Apple Tree
Far Away Places
Five Foot Two, Eyes of Blue

For King and Country
Forever & Ever
Gee But It's Great to Meet a Friend
Girl of My Dreams
Give Me Five Minutes More
Goodbye Sally
Harbour Lights
Heart of Oak
Hold Your Hand Out You Naughty Boy
I Belong to Glasgow
I Don't Want to March with the Infantry
I Lost My Heart at the Stage Door Canteen
I Wonder What Became of Sally
I Wonder Who's Kissing Her Now
I'll be Home For Christmas
I'll Be Seeing You
I'll Never Smile Again
I'll Think of You
I'll Walk Alone
I'm Forever Blowing Bubbles
I've Been Working on the Railroad
I've Got a Lovely Bunch of Coconuts
I've Got Sixpence
I've Got Spurs that Jingle Jangle Jingle
If the Sergeant Steals Your Beer
In an Old Dutch Garden
In Old Shanty Town
In the Good Old Summertime
In the Shade of an Old Apple Tree
It Looks Like Rain in Apple Blossom Time
Jeanie with the Light Brown Hair

Jersey Bounce
Juke-Box Saturday Night
Kiss the Boys Goodbye
Knees Up, Mother Brown
Lili Marlene
Long Ago and Far Away
Ma, I Miss Your Apple Pie
Marching Along Together
Mares Eat Oats and Does Eat Oats
Margie
Marine Corps Hymn
Moonlight Serenade
My Girl's a Corker, She's a New
    Yorker
My Tunic is out at the Elbows
Now is the Hour
Oh You Beautiful Doll
One of Our Planes is Missing
Paper Doll
Pistol Packin' Momma
Praise the Lord and Pass the
    Ammunition
Road to the Isle
Roll a Bowl a Ball
Roll Along Wavy Navy, Roll Along
Roll Me Over
Roll Out the Barrel (Beer Barrel
    Polka)
Roseanne of Charing Cross
Rum & Coca Cola
Sailing Up the Clyde
San Antonia Rose
Saturday Night is the Loneliest
    Night
She Likes His Eyes
She'll Be Coming Round the
    Mountain
Shoo Shoo Baby
Show Me the Way to Go Home
Side by Side
Smiles

So Close Your Eyes, My Little
    Drummer Boy
Somebody Stole My Gal
Somewhere a Voice is Calling
Somewhere in France with You
Stardust
Stick Your Thumbs Up and Sing a
    Tickety Boo
Sweet Eyes of Blue
Sweet Rosie O'Grady
Sweet Violets
The Caissons Go Rolling Along
The Darktown Strutters Ball
The D-Day Dodgers
The Grasshopper Song
The Irish Washerwoman
The Last Time I Saw Paris
The Lord's Prayer
The Man Who Did It the Last
    Time
The More We Are Together
The Red, White, and Blue
The Sailor with the Navy Blue
    Eyes
The Wedding of Lili Marlene
The Whiffenpool
The White Cliffs of Dover
There'll Always be an England
There's Something About a Sailor
Three O'clock in the Morning
Trumpeter (The)
Wait Till the Sun Shines, Nellie
Waltzing Matilda
Wash Me in the Water that You
    Washed the Colonel's Daughter
We'll Hang out the Washing on
    the Siegfried Line
We'll Meet Again
When the Lights Go On Again All
    Over the World

When There's a Breeze on Lake
  Louise
When They Sound the Last All
  Clear
When This Blasted War is Over
Whispering
White Christmas
Wish Me Luck as You Wave Me
  Goodbye

Wunderbar
Yankee Doodle Dandy
You Are Always in My Heart
You'll Never Know
You're in the Army Mr. Jones
Yours
Yours Till the Stars Lose Their
  Glory

Appendix A

Military Band Instrumentation Chart 1869 - 1998

The chart information is obtained from band photographs. The horns include Eb Alto Horns, Mellophones and French Horns. The instruments listed below correspond with the numbers at the top of the chart:

1. Flute   2. Oboe   3. Bassoon   4. Clarinet   5. Saxophone
6. Trumpet   7. Horns   8. Trombone   9. Euphonium   10. Tuba
11. Percussion

Unit	Year	1	2	3	4	5	6	7	8	9	10	11
Fifth	1869	0	0	0	0	0	4	3	0	2	2	2
GGFG	1873	1	0	0	4	0	4	3	3	2	2	2
RCGA	1889	1	0	0	2	0	3	2	3	2	2	3
Fifteenth	1903	0	0	0	1	1	4	2	2	2	2	2
Thirteen	1908	1	0	0	3	1	5	3	3	3	2	2
103rd	1913	2	0	0	5	5	5	3	3	2	4	4
RCR	1916	2	1	1	9	2	5	2	4	1	4	3
15 Battery	1918	1	0	0	6	3	6	6	4	2	2	2
R22R	1924	2	1	1	10	2	4	3	4	2	3	2
RCHA	1928	1	0	2	5	1	4	4	3	1	2	1
RCHA	1936	1	0	0	3	2	4	3	3	1	2	1
RCR	1939	1	0	1	2	0	3	1	3	1	1	3
RCR	1941	1	0	0	5	2	4	3	1	1	2	2
2 RCA	1943	0	0	0	6	3	5	2	3	1	2	3
Armoured	1944	0	0	0	6	3	6	2	3	1	3	2
RCR	1949	0	0	0	5	2	5	2	3	1	2	3
RCAF	1952	2	1	2	10	4	6	4	4	2	3	3
PPCLI	1954	2	1	1	12	3	6	4	4	2	3	3
RCN *Naden*	1958	2	1	1	10	4	8	3	5	3	3	5
RCA	1960	2	2	2	12	4	7	3	3	2	2	2

Unit	Year	1	2	3	4	5	6	7	8	9	10	11
Royal 22nd	1964	3	1	2	16	4	7	4	5	2	3	3
PPCLI	1968	3	1	1	13	5	10	4	6	3	5	5
RCR	1970	3	2	2	16	5	10	4	6	3	5	5
Vimy	1976	2	1	1	8	4	6	3	4	1	3	3
Stadacona	1980	1	1	1	7	6	6	3	4	1	3	3
Air Command	1984	2	1	0	9	3	6	3	3	2	4	3*
CF Bands	1993	2	1	1	7	3	5	3	4	1	2	3**
Stadacona Band	1996	2	1	1	7	4	5	3	4	2	3	4
Royal Regiment	1997	2	1	3***	10	6	10	5	6	3^^	4	4

*Bass, **Piano
*** Includes Bass Clt
^^ Includes Electric Bass

Appendix B

Discography

Canada has played an important part in the recording industry since the inception of the phonograph invented by Thomas Edison in 1877. The 48th Highlanders made the earliest known band recording in 1900 which was recorded on cylinders under the direction of Captain John Slatter. He selected four Scottish pieces to kick off the band recording industry in Canada and included "The Blue Bells of Scotland," "Cock of the North," "Rob Roy" and "Comin' thru the Rye."

This list is from the author's collection. It contains only Regimental, Corps and Branch marches and is a sampling of recordings for Canadian and United Kingdom units of all services. Individual regiments normally include their marches at the beginning or end of their discs.

Official Marches of the Canadian Forces
Toronto Military Garrison (Combined Bands and Pipes and Drums)
Royal Canadian Military Institute ©1988
Directors of Music:
Major G. A. Falconi CD, Royal Regiment of Canada
Major R. A. Herriot CD, 7th Toronto Regiment RCA
Pipe Major CWO A. L. Dewar CD, 48th Highlanders of Canada

Marches of the Canadian Forces (Traditional and Contemporary)
The Regimental Band of the Princess Patricia's Canadian Light Infantry
Westmount Records WSTM 7813
Director of Music: Captain Leonard Camplin CD

Regimental Marches of the British Army
Band of the Royal Corps of Signals/Pipes and Drums of the
4th Royal Tank Regiment
Vol. 1 - Droit Music DR 71 1984
Vol. 2 - Droit Music DR 72 1985
Vol. 3 - Droit Music DR 73 1985
Vol. 4 - Droit Music DR 74 1986
Directors of Music: Major G. Turner MBE and
Pipe Major M. Harden BEM

**Regimental Marches of the British Army Volume 1 (Chan 6563)
and Volume 2 (Chan 6564)**
The Regimental Band of the Coldstream Guards
Chandos Records Ltd.: Collection Series ©1991
Director of Music: Major T. L. Sharpe MBE, (Vol. 1 & 2) and
Captain R. A. Ridings (Vol. 2)

Regimental Marches of the British Army Volume 3
The Regimental Band of the Coldstream Guards
Polydor Records - Super 2383 409   ©1976
Director of Music: Captain R. A. Ridings

Marches of the Vanishing Regiments
The Band of the Royal Military School of Music, Kneller Hall
BBC Records TRC 1033
Director of Music: Lt. Col. C. H. Jaeger OBE

Regimental Marches of the British Army
Band of The Royal Military School of Music, Kneller Hall
Angels Records - Ang 35609
Director of Music: Lieutenant Colonel D. McBain OBE

March with Armour
The Band of the Junior Leaders Regiment Royal Armoured Corps
RCA LSA 3272 1976
Director of Music: Captain D. H. Mackay

Appendix C

Song Lyrics

A Hundred Pipers
Wi' a hundred pipers an' a' an a',
Wi a hundred pipers an' a' an' a';
We'll up an' gie them a blaw a blaw,
Wi' a hundred pipers an' a' an' a'.

Oh! it's wore the Border awa', awa'
It's wore the border awa' awa',
We'll on and we'll march to Carlisle ha',
Wi' its yetts, its castell, an a' an' a'.

Oh! our sodger lads looked braw, looked braw,
Wi' their tatans, kilts an' a, an' a',
Wi' their bonnets, an feathers, an glittering gear,
An pibrochs sounding sweet and clear.

Will they a' return to their dear glen?
Will they a' return, our Hieland men?
Second-sighted Sandy looked fu' wae,
And mothers grat when they marched away.

Oh wha is foremost o' a', o' a'?
Oh wha does follow the blaw, the blaw?
Bonnie Charlie, the king o' us a', hurra!
Wi' his hundred pipers an a', an' a'.

His bonnet an' feather, he's wavin high,
His prancin' steed maist seems to fly,
The nor' wind plays wi' his curly hair,
While the pipers in an unco flare.

The Esk was swollen, sae red and sae deep,
But shouther the brave lads keep;
Twa thousand swam owre to fell English ground,
An' danced themselves dry to the pibroch's sound.

Dumfounder'd the English saw — they saw —
Dumfounder'd, they heard the blaw, the blaw;
Dumfounder, they a' ran awa', awa',
From the hundred pipers an' a', an' a'

The Banks of Newfoundland
You ramblin boys of Liverpool, I'll have you to beware,
When you go in a Yankee packet ship, no dungarees to wear,
But have your monkey jacket always at your command,
For beware of the cold nor' westers on the Banks of Newfoundland.

Chorus
We'll wash her and we'll scrub her with holy stone and sand,
And we'll bid adieu to Virgin Rocks on the Banks of Newfoundland.

We had some Irishman on board, Jim Dayle and Michael Moore,
'Twas in the winter of '56 our sailors suffered sore,
Thye pawned their clothes in Liverpool and sold them out of hand,
Not thinking of those cruel winds on the Banks of Newfoundland.

One night as I lay on my bed a dreaming of my home,
I dreamt I wa in Liverpool way down in Marabone,
With my true love beside me and a jug of ale in hand—
But I woke quite broken-hearted on the Banks of Newfoundland.

We had one female kind on board, Mary Murphy was her name
To her I promised marriage, on me she laid a claim,
She tore her flannel petticoats to make mittens for my hands,
Saying "I can't see my true love freeze on the Banks of Newfoundland."

It's now we're passing Sandy Hook and cold winds they still blow
The tug-boat she's ahead of us to New York we will go,
We'll fill our glasses brimming full with a jug of rum in hand,
And bid adieu to the hardships and the Banks of Newfoundland.

So, Boys, fill up your glasses, and merrily they'll go round
And we'll drink a health to the Captain and the girls of New York Town.

Blue Bonnets Are Over The Border
March! March! Ettrich and Teviotdale,
Why, the deil, dinna ye march forward in order?
March! March! Eskdale and Liddesdale.
All the Bonnets are over the Border.

Many a banner spread flutters above your head,
Many a crest that is famous in story;
Mount and make ready then, sons of the mountain glen,
Fight for your king and the old Scottish glory.

Come from the hills where your hirsels are grazing,
Come from the glen of the buck and the roe;
Come to the crag where the beacon is blazing,
Come with the buckler, the lance and the bow.

Trumpets are sounding, warsteeds are bounding,
Stand to your arms, and march in good order;
England shall many tell of the bloody frag,
When the Blue Bonnets came over the border.

Bonnie Dundee
To the Lairds of Convention 'twas Claverhouse spoke:
"Ere the King's crown go down there are crowns to be broke,
Then let each cavalier who honour and me,
Let him follow the bonnets of Bonnie Dundee."

Chorus: (after each verse)
Come fill up my cup, come fill up my can,
Saddle my horse and call up my men;
Then awa' to the west port and let us go free,
For it's up wi' the bonnets of Bonnie Dundee.

Dundee he is mounted, he rides up the street,
The bells they ring backwards, the drums they are beat,
But the Provost said, "Just e'en let em be,
For this town is weel rid o' that de'il of Dundee."

There are hills beyond Pentland, and lands beyond Forth,
Be there lords in the south, there are chiefs in the north;
There are brave Duinnewassels three thousand times three,
Will cry "Hey for the bonnets o' Bonnie Dundee."

Then awa' to the hills, to the lea, to the rocks,
Ere I own a usurper I'll crouch with the fox,

And tremble, false Whigs, in the midst o' your glee,
Ye hae no seen the last o' my bonnets and me.

British Grenadiers
Some talk of Alexander,
And some of Hercules,
Of Hector and Lysander,
And such great names as these.
But of all the world's brave heroes,
There's none that can compare,
With a tow row row row row row
To the British Grenadiers.

When ever we are commanded
To storm the palisades,
Our leaders march with fuses
And we with hand grenades.
We throw them from the glacis
About the enemy's ears,
With a tow row row row row row
To the British Grenadiers.

And when the siege is over,
We to the town repair
The townsmen cry hurrah boys
Here comes a Grenadier,
Here comes a Grenadier, my boys
Who know no doubts or fears,
Then sing a tow row row row row row
For the British Grenadiers.

Then let us fill a bumper
And drink a health to those
Who carry caps and pouches
And wear the Louped Clothes,
May they and their Commanders
Live happy all their years,
With a tow row row row row row
For the British Grenadiers.

Ça Ira
Everything will go, it will go.
Hang the noble lords on every lamppost!

Yes, it will go, it will go, it will go.
All the noble lords in the streets shall swing!
Hang them and burn them and break their bones,
Down with 'em all from altars and thrones!
Yes, it will go, it will go, it will go,
Hang the noble lords on every lamppost—
Lords in the streets shall swing!

Ah! Ça ira, ça ira, ça ira
Les aristocrats à la lanterne!
Ah! Ça ira, ça ira, ça ira
Les aristocrats on les pendra!
Si'on n'les pend, on les romp'ra,
Si'on n'les pend, on les brûl'ra!

Ah! Ça ira, ça ira, ça ira
Les aristocrats à la lanterne!
Ah! Ça ira, ça ira, ça ira
Les aristocrats on.

The Campbells are Coming
The Campbells are Coming, O-OH, O-OH,
The Campbells are Coming, O-OH, O-OH,
The Campbells are coming, to Bonnie Lochleven,
Upon the Lomonds I lay, I lay,
Upon the Lomonds I lay, I Lay,
I looked down to Bonnie Lochleven,
And saw three bonnie pipers play.

The Campbells are coming, O-OH, O-OH,
The Campbells are coming, O-OH,O-OH,
The Campbells are coming to bonnie Lochkeven,
The great Argyle he guns before,
He makes the cannons and guns to roar;
Wi' sound O' trumpet, pipe and drum,
The Campbells are coming, O-OH, O-OH.

The Campbells are coming, O-OH, O-OH,
The Campbells are coming, O-OH, O-OH,
The Campbells are coming, to bonnie Lochleven,
The Campbells they are a' in arms,
Their loyal faith and truth to show;
Wi' banners rattin' in the wind,
The Campbells are coming, O-OH, O-OH.

Colonel Bogey
Good Luck, and the same to you,
Good Luck in everything you do,
Black outs can never blot out
The silver lining that comes shining through
(No we're not downhearted)
Britain is going to smile and grin,
Britain is going to fight and win,
Cheer up, the skies will clear up
And soon our boys will be home once again.

Corps March of the Royal Canadian Corps of Signals (Begone Dull Care)
Begone, Dull Care! I prithee be gone from me!
Begone, Dull Care! You and I shall never agree.
Long time hast thou been tarrying here, and fain thou wouldst me kill;
But' faith, dull care! Thou never shalt have thy will.

Too much care will make a young man turn grey,
And too much care will turn an old man to clay.
My wife shall dance and I will sing, so merrily pass the day,
For I hold it one of the wisest things, to drive dull care away.

Begone, dull care! I'll none of thy company;
Begone, dull care! Thou art no pair for me.
We'll pass the cheerful word along, As merrily goes the day,
And then at night, in a cheerful song, We'll drive dull care away.

El Abanico (The Fan)
Roll up your blankets, ready for kit inspection
Here comes the Major bloke looking in my direction
Buttons and bootblack, somebody swiped me razor
Blooming great pack
Breaking me back;
Ain't it grand!

Chorus:
We'd be for better off in the band
We'd be for better off in the band
Oh ain't it a lovely game.
Every the same.
We'd be far better off in the band.

We've got our orders, moving away at daybreak;
No where and back again, only to make your heart ache;

270

Seems sort of stupid, wearing the army's boots out,
Walking around,
Spoiling the ground
Every day.

Loaded with a pack and a rifle, march and march again.
Halting in the dust and sunshine; marching in the rain
When we're feeling and weary, still the same old cry;
Left right, left right in step, We'll rest in the sweet bye and bye.

World War II version:
Roll up you tarp, ready for inspection,
Here comes the Major-bloke looking in my direction,
Track jack — jerry can — somebody swiped me greaser!
Smeared to hell with p.o.i.
Ain't life grand.

Oh, for we wouldn't be infantr'ee
Nor we wouldn't want to Ar-tilr'ee
We would rather by far, stay as we are,
The boys of the R.C.A.C.

What's that urgent call
That's coming on the blower,
What's that he says—
We attack tomorrow

Lets down the beer!
Pack up your gear!

We've got our orders, moving away at daybreak,
Garry's in the load again. Up for another clambake,
Things are impeded, that's why we are needed—
Up the Garrys! Roll-l-l- the Garry's!!
We're on our way.

When you see a tank take a hull down, boy, you'd better jump,
For we mean to put the infantier boys on their final hump,
Then into the forward rally, ready—to do it again,
Re-stock ammo, check your guns,
We'll rest in the dear bye and bye.

But we sure wouldn't be Infatr'ee,
Nor would we want to be artillr'ee.
We would rather stay as we are,
The boys of the R.C.A.C

Fare Thee Well Enniskillen

Our troop was made ready at the dawn of the day
From lovely Enniskillen they were marching us away
They put us then on aboard a ship to cross the raging main
To fight in bloody battle in the sunny land of Spain.

Chorus (after each verse)
Fare thee well Enniskillen, fare thee well for a while
All around the borders of Erin's green isle
And when the was is over we'll return in full bloom
And you'll welcome home your Enniskillen Dragoon.

Oh Spain it is a gallant land where wine and ale flow free
There's lots of lovely women there to dangle on your knee
And often in a tavern there we'd make the rafters ring
When every soldier in the house would raise his glass and sing.

Well we fought for Ireland's glory there and many a man did fall
From musket and from bayonet and from thundering cannonball
And many a foeman we laid upon the battle ground
And as prepare for action you would hear us sing this song.

Well now the fighting's over and for home we have set sail
The flag above this lofty ship is fluttering in the gale
They're giving us a pension when the ship docks at the quay
And when we reach Enniskillen never more we'll have to sing.

Farmer's Boy

The sun went down, beyond the hills
Across yon dreary moor
When weary and lame, a boy there came,
Up to the farmer's door
May I ask you, if any there be
That will give me employ?
To plough and sow, to reap and mow
And to be a farmer's boy.
May I ask you, if any there be
That will give me employ?
To plough and sow, to reap and mow
And to be a farmer's boy.

And if that thou won't me employ
One thing I have to ask
Will you shelter me, till break of day

From this cold wintry blast?
At break of day I'll trudge away
Elsewhere to seek employ
To plough and sow, to reap and mow
And to be a farmer's boy
At break of day I'll trudge away
Elsewhere to seek employ
To plough and sow, to reap and mow
And to be a farmer's boy

My father's dead, my mother's left
With her five children small
And what is worse for mother still
I'm the eldest of them all
Though little I be, I fear not work
It thou wilt me employ?
To plough and sow, to reap and mow
And to be a farmer's boy
Though little I be, I fear not work
It thou wilt me employ?
To plough and sow, to reap and mow
And to be a farmer's boy

In course of time, he grew a man
The good old farmer died
And left the boy the farm now has
And his daughter for his bride
That boy that was, the farm now has
He thanks and smiles with joy
Of the lucky day, he came that way
For to be a farmer's boy.
That boy that was, the farm now has
He thanks and smiles with joy
Of the lucky day, he came that way
For to be a farmer's boy.

Garry Owen
Let Bacchus' sons be not dismayed,
But join with me each jovial blade;
Come, booze and sing and lend me aid,
To help me with the chorus.

Chorus (after each verse)
Instead of spa we'll drink down ale,
And pay the reckoning on the nail,
For debt no man shall go to jail
From Garryowen in glory!

We are the boys who take delight in
Smashing the Limerick lamps when lighting,
Through the street like sporters fighting
And tearing all before us.

We'll break windows, we'll break doors,
The watch knock down by threes and fours,
Then let the doctors work their cures,
And tinker up our bruises.

We'll beat the bailiffs out of fun,
We'll make the mayor and sheriffs run,
We are the boys no man dares dun,
If he regards a whole skin.

Our hearts, so stout, have got us fame,
For soon 'tis known from whence we came;
Where'er we go they dread the name,
Of Garryowen in glory.

Johnny Connell's tall and straight,
And in his limbs he is complete;
He'll pitch a bar of any weight,
From Garryowen to Thomond Gate.

Garryowen is gone to wrack
Since Johnny Connell went to Cork,
Though Darby O'Brien leaped over the dock,
In spite of all the soldiers.

God Bless The Prince of Wales
There was born one day
To our Gracious Queen
And her Consort fair and wise,
A Prince who brought
Such infinite joy
As the Heir to an Ancient Line.
This much beloved Prince
In whose veins there run

Many bloods side by side
Has been chosen by God
To serve in his time
Over peoples far and wide.

After his training long we sing this song
As he stands on the threshold of life.
In this year of grace he can show his face
To the ever eager crowds
As The Prince of Wales he now is acclaimed
And we wish him all happiness.

God bless our Prince
Our fine young Prince
God bless The Prince of Wales.
We wish him health
We wish him wealth
God bless the Prince of Wales.

May his future be bright
And free from strife
In his time may he see
All peoples on earth to agree.
Living side by side contentedly
And so fulfill his destiny.

God bless our Prince
Our fine young Prince
God bless The Prince of Wales.
We wish him health
We wish him wealth
God bless the Prince of Wales

Greensleeves
Alas my love, you do me wrong
To cast me off, discourteously
And I have loved you so long
Delight in your company.

Chorus
Greensleeves was all my joy
Greensleeves was all my delight
Greensleeves my heart of gold
And but my Lady Greensleeves

I have been ready at your hand
To grant whatever you would crave;
I have both waged life and land,
Your love and good will for it have.

I bought kerchers to thy head,
That were wrought fine and gallantly;
I kept thee both at board and bed,
Which cost my purse well favouredly.

I bought thee petticoats of the best,
The cloth so fine as fine might be;
I gave thee jewels for thy chest,
And all this cost I spent on thee.

Thy purse and eke thy agy gilt knives,
Thy pincase gallant to the eye;
No better wore the burgess wives,
And yet thou wouldst not love me.

The Grenadiers' March
First and third verses:
Come my lads, let's march away,
Let drums beat and pipes play.
I think it a twelvemonth every day,
Till the rebels are confounded.

We'll drown Argyle in the raging sea
Bring rampant Monmouth to his knee
And cuckold Grey to triple tree,
With a number of lay elders.

Heart of Oak
Chorus (after each verse)
Heart of Oak are our ships,
Heart of Oak are our men,
We always are ready,
Steady boys steady,
We'll fight and well conquer again and again.

Come, cheer up, my lads tis to glory we steer,
To add something more to this wonderful year,
To honour we call you, not press you like slaves,
For who are so free as the sons of the waves?

276

We ne'er see our foes but we wish 'em to stay,
They never see us but they wish us away,
If they run, why we follow and run 'em ashore,
If they won't fight us, we cannot do more.

They swear they'll invade us, these terrible foes,
They frighten our women, our children and beaux,
But should their flat bottoms in darkness get o'er,
Still Britons they'll find to receive them on shore.

We'll still make 'em run and we'll still make 'em sweat
In spite of the devil and Brussels Gazette.
Then cheer up lads, with one heart let us sing,
Our soldiers, our sailors, our statesmen and King.

Here's to the Maiden
Here's to the maiden of bashful fifteen,
Now to the widow of fifty;
Here's to the flaunting extravagant queen,
And here's to the housewife that's thrifty.

Chorus
Let the toast pass, Drink to the lass,
I warrant she'll prove an excuse for the glass.
Let the toast pass, Drink to the lass,
I warrant she'll prove an excuse for the glass.

Here's to the chamer whose dimples we prize,
Now to the damsel with none, sir,
Here's to the girl with a pair of blue eyes,
And now to the nymph with but one, sir.

Here's to maid with bosom of snow,
Now to her that's as brown as a berry,
Here's to the wife with a face full of woe,
And now to the damsel that's merry.

For let her be clumsy, or let her be slim,
Young or ancient, I care not a feather;
So fill up a bumper, nay, fill to the brim,
And let us e'en toast'em together.

Highland Laddie or Hielan Laddie

The bonniest lad that e'er I saw,
Bonnie laddie, Highland laddie;
Wore a plaid and was fu' braw,
Bonnie Highland laddie.
On his head a bonnet blue,
Bonnie laddie, Highland laddie;
His loyal heart was firm and true,
Bonnie Highland laddie.

Trumpets sound, and cannons roar,
Bonnie lassie, Lowland lassie;
And a' the hills wi' echoes roar,
Bonnie Lowland lassie.
Glory, honour, now invite,
Bonnie lassie, Lowland lassie,
For freedom and my king to fight,
Bonnie Lowland lassie.

The sun a backward course shall take,
Bonnie laddie, Highland laddie;
Ere aught thy manly courage shake
Bonnie Highland laddie
Go! for yoursel' procure renown,
Bonnie laddie, Highland laddie
And for your lawful king, his crown,
Bonnie Highland laddie.

I'm Ninety-Five

I'm ninety-five, I'm ninety-five,
And to keep single I'll contrive.
I'll not get married — no, not I —
To have five brats to squall and cry.
A fortune teller told me so
But I'll resist her tale of woe.

I'm ninety-five, I'm ninety-five,
And to keep single I'll contrive.
I'll not be bound, to be for life,
Some man's mere toy or wedded wife,
To bake and brew, to screw and save,
And be my husband humble slave.

I'm ninety-five, I'm ninety-five,
And to keep single I'll contrive.
And I will let the fellows see,
That none make a fool of me;
To darn their socks and mend their clothes,
To suit their whims and take their blows.

John Peel

D'ye ken John Peel with his coat so gay?
D'ye ken John Peel at the break of the day?
D'ye ken John Peel when he's far, far away,
With his hounds and his horn in the morning.

Twas the sound of his horn brought me from my bed
And the cry of his hounds which he of times led
For Peel's view holloa would awaken the dead
Or the fox from his lair in the morning.

Do ye ken that hound whose voice is death?
Do ye ken her sons of peerless faith
Do ye ken that a fox with his breath
Cursed them all as he died in the morning?

Yes, I ken John Peel and auld Ruby, too
Ranter and Royal and Bellman so true,
From the drag to the chase, from the chase to the view
From a view to the death in the morning.

And I've followed John Peel both often and far
O'er the rasper fence and the gate and the bar
From Low Denton Holme to the Scratchmere Scar
When we vied for the brush in the morning.

Then here's to John Peel with my heart and soul,
Come fill, fill to him a brimming bowl
for we'll follow John Peel thro fair or thro foul,
While we're waked by his horn in the morning.

Keel Row

As I came thro' Sandgate,
Thro' Sandgate, thro' Sandgate
I came thro' Sandgate
I Heard a lassie sing:
"O weel may The Keel Row

The Keel Row, The Keel Row
O weel may The Keel Row,
That my laddie's in.

O wae's like my Johnny,
Sae liesh, sae blithe, sae Johhny?
He's foremost amony the mony
Keel lads O'coaly tyne;
He'll set and row so tightly
Or in the dance—so sprightly
He'll cut and shuffle slightly
"Tis true—were he not mine

He wears a Blue Bonnet
Blue Bonnet, Blue Bonnet;
He wears a Blue Bonnet,
A dimple in his chin;
And weel may the Keel Row
The Keel Row The Keel Row;
And weel may The Keel Row
That my Laddie's in.

Lili Marlene

Underneath the lantern by the barrack gate,
Darling I remember the way you used to wait;
"Twas there that you whispered tenderly,
That you loved me, you'd always be,
My Lilli of the lamplight,
My own Lilli Marlene

Time would come for roll call, time for us to part,
Darling I'd caress you and press you to my heart
And there 'neath that far off lantern light,
I'd hold you tight, we'd kiss "Good-night",
My Lilli of the lamplight,
My own Lilli Marlene

Orders came for sailing somewhere over there
All confined to barracks was more than I could bear
I knew your were waiting in the street,
I heard your feet, But could not meet,
Resting in a billet just behind the line,
Even tho' we're parted your lips are close to mine;

Resting in a billet just behind the line,
Even tho' we're parted your lips are close to mine
You wait where that lantern softly gleams,
Your sweet face seems to haunt my dreams,
My Lilli of the lamplight,
My own Lilli Marlene.

The Lincolnshire Poacher

When I was bound apprentice, in famous Lincolnshire,
Fell well I serv'd my master for more than seven year,
Till I took up to poaching, as you will quickly hear:
Oh! tis my delight on a shining night, in the season of the year.

As me and my comrade were setting of a snare
Twas then we spied the gamekeeper, for him we did not care,
For we can wrestle and fight, my boys, and jump o'er anywhere,
Oh! tis my delight on a shining night, in the season of the year.

As me and my comrade were setting four or five
And taking on 'em up again, we caught a hare alive,
We took the alive, my boys, and thru the woods did steer
Oh! tis my delight on a shining night, in the season of the year.

I threw him on my shoulder and then we trudge home
We took him to a neighbours home, and sold him for a crown
We sold him for a crown, my boys, but I did not tell you where
Oh! tis my delight on a shining night, in the season of the year.

Success to any gentleman that live in Lincolnshire
Success to every poacher that wants to sell a hare
Bad luck to every gamekeeper that will not sell his deer
Oh! tis my delight on a shining night, in the season of the year.

Lutzow's Wild Hunt

From yonder dark forest what horsemen advance?
What sounds from the rocks are rebounding?
The sunbeams are gleaming on sword and on lance,
And loud the shrill trumpet is sounding,
And loud the shrill trumpet is sounding,
And if you ask what you there behold,
Tis the hunt of Lutzow the free and the bold.

Why roars in yon valley the deadly fight?
What glittering sounds are clashing,

Our true hearted riders maintain the right,
And the torch of freedom is flashing,
And the torch of freedom is flashing,
And if you ask what you there behold,
Tis the hunt of Lutzow the free and the bold.

Tis our hunt! the proud tyrant and dastardly slave,
Before our hunters are flying,
And weep not for us, if our country we save,
Although we have saved it dying!
Although we have saved it dying.
From age to age, it shall still be told,
Twas the hunt of Lutzow's the free and the bold.

Maple Leaf Forever
In days of yore, from Britain's shore,
Wolfe, the dauntless hero came,
And planted firm Britannia's flag
On Canada's fair domain.
Here may it wave, our boast, our pride,
And joined in love together,
The Thistle, Shamrock, Rose entwine
The Maple Leaf Forever!

Chorus (after each verse)
The Maple Leaf, our emblem dear
The Maple Leaf forever! God save our King
And Heaven bless The Maple Leaf forever!

At Queenston Heights and Lundy's Lane,
Our brave fathers, side by side,
For freedom, homes, and loved ones dear
Firmly stood and nobly died:
And those dear rights which they maintained,
We swear to yield them never!
Our watch-world ever more shall be
The Maple Leaf forever!

On merry England's far-famed land
May kind heaven sweetly smile;
God bless old Scotland ever more,
And Ireland's emerald isle!
Then swell the song, both loud and long,

Till rocks and forests quiver,
God save our King, and Heaven bless
The Maple Leaf forever.

March of the Cameron Men
In the whole of the Cameron Clan there is not one brave
youth who will not serve willingly under the banner of
Lochiel. In victory or in death, they will be faithful in
every circumstance, because a Cameron never yield.

Chorus
Do you not hear the sounding of the bagpipe approaching,
High over moorland and glen, and light footsteps tread
The heather. It is the March of the Cameron Men!
It is the March, It is the March, It is the march of the Cameron Men.

Sprightly are their although each one is aware that
he may under the sod tomorrow, but every hero is
without fear who goes with his chief to the fray, where
it was customary for them to win victory and fame.

Marianne s'en va-t-au moulin (Marianne is Going to the Mill)
Marianne wanders to the mill,
Marianne wanders to the mill,
With grain to grind her sack to fill,
With grain to grind her sack to fill,
Her donkey for a pony,
Marianne wee and bonny,
For pony just her donkey named Jill,
All wand'ring to the mill.

The miller, when he saw her,
The miller, when he saw her,
Ran up at once to say "My dear,
Ran up at once to say "My dear,
Hitch up your donkey pony,
Marianne, wee and bonny,
Hitch up your donkey pony, named Jill,
Back there behind the mill."

And while the mill the grain it ground,
And while the mill the grain it ground,
The wolf was prowling all around
The wolf was prowling all around

And ate the donkey pony,
Marianne, wee and bonny,
The wolf ate up the donkey, named Jill,
Back there behind the mill.

Marianne then in grief was drowned.
Marianne then in grief was drowned.
Her gave her a hundred pound,
Her gave her a hundred pound,
To buy a donkey pony,
Marianne, wee and bonny,
To buy another donkey, named Jill,
All going home from the mill.

Her father when he saw her near,
Her father when he saw her near,
Could only — "What have you dear.
Could only — "What have you dear.
Done with your donkey pony?
Marianne, wee and bonny,
What have you done with your donkey, named Jill,
All wandering to the mill?"

To-day, it is St. Michael's day
To-day, it is St. Michael's day
When donkeys change their skins, they say.
When donkeys change their skins, they say.
I bring the donkey pony,
Marianne, wee and bonny,
"I bring the same old donkey, named Jill,
Who brought me to the mill."

Men of Harlech
Men of Harlech, in the hollow,
Do ye hear like rushing billow?
Wave on wave that surging follow,
Battle's distant sound.

Tis the tramp of Saxon foeman,
Saxon spearmen, Saxon bowmen.
Be they knights or hinds or yeomen,
They shall bite the ground!

Loose the folds a sunder,
Flag we conquer under.
The placid sky now bright on high,
Shall launch its bolted in thunder.

Onward, 'tis our Country needs us;
He is bravest he who leads us.
Honour's self now proudly leads us,
Freedom, God and Right!

Rocky steeps, and passes narrow,
Flashes with spear and flights of arrows.
Who would think of death or sorrow?
Death is glory now!

Hurl the reeling horsemen over,
Let the earth dead foeman cover.
Fate of friend, of wife, of lover,
Trembles on a blow.

Strands of life are riven.
Blow for blow is given.
In deadly lock or battle shock,
And mercy shrieks to heaven.

Men of Harlech, young or hoary,
Would you win a name in story?
Fight for home, for life, for glory,
Freedom, God, and Right!

My Boy Willie
Oh. where have you been all the day
My boy Willie,
Oh, where have you been all the day?
Oh, Willie, won't you tell me now?
Oh, where have you been all the day?
I've been all the day courting of a lady gay
But she is too young to be taken from her mother.

Oh, can she brew and can she bake,
My boy Willie,
Oh, can she brew and can she bake?
Oh, Willie won't you tell me now?
She can brew and she can bake,

She can make a wedding cake,
But she is too young to be taken from her mother.

Oh, can she knit and can she spin
My boy Willie,
Oh, can she knit and can she spin?
Oh, Willie won't you tell me now?
She can knit and she can spin
She can do most anything
But she too young to be taken from her mother.

Oh, how old is she now
My boy Willie,
Oh, how old is she now?
Oh, Willie won't you tell me now?
Two time six, two time seven,
Two time twenty and eleven,
But she is too young to be taken from her mother.

Onward Christian Soldiers
Onward Christian Soldiers, Marching as to war,
With the cross of Jesus, going on before;
Christ, the royal master, Lads against the foe,
Forward into battle, see his banners go!

Chorus: (after each verse)
Onward Christian Soldiers, Marching as to war,
With the cross of Jesus, going on before;

Like a mighty army, Moves the church of God;
Brothers we are treading, Were the saints have trod;
We are not divided, All one body we,
One in hope, in doctrine, one in charity.

Crowns and thrones may perish, Kingdoms rise and wane,
But the Church of Jesus, Constant will remain;
Gates of hell can never, 'Gainst that Church prevail;
We have Christ's own promise, And that cannot fail.

At the sign of triumph, Satan's legions flee;
On then, Christian soldiers, on the victory!
Hell's foundation quiver, At the shout of praise;
Brothers, lift your voices, Loud your anthems raise.

Pibroch of Donuil Dhub (Piobaireach of Donald Dhu)
Pibroch of Donuil Dhu,
Pibroch of Donuil
Wake thy wild voice anew,
Summon Clan Conuil.
Come away, come away,
Hark to the summons!
Come in your war array,
Gentles and commons.

Chorus
Come away, come away,
Hark to the summons!
Come in your war array,
Gentles and commons.

Come from deep glens and
From mountain so rocky
The war pipe and pennon
Are at Inverlocky;
Come every hill-plaid, and
True heart that wears one,
Come every steel blade, and
Strong hand that bears one.

Leave untended the herd,
The flock without shelter;
Leave the corpse uninterr'd
The bride at the alter;
Leave the deer, leave the steer,
Leave nets and barges;
Come with your fighting gear,
Broadswords and targes

Come as the winds come, when
Forests are rended;
Come as the waves come, when
Navies are stranded;
Faster come, faster come,
Faster and faster
Chief, vassal, page and groom,
Tenant and master.

Faster they come, faster they come;
See how they gather!
Wide waves the eagle plume,
Blended with heather,
Cast your plaids, draw your blades
Forward each man set:
Pibroch of Donuil Dhu
Knell for the onset.

Pork, Beans & Hard Tack
Our volunteers are soldiers bold, so say the people all,
When duty call they spring to arms, responsive to the call.
With outfits old and rations clothes ill-fitted for the strife,
They leave their homes on starving pay to take the nitchies life.

Faint, cold, and weary we're packed on an open car,
Arriving our fate and grumbling as soldiers ever are.
Hanging and thirsty over the CPR, we go,
Instead of by the all-rail route, Detroit & Chicago.

On half-cooked beans and fat pork we've fed without relief,
Save when we get a chance of grub on hard-tack and corn beef.
On fatigue and guards all day, patrols and pickets by night,
It's this we while our time away, our duty seems ne'er to fight.

Dawns the wild Saskatchewan in rivers boats we go,
At last we reach Lake Winnipeg where a tug takes us in tow
On board a barge two regiments are shoved into the hold
Like sardines in a box we're packed, six hundred men all told.

Dawn the length of Winnipeg Lake we roll throughout the night,
And on we're towed along the Lake till Selkirk is in sight.
We disembark in double-quick time, we once more board a train;
We're on our way for Winnipeg, we're getting near home again.

In rags we march the prairie most eager for the fray'
But when we near the enemy they always run away.
As Corporation labourers with fatigue each day
We dig and scrape and hoe and rake for fifty cents a day.

Refrain: (after each verse)
Pork, beans and hard tack Tra la la la la la la
Poor hungry soldiers Tra la la la la la la.

288

In rags we march the prairie, most eager for the fray,
But when we near the enemy they always run away.
As Corporation labourers with fatigue each day,
We dig and scrape and hoe and rake for fifty cents a day.

Princess Patricia's Canadian Light Infantry Regimental March
(Has Anyone Seen The Colonel?, It's a Long Way to Tipperary,
Mademoiselle from Armentieres)
Has Anyone Seen The Colonel
Has anyone seen the Colonel?
I know where he is,
I know where he is, I know where he is,
Has anyone seen the Colonel?
I know where he is,
He's dining with the Brigadier.
How do you know?
I saw him, I saw him, dining with the Brigadier,
I saw him, dining with the Brigadier.

Has anyone seen the Major?
I know where he is,
I know where he is, I know where he is,
Has anyone seen the Major?
I know where he is,
He's down in the deep dug-out.
How do you know?
I saw him, I saw him, down in the deep dug-out,
I saw him, down in the deep dug-out.

Has anyone seen the Captain?
I know where he is,
I know where he is, I know where he is,
Has anyone seen the Captain?
I know where he is,
He's away on six weeks leave.
How do you know?
I saw him, I saw him, away on six weeks' leave,
I saw him, away on six weeks' leave.

Has anyone seen the Subaltern?
I know where he is,
I know where he is, I know where he is,
Has anyone seen the Subaltern?

I know where he is,
He's out on a night patrol
How do you know?
I saw him, I saw him, out on a night patrol,
I saw him, out on a night patrol.

Has anyone seen the Sergeant-Major?
I know where he is,
I know where he is, I know where he is,
Has anyone seen the Sergeant-Major?
I know where he is,
He's drinking up the private's rum.
How do you know?
I saw him, I saw him, drinking up the Private's rum,
I saw him, drinking up the Private's rum.

Has anyone seen the Sergeant?
I know where he is,
I know where he is, I know where he is,
Has anyone seen the Sergeant?
I know where is he is.
He's lying on the canteen floor.
How do you know?
I saw him, I saw him, lying on the canteen floor
I saw him, lying on the canteen floor.

Has anyone seen the Corporal?
I know where he is,
I know where he is, I know where he is,
Has anyone seen the Corporal?
I know where he is,
He's hanging on the old barbed wire.
How do you know?
I saw him, I saw him, hanging on the old barbed wire,
I saw him, hanging on the old barbed wire.

Has anyone seen the Private?
I know where he is,
I know where he is, I know where he is,
Has anyone seen the Corporal?
I know where he is,
He's holding up the damn line.
How do you know?

I saw him, I saw him, holding up the whole damn line,
I saw him, holding up the whole damn line.

It's a Long Way To Tipperary
Up to mighty London came an Irishman one day,
As the streets are paved with gold, sure, ev'ry one was gay;
Singing songs of Piccadilly, Strand and Leicester Square,
Till Paddy got excited, then he shouted to them there:

Chorus (after each verse):
It's a long way to Tipperary,
It's a long way to go;
It's a long way to Tipperary
To the sweetest girl I know!
Goodbye-Piccadilly,
Farewell Leicester Square,
It's a long, long way to Tipperary
But my heart's right there!

Paddy wrote a letter to his Irish Molly O',
Saying "should you not receive it, write and let me know!
If I make mistakes in spelling, Molly dear," said he,
"Remember it's the pen that's bad, don't lay the blame on me."

Molly wrote a neat reply to Paddy O',
Saying "Mike Maloney wants to marry me, and so
Leave the Strand and Piccadilly, or you'll be to blame,
For love has fairly drove me silly — hoping you'll the same."

Mademoiselle From Armentieres
Mademoiselle from Armentieres, Parley-voo?
Mademoiselle from Armentieres, Parley-voo?
Mademoiselle from Armentieres,
She hasn't been kissed for forty years,
Hinky, dinky, parley-voo.

O Madame, have you a daughter fine, parlez-vous?
O Madame, have you a daughter fine, parlez-vous?
O Madame, have you a daughter fine,
Fit for a soldier of the line—
And his hinky pinky parlez-vous.

Mademoiselle has eyes of brown, parlez-vous.
Her golden hair is hanging down, parlez-vous.

With her golden hair and eyes of brown,
She's been kissed by all the troops in town—
And their hinky pinky parlez-vous.

The Colonel called on Mademoiselle, parlez-vous.
His carriage erect and his head as well, parlez-vous.
The Colonel called on Mademoiselle,
But she told him to go to hell—
With his hinky pinky parlez-vous.

Red River Valley
It was raining and hailing this morning
On the corner of Portage and Main;
Now it's noon and the basements are flooded
And the dust storms are starting again.

(*The words based on a Canadian version*):
From this valley they say you are going;
I will miss your bright eyes and sweet smile,
For they say you are taking the sunshine
That brightened our pathway awhile.

Chorus:
Come and sit by my side if you love me,
Do not hasten to bid me adieu,
But remember the Red River Valley,
And the cowboy who loved you so true.

I have promised you, darling, that never
Shall the words from my lips cause you pain,
And I swear I will love you forever
If you only will love me again.

As you go to your home by the ocean,
May you never forget those sweet hours,
That we spent in the Red River Valley,
And the love we exchanged 'mid the flowers.

REME Corps Marchpast (Aupres de ma Blonde and Lillibulero)

Aupres de ma Blonde
Oh, in my father's garden
The lilacs are in bloom,
Oh, in my fathers garden

The lilacs are in bloom
And all the birds are singing
To make their nests they come.

Chorus
Near to my fair one,
Oh, it's good, its good, it's good,
Near to my fair one,
Oh it's good to be!

The turtle-dove and quail
And partridge bright and gay,
The turtle-dove and quail
And partridge bright and gay,
And my white dove is singing,
She's singing night and day.

She's singing for the maidens,
For maids with husbands none,
She's singing for the maidens,
For maids with husbands none,
It's not for me she's singing,
For I've a handsome one.

But he is now in Holland,
A prisoner is he;
But he is now in Holland,
A prisoner is he;
"What would you give, my fine girl,
To have him back with thee?"

Oh, I would give Versailles,
Paris and St. Denis,
Oh, I would give Versailles,
Paris and St. Denis,
The towers of Notre Dame
And the bells of my country.

Lillibulero
Ho! brother Teague, dost hear the decree?
Lilli bulero, bullen a la;
Dat we shall have a new deputy,
Lilli bulero, bullen a la.

Chorus: (after each verse)
Lero, lero, lilli burlero,
Lilli burlero, bullen a la
Lero, lero, lero lero,
Lilli burlero, bullen a la.

Ho! by my soul, it is de Talbot,
Lilli bulero, bullen a la;
And he will cut all de English throat,
Lilli bulero, bullen a la.

Though, by my shoul, de English do praat,
Lilli bulero, bullen a la;
De law's on dare side, and creish knows what,
Lilli bulero, bullen a la.

But if dipense do come from de Pope
Lilli bulero, bullen a la;
We'll hang Magna Charta and dem in a rope
Lilli bulero, bullen a la.

And de good Talbot is made a lord,
Lilli bulero, bullen a la;
And he with brave lads is coming abroad.
Lilli bulero, bullen a la.

Who all in France have tauken a sware
Lilli bulero, bullen a la;
Dat de will have Protestant heir.
Lilli bulero, bullen a la.

Ara!, but why does he stay behind?
Lilli bulero, bullen a la;
Ho! by my shoul 'tis a Protestant wind.
Lilli bulero, bullen a la.

But see, de Tyrconnel is come ashore,
Lilli bulero, bullen a la;
And we shall have commissions gillore;
Lilli bulero, bullen a la.

And he dat will not go to mass
Lilli bulero, bullen a la;
Shall turn out, and look like an ass.
Lilli bulero, bullen a la.

But now de heretics all go down,
Lilli bulero, bullen a la;
By Creish and St. Patrick, de nation's our own.
Lilli bulero, bullen a la.

Dare was an old prophecy found ina bog,
Lilli bulero, bullen a la;
"Ireland shall be rules by an ass and a dog."
Lilli bulero, bullen a la.

And now dis prophecy is come to pass,
Lilli bulero, bullen a la;
For Talbot's de dog, and James is de ass.
Lilli bulero, bullen a la.

Rêves Canadiens

Sur les bords du Saint-Laurent Vit une autre France,
Tout un peuple jeune, ardent Remplide vaillance;
Qui prépare sa carrière Lirelon lirelon laire
Fait les rêves les plus beaux,
Lire lon laire, lire lon lo,
Qui prépare sa carrière,
Lire lon lire lon laire,
Fait les rêves les plus beaux,
Lire lon laire lon laire lo.

Royal Canadian Air Force Marchpast

RCAF Marchpast Trio:
Through adversities we'll conquer.
Blaze into the stars
A trail of glory
We'll live on land and sea
'till victory is won
Men in blue the skies are winging,
In each heart one thought is ringing.
Fight got the right
God is our might,
We shall be free.

The Royal Canadian Regiment

Oh! were crushing the gravel again to day.
And wearing out boots in the same old way,

For that is how we earn our pay, in the good old RCR.
With a Left, Right, Left, Oh! soon there'll be the devil to pay,
With a Left, Right, Left, Oh! gee what a rollicking lay.
And where ever we are we'll all ways sing,
As we march along with the same old swing,
That we don't give a hang for any thing in the good old RCR

Oh! we walk all other corps clean off their feet,
For our pace is a killer that none can beat,
Sure! mud pushing to us is no more than a treat in good old RCR.
With a left, right, left, with our bottles filled with something neat.
With a left, right, left, the smile on our faces is sweet,
Now the man on the 'orse is only a trotter,
The gunner of course is a noisy old rotter;
What we have and we'll hold is the tramp of the sodger in the good old RCR

We 're modest you know, so don't like to boast,
Of the time when we had poor Cronjie toast,
Anf Kruger went lickity pelt for the coast, Hooray for the RCR.
With a left, right, left, he very soon after did give up the ghost,
With a left, right, left, he reckoned without his host.
So take heed other nations and don't get us cross,
For we're armed with a rifle known as the Ross;
She shoots like a daisy and kicks like a hoss Hip, hip, for the RCR.

To the pathway of glory, we've ne'er had a rest,
Since the rebellion we quelled in the wolly Northwest,
Where Saskatchewan first claimed the blood our best, in the Good old RCR.
With a left, right, left, the rebels got more than they could digest
With a left, right, left, we fight like devils possessed,
As higher we mount on the scroll of fame
We hope for our country to fight yet again;
And still further glory and honour obtain, for the good old RCR.

Now there's one thing more we should like to say,
While we're pounding your bally old roads today
We wouldn't object to a little more pay in the good old RCR.
With a left, right, left, we're guarding your frontiers, night and day
With a left, right, left, we're keeping your foes at bay,
So when tucked up at night and cosy in bed,
With tummies well filled and your kiddles all fed,
Think of those who for you will face fire and lead in the good old RCR.

Scotland the Brave

Hark when the night is falling,
Hear, hear the pipes are calling,
Loudly and proudly calling,
Down through the glen.
There where the hills are sleeping,
Now feel the blood a-leaping,
High as the spirits of the old Highland men.

Towering in gallant fame,
Scotland, my mountain home
High may your proud standards gloriously wave.
Land of the high endeavour,
Land of the shining river,
Land of my heart for ever,
Scotland the Brave.

High in the misty Highlands,
Out by the purple islands,
Brave are the hearts that beat
Beneath Scottish skies.
Wild are the winds to meet you,
Staunch are the friends that greet you,
Kind as the love that shines
From fair maidens' eyes.

Soldiers of the Queen

Britons always loyally declaim, about the way we rule the waves.
Every Briton's song is just the same, when singing of our soldiers brave
All the world has heard it, wonders why we sing, and some learned the
reason why.
We're not forgetting it, we're not letting it
Fade away or gradually die; fade away or gradually die.
So when we say that England's master, remember who made her so.

Chorus (after each verse)
It's the soldier's of the Queen, my lads,
Who've been, my lads, who've seen, my lads,
In the fight for England's glory lads,
Of its world wide glory let us sing.
And when we say we've always won,
And when they ask us how it's done,
We'll proudly point to every one
Of England's soldiers of the Queen.

War clouds gather over land, our treaties threatened east and west.
Nations that we've shaken by the hand, our honoured pledges try to test.
They may have thought us sleeping, though us unprepared, because we
have our party wars.
But Britons all unite, when they're called to fight
The battle for old England's cause; the battle for old England's cause.
So when we say that England's master, remember who has made her so.

When we've roused we buckle on our swords, we've done with diplomatic
lingo.
We do deeds to hollow our words, we show we've something more than
jingo
The sons of merry England answered duty's call, and military duties do,
And though new at the game, they show them all the same,
An Englishman can be a soldier too; an Englishman can be a soldier too.
So when we say that England's master, remember who made her so.

St. Patrick's Day
Oh! blest be the days when the green banner floated,
Sublime o'er the mountains of free Innisfail;
Her sons to her glory and freedom devoted,
Defied the invader to tread her soul,
When back o'er the main they chas'd the Dane,
And gave to religion and learning their spoil:
But wherefore lament o'er the glories departed?
Her star shall sine out with as vivid a ray,
For ne'er had she children so brave and true-hearted,
As those she now sees on St. Patrick's Day.

Her sceptre, alas! pass'd away to the stranger,
And treason surrender'd where valour had held;
But true hearts remained amid darkness and danger;
Which spite of her tyrants would not be quell'd.
Oft', oft' thro' the night flashed gleams of light,
Which almost the darkness of bondage dispell'd;
But a star now is near her heaven to cheer,
Not like the wild gleams which so fitfully darted,
But long to shine out with a hallowing ray
On daughters as fair and sons as true-hearted,

As Erin beholds on St. Patrick's Day.
Oh! blest be the hour when begirt by her cannon,
And hail'd as it rose by anation's applause,

That falg wav'd aloft o'er the spire of Dungannon,
Asserting for Irishmen Irish laws.
Once more for shall it wave o'er hearts as brave,
Despite of the dastards who mock at her cause;
And like brothers agreed, whatever their creed,
Her children inspir'd by those desponding will stay,
No longer in darkness desponding will stay,
But join in her cause like the brave and true-hearted,
Who rise for their rights on St. Patrick's Day.

Vive la Canadienne

Pledge the Canadian maiden!
Soar my heart, oh soar on!
Pledge the Canadian maiden
And her sweet eyes that glow,
And her sweet eyes that glow, glow, glow,
And her sweet eyes that glow, and glow

We to wedding drive her,
Soar, my heart, oh soar on!
We to the wedding drive her,
At tired in fine trousseau,
At tired in fine trousseau, seau, seau,
At tired in fine trouseau, at seau.

There we chat on so freely,
Soar, my heart, oh soar on!
There we chat on so freely,
All have a good time too, etc

Good is the cheer they give us,
Soar, my heart, oh soar on!
Good is the cheer they give us,
We know our taste is true, etc

We and girls are dancing,
Soar, my heart, oh soar on!
We and blondes are dancing
And change our partners too, etc

So goes the time a-passing,
Soar, my heart, oh soar on!
So goes the time a-passing,
How sweet it is you know, etc.

Waltzing Matilda

Oh! there once was a swagman camped in the Billabong,
Under the shade of a Coolabah tree,
And he sang as he looked at his old billy boiling
"Who'll come a-waltzing Matilda with me?"

Who'll come a-waltzing Matilda my darling
Who'll come a-waltzing Matilda with me?
Waltzing Matilda and leading a waterbag,
Who'll come a-waltzing Matilda with me?

Down came a jumbuck to drink at the waterhole,
Up jumped the swagman and grabbed him in glee;
And he sang as he put him away in his tuckerbag,
"You'll come a-waltzing Matilda with me."

Down came the squatter a-riding his thoroughbred;
Down came the policeman - one, two, three.
"Whose is jumbuck you've got in the tuckerbag?
You'll came a waltzing Matilda with me."

But the swagman, he up and he jumped into the waterhole.
Drowning himself by the Coolabah tree.
And his ghost may be heard as it sings in the Billabong,
"Who'll come a-waltzing Matilda with me?"

Warwickshire Lads

Ye Warwickshire lads and ye lasses
See what at our Jubilee passes,
Come revel away, rejoice and be glad,
For the lad of all was a Warwickshire lad,
Warwickshire lad, Ever be glad,
For the lad of all was a Warwickshire lad.

Be proud of the charms of your country,
When nature has lavished her bounty;
Where much she has given, and some to be spared,
For the bard of all bards was a Warwickshire bard
Warwickshire bard, never paired,
For the bard of all bards was a Warwickshire bard.

Wings

Wings to bear me over mountains and vale away,
Wings to bathe my spirit in morning's sunny ray;
Wings that I might hover at morn above the sea,
Wings through life to bear me, and Death triumphantly.

Wings! like youth's fleet moments which swiftly o'er me passed
Wings! like my early visions, too bright too fair to last;
Wings! that I might recall them, the loved, the lost, the dead;
Wings! that I might fly after the past, long vanished.

Glossary

Canadian Forces present day ranks

Navy	Army	Air Force
Ordinary Seaman	Private	Private
Leading Seaman	Corporal	Corporal
Master Seaman	Master Corporal	Master Corporal
Petty Officer 2	Sergeant	Sergeant
Petty Officer 1	Warrant Officer	Warrant Officer
Chief Petty Officer 2	Master Warrant Officer	Master Warrant Officer
Chief Petty Officer 1	Chief Warrant Officer	Chief Warrant Officer
Officer Cadet	Officer Cadet	Officer Cadet
Sub Lieutenant	Lieutenant	Lieutenant
Lieutenant	Captain	Captain
Lieutenant Commander	Major	Major
Commander	Lieutenant Colonel	Lieutenant Colonel
Captain	Colonel	Colonel
Commodore	Brigadier General	Brigadier General
Rear Admiral	Major General	Major General
Vice Admiral	Lieutenant General	Lieutenant General
Admiral	General	General

Canadian Forces Ranks (Pre-Unification)

Navy	Army	Air Force
—	—	Aircraftman Second Class
—	Private	Aircraftman First Class
Ordinary Seaman	Lance Corporal	Leading Aircraftman
Able Seaman	Corporal	Corporal
Leading Seaman	Sergeant	Sergeant
Petty Officer	Staff Sergeant	Flight Sergeant
Chief Petty Officer	Warrant Officer II	Warrant Officer II
—	Warrant Officer I	Warrant Officer I
Midshipman	2nd Lieutenant	Pilot Officer
Sub Lieutenant	Lieutenant	Flying Officer
Lieutenant	Captain	Flight Lieutenant
Lieutenant Commander	Major	Squadron Leader
Commander	Lieutenant Colonel	Wing Commander
Captain	Colonel	Group Captain
Commodore	Brigadier	Air Commodore
Rear Admiral	Major General	Air Vice Marshal
Vice Admiral	Lieutenant General	Air Marshal
Admiral	General	Air Chief Marshal

Music Establishments and Degrees

AmusLCM	Associate in Music, London College of Music
AmusTCL	Associate in Music, Trinity College of Music
ARCM	Associate, Royal College of Music
BA	Bachelor of Arts
BMus	Bachelor of Music
CFSMUS	Canadian Forces School of Music
FLCM	Fellow London of Music
FRAM	Fellow Royal Academy of Music
FRSA	Fellow Royal Society of Arts
FTCL	Fellow Trinity College of Music
FVCM	Fellow Victoria College of Music
LGSM	Licentiate Guildhall School of Music
LmusLCM	Licentiate in Music, London College of Music
LmusTCL	Licentiate in Music, Trinity College of Music
LRAM	Licentiate Royal Academy of Music
LTCL	Licentiate Trinity College of Music
Mus Doc	Doctor of Music
psm	passed school of music (Royal Military School of Music)
Std BM	Student Band Master (Kneller Hall)

Musical Abbreviations

arr	Musical arranger/arrangement
Bdmn	Bandsman
BM	Bandmaster
BMjr	Bugle Major
bn/bsn	Bassoon
bs clt	Bass clarinet
BSgt	Band Sergeant
BSM	Band Sergeant Major
Civ BM	Civilian Bandmaster
cl/clar	Clarinet
DMjr	Drum Major
DoM	Director of Music
dr/drm	Drums, parade or taps
eu	Euphonium
fh/fhon	French Horn
fl	Flute
inst	Instrument/instrumental/instrumentation
Instr	Instructor
MoB	Master of Band
Mus Bac	Bachelor of Music
Musn	Musician
ob	oboe

perc	percussion
Pmajor or P/M	Pipe Major
SSgt	Staff Sergeant
sx/sax	alto/tenor/baritone
tb/tba	tuba
TMjr	Trumpet Major
tr/trb	trombone
ww	woodwinds

Other titles

ADC	Aide-de-Camp
Adjt	Adjutant
Bn	Battalion
Capt.	Captain
CBC	Canadian Broadcasting Corporation
CDS	Chief of the Defence Staff
CF	Canadian Forces
CFB	Canadian Forces Base
Cmdr	Commander
CO	Commanding Officer
Col	Colonel
Cpl	Corporal
CQSM	Company Quartermaster Sergeant
CSM	Company Sergeant Major
CWO	Chief Warrant Officer
DC	Director of Ceremonial
DND	Department of National Defence
Flt Lt	Flight Lieutenant
Gen	General
HM	His/Her Majesty
HMCS	Her/His Majesty's Canadian Ship
HMS	Her/His Majesty's Ship
HRH	His/Her Royal Highness
LCpl	Lance Corporal
Lt.	Lieutenant
Lt-Col	Lieutenant Colonel
Maj.	Major
Maj-Gen	Major General
MG	Machine Gun
MWO	Master Warrant Officer
NCO	Non Commissioned Officer
NDHQ	National Defence Headquarters, Ottawa
OC	Officer Commanding
Pte	Private
Regt	Regiment

Ret	Retired
RHQ	Regimental Headquarters
RQMS	Regimental Quartermaster Sergeant
RSM	Regimental Sergeant Major
S/Sgt	Staff Sergeant
Sgt	Sergeant
SHAEF	Supreme Headquarters, Allied Expeditionary Force
Sqn	Squadron
Tpr	Trooper
WO	Warrant Officer
WO1	Warrant Officer Class One
WO2	Warrant Officer Second Class

Awards and Decorations

CB	Companion of the Bath
CBE	Commander of the Order of British Empire
CD	Canadian Forces Decoration
CM	Member of the Order of Canada
CMG	Companion of the Order of St. Michael and St. George
CVO	Commander of the Royal Victorian Order
DCM	Distinguished Conduct Metal
DSO	Distinguished Service Order
ED	Efficiency Decoration
GC	George Cross
GCVO	Knight Grand Cross of the Victorian Order
IODE	Imperial Order of Daughters of the Empire
KCB	Knight Commander of the Bath
KT	Knight of the Thistle
LVO	Lieutenant of the Royal Victorian Order
MBE	Member of the Order of the British Empire
MC	Military Cross
MM	Military Metal
MMM	Member of the Order of Military Merit
MVO	Member of the Royal Victorian Order
OBE	Officer of the Order of the British Empire
OMM	Officer of the Order of Military Merit
TD	Territorial Army Decoration
VC	Victoria Cross
VD	Volunteer Officers' Decoration

List of units

1 RNBR	1st Battalion, The Royal New Brunswick Regiment
12e RBC	Le 12e Régiment blinde du Canada
1H	1st Hussars
2 Irish R of C	2nd Battalion, The Irish Regiment of Canada

2 RNBR (NS)	2nd Battalion, The Royal New Brunswick Regiment
4 R22eR	4e Bataillon, Royal 22e Régiment (Chateauguay)
4 RCR	4th Battalion, The Royal Canadian Regiment
48 Highrs	48th Highlanders of Canada
6 R22eR	6e Bataillon, Royal 22e Régiment
8CH	8th Canadian Hussars (Princess Louise's)
8th Recce	8th Reconnaissance Regiment (14th Canadian Hussars)
A & SH of C	Argyll and Sutherland Highlanders of Canada (Princess Louise's)
ALQ R	Algonquin Regiment
BCD	British Columbia Dragoons
BCR	British Columbia Regiment (Duke of Connaught's Own) (RCAC)
Brock Rif	Brockville Rifles
C Scot R	Canadian Scottish Regiment (Princess Mary's)
CAB	Canadian Armoured Brigade
CAC	Canadian Armoured Corps
Calg Highrs	Calgary Highlanders
Calg R	Calgary Regiment
Camerons of C	Queen's Own Cameron Highlanders of Canada
CAR	Canadian Armoured Regiment
CASF	Canadian Active Service Force (WW2)
CASF	Canadian Army Special Force (Korea)
Cdn AB Regt	Canadian Airborne Regiment
CEF	Canadian Expeditionary Force
CELE	Communications & Electronics Engineering Branch
CGG	Canadian Grenadier Guards
CH of O	Cameron Highlanders of Ottawa
CIC	Canadian Intelligence Corps
CPC	Canadian Provost Corps
CWAC	Canadian Women's Army Corps
E & K Scot	Essex and Kent Scottish Regiment
Elgin R	Elgin Regiment (RCAC)
FGH	Fort Garry Horse
Fus de Sher	Les Fusiliers de Sherbrooke
Fus du St-L	Les Fusiliers du St-Laurent
Fus MR	Les Fusiliers Mont-Royal
GGFG	Governor General's Foot Guards
GGHG	Governor General's Horse Guards
Grey & Sim For	Grey and Simcoe Foresters
Hast & PER	Hastings and Prince Edward Regiment
HF of C	Royal Highland Fusiliers of Canada
KOCR	King's Own Calgary Regiment (RCAC)
L & R Scot R	Lanark and Renfrew Scottish Regiment

L Edmn R	Loyal Edmonton Regiment (4th Battalion PPCLI)
Lake Sup Scot R	Lake Superior Scottish Regiment
LdSH	Lord Strathcona's Horse (Royal Canadians)
Linc Welld R	Lincoln and Welland Regiment
N Sask R	North Saskatchewan Regiment
NS Highrs	Nova Scotia Highlanders
Ont R	Ontario Regiment (RCAC)
PEIR	Prince Edward Island Regiment (RCAC)
PLF	Princess Louise Fusiliers
PPCLI	Princess Patricia's Canadian Light Infantry
PWOR	Princess of Wales' Own Regiment
QOR of C	Queen's Own Rifles of Canada
QRY	Queen's York Rangers (1st American Regiment) (RCAC)
R 22e R	Royal 22e Régiment
R de Chaud	Le Régiment de la Chaudiére
R de Hull	Le Régiment de Hull (RCAC)
R de Mais	Le Régiment de Maisonneuve
R du Sag	Le Régiment du Saguenay
R Nfld R	Royal Newfoundland Regiment
R Regt C	Royal Regiment of Canada
R Westmr R	Royal Westminster Regiment
R Wpg Rif	Royal Winnipeg Rifles
RAC	Royal Armoured Corps
RCA	Royal Regiment of Canadian Artillery
RCAC	Royal Canadian Armoured Corps
RCACC	Royal Canadian Army Chaplain Corps
RCADC	Royal Canadian Army Dental Corps
RCAF	Royal Canadian Air Force
RCAMC	Royal Canadian Army Medical Corps
RCAPC	Royal Canadian Army Pay Corps
RCASC	Royal Canadian Army Service Corps
RCCS	Royal Canadian Corps of Signals
RCD	Royal Canadian Dragoons
RCE	Corps of Royal Canadian Engineers
RCEME	Corps of Royal Canadian Electrical and Mechanical Engineers
RCH	Royal Canadian Hussars (Montreal)
RCHA	Royal Canadian Horse Artillery
RCIC	Royal Canadian Infantry Corps
RCN	Royal Canadian Navy
RCNVR	Royal Canadian Navy Volunteer Reserve
RCOC	Royal Canadian Ordnance Corps
RCPC	Royal Canadian Postal Corps
RCR	Royal Canadian Regiment

RHC	Black Watch (Royal Highland Regiment of Canada)
RHLI	Royal Hamilton Light Infantry
RM Rang	Rocky Mountain Rangers
RMR	Royal Montreal Regiment
RNBR	Royal New Brunswick Regiment
RNfldR	Royal Newfoundland Regiment
RRR	Royal Regina Rifles
SALH	South Alberta Light Horse
SaskD	Saskatchewan Dragoons
SD&G Highers	Stormont, Dundas and Glengarry Highlanders
Seaforth of C	Seaforth Highlanders of Canada
SherH	Sherbrooke Hussars (RCAC)
The Lorne Scots	Lorne Scots (Pell, Dufferin and Halton Regiment)
Tor Scot R	Toronto Scottish Regiment
VOLTIGEURS	Les Voltigeurs de Québec
West NSR	West Nova Scotia Regiment
WindR	Windsor Regiment (RCAC)

Bibliography

Adam, F. *Clans, Septs and Regiments of the Scottish Highlands*. (W&AK Johnston & GW Bacon Ltd.).

Adkins, H.E. *Treatise on the Military Band* (London: Boosey & Co.,1958).

Friedman, Albert B. *Viking Book of Folk Ballads of the English Speaking World*. (New York: Penquin Books, 1976).

Arbuckle, G. *Customs and Traditions of the Canadian Navy*. (Halifax, NS: Nimbus Publishing Ltd, 1984).

Barnard, W.T. *One Hundred Years of Canada 1860-1960*. (Don Mills, Ontario: Ontario Publishing Company Ltd.).

Baxter, James. *New Brunswick Regiment of Artillery 1793-1896*. (St. John, NB: The Sun Publishing, 1898).

Binns, P.L. *A Hundred Years of Military Music*. (Dorset, UK: Blackmore Press, 1959).

Binns, P.L. *The Story of the Royal Tournament*. (Aldershot, UK: Gale & Polden, 1952).

Boon, Brindley. *Play the Music*. (London: Salvationist Publishing & Supplies Ltd, 1978).

Brown, Brian A. *The Foresters*. (Erin, Ontario: Boston Mills Press, 1991).

Bull, Stewart H. *Queen's York Rangers*. (Erin, Ontario: The Boston Mills Press, 1984).

Campbell, D.A. *Dress of the Royal Artillery*. (London: Arms and Armour Press, 1971).

Campbell, William. *Popular Music of Old Times Volumes 1 & 2*. (Dover Publications, 1965).

Canadian Defence Information. (Department of National Defence, May 1993).

Canadian Forces Administrative Orders. (Department of National Defence. 1987).

Chambers, BJ. *Histoire du 65me Regiment Carabiniers Mont-Royal*. (Guertin Publishing, 1907).

Chambers, Ernest J. *Prince of Wales Regiment*. (Montreal: EL Ruddy, 1897).

Chambers, Ernest J. *Forty-Third Regiment*. (Ottawa: EL Ruddy, 1903).

Cole, William. *Folk Songs of England, Ireland, Scotland & Wales*. (New York: Doubleday Inc., 1961).

Cook, E.D. and J.K. Marteinson. *125 Years of Service 1843-1973*. (8th Canadian Hussars Regimental Association, 1973).

Cooke, James F. *Standard History of Music*. (Philadelphia: Theodore Presser Co).

Curchin, A. and Lt. B.D. Sim. *The Elgins.* (St. Thomas, Ontario: Sutherland Press, 1977).

Denison, George. *Soldiering in Canada.* (Toronto: George N. Morrang & Company Ltd, 1901).

Edwards, T. J. *Military Customs.* (Aldershot, UK: Gale and Polden Ltd, 1954).

Elliot, R. S. R. *Scarlet to Green.* (Toronto: Canadian Intelligence and Security Association, 1981).

Facey-Crowther, David. *The New Brunswick Militia 1787-1867.* (New Brunswick: New Brunswick Historical Society and New Ireland Press, 1990).

Famous Songs and Those Who Made Them. (New York: University Society, 1899).

Farmer, Henry George. *History of the Royal Artillery Band.* (RA Bands Executive Committee, 1954).

Farmer, Henry George. *Military Music.* (New York: Chanticleer Press, 1950).

Farmer, Henry George. *Rise and Development of Military Music.* (London: W.M. Reeves)

Fetherstonhaugh, R.C. *The Royal Canadian Regiment 1883-1933 Vol. 1.* (London, Ontario: The Royal Canadian Regiment, 1981).

Frost, Sydney. *Once a Patricia.* (St. Catharines, Ontario: Vanwell Publishing Ltd, 1988).

Giddings, Robert. *War Poets.* (New York: Orion Books, 1988).

Glass, Paul, and Louis C. Singer. *Singing Soldier.* (New York: Da Capo Press, 1988).

Gordon, L. L. *Military Origins.* (New York: A.S. Barnes & Co., 1971).

Goss, John. *Daily Express Community Song Book.* (London: Daily Express, 1927).

Greenhous, Brereton. *Dragoon.* (Belleville: Guild of the Royal Canadian Dragoons, 1983).

Greenhous, Brereton. *Semper Paratus.* (Hamilton, Ontario: Royal Highland Light Infantry Historical Association, 1977).

Guide Book of Official Marches of the CF. (Toronto: Royal Canadian Military Institute, 1989).

Hallows, Ian S. *Regiments and Corps of the British Army.* (London: Arms & Armour Press, 1991).

Heinl, R.D. Jr. *Dictionary of Military and Naval Quotations.* (Maryland: Naval Institute Press, 1966).

Henderson, Dianna M. *The Scottish Regiments.* (Glasgow: Harper Collins, 1993).

Hering, P.G. *Customs and Traditions of the Royal Air Force.* (Aldershot, UK: Gale and Polden Press, 1960).

Hopkins, Anthony. *Songs from the Front and Rear.* (Edmonton: Hurtig Publishers, 1979).

Hughes, G. W. *A Marchpast of the Canadian Army Past & Present.* (Calgary: G. W. Hughes, nd).

Hugill, Stan. *Shanties from the Seven Seas.* (London: Routledge & Kegan Paul Ltd, 1961).

Hunter, A. T. *The Twelfth York Rangers.* (Toronto: Murray Printing).

Hutchison, Paul P. *Canada's Black Watch.* (Montreal: The Royal Highlanders of Canada Association, 1962).

Jackson, H. M. *Princess Louise IV Dragoon Guards of Canada.* (Regimental Publication nd).

Jackson, H.M. *Argyll and Sutherland Highlanders.*

Johnston, Murray. *Canada's Craftsmen.* (LORE Association, 1984).

Kerry, A.J. , and W.A. McDill. *History of The Corps of Royal Canadian Engineers,* Vol. 1&2. (Ottawa: The Military Engineers Association of Canada, 1962).

Kilpatrick, Bill. *The Story of the March,* Vol. 3. (Longines Symphonette Society, nd)

Kopstein, Jack. *When the Band Begins to Play.* (Kingston, Ontario Apple Jack Publishers, 1992).

Lawn, G.R. *Music in State Clothing.* (London: Leo Cooper, 1995).

Malcolm, C.A. *Piper in Peace and War.* (London: Hardwicke Press, 1993).

Marteinson, John. *We Stand on Guard.* (Montreal: Ovale Publications, 1992).

McAvity, J.M. *Strathcona's 39-45.* (Toronto: Brigdens Limited, 1947).

McBain, D. *Regimental Marches of the British Army.* (RMSM, Kneller Hall and Angel Records 1957).

McDayter/Purvis. *Military Music of the War of 1812.* (Toronto Historical Board, 1993).

Military Band Journal, Vol. 4. (1965).

Mirtle, Jack. *Naden Band.* (Victoria: Jackstays Publishing and The Naden Band, 1990).

Mitchell, G. D. *RCHA — Right of the Line, Major.* (Ottawa: RCHA History Committee, 1968).

Mitchell, M. *Ducimus (Regiments of Canadian Infantry).* (Ottawa: Canadian War Museum, 1992)

Mulvey, C. P. and W. E. Carger. *Toronto Past and Present.* (Reprint Coles Book Stores, 1884).

Music Unites the People. Canadian Edition. (Boston: C.C. Birchard & Company, 1917).

New Grove Dictionary of Music and Musicians. (MacMillan Publishers Ltd, 1980).

New Treasury of Irish Songs and Ballads 2. (Dublin: Walton's Ltd., Fodhla Printing, 1966).

Nicholson, G.W.L. *The Fighting Newfoundlanders.* (Government of Newfoundland).

Nicholson, G.W.L. *More Fighting Newfoundlanders.* (Government of Newfoundland)

Patterson, William, and Alasdair Gray. *Songs of Scotland.* (Edinburgh: Mainstream Publishing, 1996).

Preston, Richard A. *Canada's RMC — A History of the Royal Military College.* (Toronto: University of Toronto Press, 1969).

Quigley, John. *The Halifax Rifles 1860-1960.* (Halifax: W. McNab)

Railsback, Thomas C. and John P. Langellier. *Drums Would Roll.* (Dorset, UK: Arms & Armour Press, 1987).

Regiment Magazine. (Kent, UK: Nexus Special Interest, Nexus House), various issues.

"Regimental Marches." (*Canadian Army Journal,* Department of National Defence, September, 1951).

Regiments and Corps of The Canadian Army. (Ottawa: Queen's Printer, 1964).

Richardsons War of 1812. (Facsimile, Coles Press, 1972).

The Rise and Development of the Wind Band. (London: William Reeves, 1912).

Robertson, Donald Struan. *Scots Guards, Standard Setting of Pipe Music.* (The Scots Guards, 1954).

Rogers R. L. *History of the Lincoln and Welland Regiment.* (Privately published, 1954)

Roy, R. H. *Seaforth Highlanders of Canada.* (Seaforth Highlanders of Canada, 1969).

Roy, R.H. *Sinews of Steel.* (Toronto: Charters Publishing Co Ltd, 1965).

Russel, E.C. *Customs & Traditions of the Canadian Forces.* (Government of Canada Press, 1980).

Skilton, Wendy. *British Military Band Uniforms* Vol. 1 and 2. (Leic, UK: Midland Publishing, 1992).

Smith, Norman E. *March Music Notes.* (Louisiana: Program Note Press).

Songs of Scotland. (Midlothian, Scotland: Lang Syne Publishers Ltd., 1978).

Standing Orders of the Royal Canadian Dragoons 1907. (Government Printing Bureau, 1907)

Standing Orders Queen's Own Rifles of Canada. (Toronto: Brown Brothers, 1884).

Stephens, W. Ray. *Memories and Melodies of World War II.* (Erin, Ontario: Boston Mills Press, 1987).

Stevens, G.R. *Royal Canadian Regiment* Vol.2. (London, Ontario: London Printing & Lithographing Co Ltd, 1967).

Stevens, GR. *Princess Patricia Light Infantry* Vol. 3. (Regimental Publications).

Sutton, D.J. (ed.) *Story of the RASC and RCT 1945-1982.* (London: Leo Cooper, 1983)

Swinson, Arthur (ed.) *Register /Regiments/Corps of the British Army.* (London: The Archive Press, 1972).

Tawney, Cyril. *Grey Funnels Lines.* (London: Routledge & Kegan Paul, 1987).

Telford, M. M., *Scarlet to Grey.* (Erin, Ontario: Boston Mills Press, 1987).

Tooley, Robert. *Invicta.* (Fredericton: New Ireland Press, 1989).

Traditions and Customs of the Canadian Forces, Part 3 — Bands and Music. (Department of National Defence, Ottawa, 1991).

Trendell, John. *Colonel Bogey to the Fore.* (The Blue Band Magazine, 1991).

Turner, Gordon and Alwyn Turner. *History of British Military Bands* Vol. 1, 2, 3. (Kent, UK: Spellmount Publishers, 1997).

Turner, Gordon and Alwyn Turner. *Trumpets Will Sound.* (Kent, UK: Parapress Limited, 1996).

Various authors. *Band International.* Vol. 3 #2, Vol. 9 #1, Vol. 9 #1, Vol. 14 (International Military Music Society)

Walton's New Treasury of Irish Songs and Ballads. (Ireland: Walton's Ltd, 1966).

Ware, Frances. *The Story of the 7th Regiment Fusiliers.* (London, Ontario: Hunter Publishing).

Warren, Arnold. *Wait for the Wagon.* (Toronto: McClelland & Stewart, 1961).

Weir, Christopher. *Village and Town Bands.* (Bucks, UK: Shire Publications, 1981)

Westrup, J.A. & F.L.I. Harrison. *New College Encyclopedia of Music.* (New York: WW Norton & Co Inc, 1960).

White E.L. *A Collection of Secular Melodies, 4th Edition.* (Cornhill, Mass: Elias Howe, 1846)

Whitman, W.W. *Songs that Changed the World.* (New York: Crown Publishers, 1969).

Wicks, H.L. *Regiments of Foot.* (Berkshire, UK: Osprey Books, 1974).

Wild, Walter. *Romance of Regimental Marches.* (London: William Clowes & Sons, 1932).

Willes, John A. *Out of the Clouds.* (Port Perry, Ontario: Port Perry Printing Ltd, 1995)

Wilson, Barbara. *Ontario and the First World War.* (Toronto: University of Toronto Press).

Winstock, Lewis. *Songs and Music of the Redcoats 1642-1902.* (London: Leo Cooper, 1970)

The Years of Agony: John Craig's Canada. (Jack McCelland: Illustrated Heritage Series).

Zeally, Alfred. *Famous Bands of the British Empire.* (J P. Hull, 1926).

Zeally, A.E. *Music Ashore and Afloat, (Famous Bands of the RCN).* (Wallaceburg, Ontario: The Standard Press, 1943).

Documents

Annual Reports of the Department of Militia and Defence, 1867-1913.

Dornbusch, C.E. The Canadian Army 1955-1958. Regimental Histories. (New York: Cornwallville Press, 1959).

The Official History of the Canadian Forces in the Great War. (1938).

General Surveys

"A Concise History of the PPCLI Band," PPCLI Museum, Jack Kopstein.

"A Concise History of the Royal Canadian Regiment Band," RCR Museum, Jack Kopstein.

"A Famous Military Band," Zeally, Etude 65, c1947.

Band of the Canadian Grenadier Guards, Historical Notes, c1979.

British Regimental Marches, Ernest Hart.

Musical Quarterly 4, c1918.

Canadian Music and Trades Journal (1900), Band of the 48th Highlanders.

Canadian Women's Army Corps, Various Newsletters.

Military Bands and Military Music, McKenzie Rogin.

"Bands and Their Usefulness," Musical Canada (July 1932).

The 48th Highlanders, Newsletter/International Military Music Society Canadian Branch.

Notes on early military bands, C. Fouldes, Society for Military Research, c1938.

Police Court Case Rex vs Union 1929, St. Catharines, Ontario.

Report Number 47, Historical Section Army Headquarters, J. R. Madden, c1952.

Royal Canadian Army Service Corps Band War Diary 1944/45. A. Hollick, Bandmaster.

The Aldershot News, (Aug 1943 and July 1943).

The Canadian Bandmaster (Fall 1961), National Library of Canada.

The Canadian Military Journal (Sept 1952 and Jan 1956).

The Guide (A Manual for the Canadian Militia), Major General Otter, 1914.

The History of the Governor General's Foot Guards, Jim Milne Manuscript, c1979.

The Ontario Weekly Notes 1930, Supreme Court of Ontario Vol. 39, P 89.

Index

Music Titles appear in Italics

Year of Victories 190
York and Lancaster Regiment 212
York Rangers Regiment 24
Yorkshire Lass (The) 203, 209
Young May Moon 198, 250
Young, Sergeant 52

Zeally, Alfred 93, 94, 95, 96, 167, 175, 176
Zinken 14
Ziska, Maurice 115, 176